END TO
BEGINNING

ISBN: 979-8-9997159-2-0
LCCN: 2025916596
Front cover by Tanner Critz

www.tannercritz.com

END TO BEGINNING

A Healing Story of Ayahuasca

by Tanner Critz

Acknowledgements

After writing a book about gratitude, I'm compelled to thank everyone who ever helped guide me to this point. Rather than write a second book before starting this one, I'll simply say I asked a small army of friends to look over this memoir to be sure it didn't come off as the ravings of a lunatic.

Thanks to Melanie and my boys for not only being generally amazing, but also talking with me about what they remembered and deeply considering what they wanted to share.

Thanks to David, Mark, Taran, Jean, and MJ for your speedy and enormously helpful comments on the first draft.

Thanks to my author schoolmate, Kevin Brockmeier, for so generously giving your time for detailed notes and insightful suggestions. Readers should absolutely seek out your books, which have long inspired me with your distinctive voice. Judy Goss's creative writing class at Parkview High produced four published authors from that year alone — there was a special chemistry to that angsty brew of teen writing.

Thanks to every volunteer who held space for me during ceremony, particularly Brandon, whose light continues to shine bright over this experience for both Wayah and me.

Thanks to my students, my teachers, my amazing lifelong friends, and of course, my magical, loving Granny.

End to Beginning

Part 1
Ends

Chapter 1

Stillness

I could see my shallow breath twist into the light as I sat in the sun behind my house. On the playground we called it dragon's breath, and its mastery was sought after. At the edge of the deck it swirled into the sun to vanish in the light. I lay almost flat in a deck chair, looking at the sky and wondering where my body had gone. It's a thick, heavy body that usually felt warm and meaty, with some soreness and strains telling the story of the last week's activity. Now it felt like the engine was purring in some sort of low-power, economy mode. I felt hollow and less than whole, like a partially deflated beach ball. My mind was slow and my thoughts thin. The cold air stung my nostrils where they were still raw and cracked from the hospital tubes.

Arkansas winters are laughable to people who need electric blankets to keep their engines from freezing and snow rooms to take off all of their winter gear before entering the house. We are just as likely to wear short sleeves to Christmas dinner as a coat, but it does get cold in manic spurts that can fall anytime from November through March. February is the most reliably cold Arkansas month. If there's going to be lasting snow and ice, power outages, or frozen pipes, it's almost certainly in February. The month itself has shriveled from the cold to be the shortest of the year.

Our home sat on the slope of a hill, so the deck was twenty feet off the ground to my left, with only a seven foot drop to my right where it butted up to the kitchen with a car tucked underneath, remembering a time when I had places to go. I was wrapped in blankets and winter clothes with my legs propped up on a second deck chair. My hands were gloved and tucked loosely into my blankets with a half full bottle of water balanced on my chest. My face was uncovered to catch as much sun as I could, but I felt the fur of my big Icelandic snow hat stirring in the air. That's why I was out there. Sun and fresh air.

My breaths were shallow. The neighborhood breeze smelled like ice and burnt wood with a hint of mulching leaves. I was still having trouble taking full breaths. It had been a little more than two weeks since they sent me home from the hospital because I was finally able to stand up for thirty seconds, but really because they badly needed the room. I had thought I'd need just a week to recover. It was going to be longer. I hoped not more than a month.

It was February of 2021 and we were ten months into the Covid pandemic. The normally busy neighborhood road by my house stood quiet, watching the light flicker aimlessly from green to yellow to red. Its faint, electrical buzz was audible in wide emptiness of the intersection. Vaccines had been given to doctors but the general population couldn't have them yet. An angry crowd had stormed the capitol in DC, but I was in bed fighting to breathe and no one wanted to burden me with news of the world.

I had been nearly forced to close down my karate school when all of this first started. To adapt to the sudden loss of more than half of our students, we started offering our new building as a place for kids to do virtual schooling during the day, and holding touchless martial arts classes for those willing to risk it in the evening. People's kids could get out of the house leaving their parents with some peace as they learned to work remotely, and we tried to scrape together enough money to keep our building, home, and staff. We'd all been working twelve hour days and figuring it out as we went. My advanced students had been there running it without me since I got sick. I didn't have the energy to wonder how it was going.

My wife and two sons were at home all day. I had suddenly been home with them when everything first shut down and we could only hold video classes. Despite the stress of the outer world, we were all together in a way we had never been able to achieve before being locked in. I had started cooking a lot since I was home in the evening and no restaurants were open, but not any more. All of the noise, whether pleasant or terrifying, had blurred to a low muffled hum. I thought my childhood when the shuttle blew up and the wall came down was the craziest time in human history. The last few years had seen a level of madness that made the Cold War 80s seem like an episode of Sesame Street. Then, in an instant, pandemics and protests and culture wars had fallen to a distant buzz that I was vaguely aware of somewhere in the periphery of the wind. A host of worries rendered impotent by the kiss of death's razor.

The sun held my heavy face gently as a breeze light as a leaf's twist kissed my closed eyelids. It was like relaxing in many ways, but in reverse. Normally my days were full of movement. The life of a karate teacher is challenge, exercise, and motivation. Sleep came easy. My preferred days off let me recline and recharge, but this weariness was something I'd never experienced. Normally recovery would allow energy to refill a drained vessel. My body wasn't drained from exhaustion now. I was actually very rested, but my tank on full was now a tiny fraction of what my tank on empty had been before I got sick. Reclining there in the sun was about healing so that there was a tank to fill.

The day before, I had tried to take a shower, but the effort of both standing and also scrubbing my fingers through my hair made me have to sit and recover, finishing the shower sitting on the floor of the tub. Earlier that day I had managed to climb a flight of stairs without having to sit on the middle step to recover like the days before. Next I hoped to walk to the end of the block and back with Melanie's help, but that would probably have to wait a day or two. Everything was conscious intentional work: my thoughts, my breath, every movement. It was all challenging, but I was prodded by the patient urgency of my own memory of all I needed to do before this started. That spectre of my unfettered self, looming at my periphery, was eager to get back to work as if nothing had happened.

My phone sat near me where I could see it ring, but I couldn't hold it up for more than a minute or focus my eyes on it for long. When people called, I would put it on speaker, lay it on my shoulder, and close my eyes. I preferred talking to friends that had energy to give. I couldn't answer a lot of questions or think hard about anything. I normally had a great reservoir of patience that let me teach kids for hours or listen to someone that had problems to solve, but not anymore. I hadn't realized how much energy I was spending on patience until the battery ran dry. Now I felt my attention pumping like a muscle, and heavy weights would wear it out fast.

An hour earlier, the owner of the Pantry, a restaurant where Melanie and I had spent date night every Wednesday for the last ten years, stopped by to bring me some food and express how relieved he was that I survived. Someone had told him how close it was. I could tell that he was exhausted. He was hustling to keep his business and not let go of his employees through the waves of instability. Like me, he was feeling those strings of human connection more powerfully. The ones that give and the ones that take stood out sharply through the weariness. I looked forward to getting the strength back so that I could rejoin the work. We determined to keep each other going even when the world crumbles around us. As weak as I felt, the power of this need and connection called to me.

The day before September 11, 2001, was the only time I've ever been fired from a job. The multimedia wing of a company that I'd been hired to build got lopped off as the dot com bubble erupted and web designers and salespeople scattered from the blinding light of change. The next morning, sitting in a Waffle House with my dad and wondering what to do next in my life, I felt a shudder go through a waitress as she stood transfixed by a tiny television. It didn't seem right to look for another web design job after the planes crashed and the towers fell. There was something in the air that felt more essential and more driven to purpose. That was when I decided to take my lifelong love of the martial arts and find a way to forge that path into a career. It was that charged person-to-person connection kindled in sweeping uncertainty that set me on my path. I could feel it swirling around me as I sat on the porch, but I couldn't move. I couldn't take a full breath. I wasn't in my late twenties wondering what kind of life I wanted to build. I was almost fifty with a family and a life I feared to lose.

Josh texted that he would come by and sit for a while. We still couldn't know exactly what was safe with Covid. It seemed clear that sitting outside with some distance was safe as long as we didn't sneeze or cough at each other. Having just left the hospital, I would hope to be super-charged with antibodies, but the chair ten feet across the deck is where we drew our magical safety line. Josh was already a friend before all of this. His children had trained with me for years, and then he'd begun taking my classes also. He had been my kids' pediatrician, sometimes coming over at night or on the weekend to check on a wound or bring over a prescription so that our lives weren't full of unnecessary emergency room visits. My being sick, though, had triggered something new in our friendship. He was able to provide and care for me on a new level. Our relationship had become more balanced. Starting out with me as the teacher had kept a distance between us, but two weeks ago, that had changed.

The hospital had been a sudden and surprising transition. I had gotten Covid after so many months of masks, and distancing, and careful protocols. Even though we stayed away from the Christmas gatherings that my extended family cavalierly decided to hold, it wasn't enough. Tendrils of incubating virus had quietly slipped from these parties in all directions and assaulted our wearied defenses.

When I learned I had been infected, just a fever nagging at me one night confirmed at a clinic in the morning, I was mostly fearful about passing it on to the most vulnerable people around me. I had a student in her eighties who was finally back up to speed after beating breast cancer. What if she'd survived cancer only to die from a virus I passed on to her? I'd just had my protege Chris and his wife Ming over, newly pregnant with their highly anticipated first child. What if she got it from me and it hurt or ended the pregnancy?

I knew the hospitals were full and people were dying, but no one I knew had suffered more than a flu-like few days in quaran-tine at home. While I feared for vulnerable people around me, I was sure I was healthy and fit and would ride it out quickly, quarantined in our bedroom with Melanie setting herself up in the guest room. When my oxygen kept dropping and breathing came harder and harder over the next few days, my doctor friends became worried, and Melanie and I found ourselves waiting in a car outside the hospital for our turn.

We spent hours in the parking lot since the waiting room was full. With the engine running for heat, nurses would come by periodically to check oxygen levels. The hospitals were so short on staff and space that they would send home all but the most dire cases, but they also had to keep checking the scattered cars and be on the lookout for anyone suddenly worsening. Those hours of waiting in the car are probably when Melanie caught it from me. We passed the time listening to music but I was nearly unconscious and she was in emergency advocate mode. When, four hours into waiting, she asked a nurse if she could drive us to get food and refill gas, they told her we'd lose our place.

We were finally ushered from the car and allowed into a tiny curtained partition inside where the seriousness of my symptoms could be evaluated past what a thermometer and a pulse oximeter through a car window could tell. I could hear the muffled swarm of aching humanity pressing in from just past the curtains and temporary walls in all directions. Melanie was receiving and interpreting, while I sat in an asphyxiated daze, waiting for any kind of relief. There was a break in the slow tedium, and then I was wheeling along beige hallways, the end of the bed on wheels bumping into swinging doors. Without any warning or fanfare, Melanie got peeled away as we entered the Covid ward. There, access was restricted, and doctors and nurses wore many layers of protective gear, looking more like astronauts than caregivers. We didn't get to talk about how bad the x-rays of my lungs looked, both riddled with pneumonia, or how quickly they decided to put me in a room once they'd seen them. We hadn't said goodbye. Not really. Not the way you'd want to if you thought there was any chance it could be the last time.

In the room, I was transferred to one of the heavy hospital beds, with its many moving parts and connectors. On the wall behind me were monitors, and charts, and an oxygen connection that was quickly hooked to a tube wrapped around my head to secure it up my nose. Needles introduced IV's into my left arm, and they began the steady drip of medicine and nutrients into my veins. I was mounted firmly into the care of Western medicine, and I waited eagerly for the miracles of science to begin easing my pain. The oxygen, nutrients, and pain-killers were a brief relief, but the suffering that was creeping slowly to the fore was the exertion of working with my lungs and the ache of slow asphyxiation.

Breathing was hard, so talking on the phone was hard. Even the focus of texting or looking at the screen was too much. My breathing became a battle that required constant concentration and effort. Sleep became impossible since an unfocused breath led to coughing fits that twisted my spine and raked my chest with pain. Nurses and doctors were so covered up that when they checked on me, which was seldom, I couldn't see skin or eyes or hear a clear voice through double masks and visors. They were weary, humorless, and fewer than was necessary for the task. I felt utterly alone in my struggle. I was too busy fighting to worry that I might die alone in this place without ever seeing my wife or sons again. The halls echoed day and night with the sounds of gurneys taking people to ventilators, but I didn't have time to fear it. All of my attention was committed to balancing the teetering spectre of mortality over my aching lungs.

By the fourth day, I was pierced by a ceaseless downward pressure. The medicine made me feel a little better, and I was getting all the treatments that should lead to my swift recovery, but my numbers kept slipping, and the amount of oxygen coming from the wall kept increasing. In the midst of my restless waiting, a doctor came into the room who didn't match the pattern. I normally only saw a doctor once a day and had already seen one. This one also moved awkwardly, like he wasn't sure he should stay, and then began to take off his protective layers. He might as well have been setting his hair on fire. This should not have been happening. I supposed it would make sense if I were to start hallucinating at this point, but it seemed very real. Then I saw some familiar shaped hands as gloves came off, followed by the eyes and worried brow that I knew so well. It was Josh!

"Hey, brother," he said as he peeled off his coat and came a little closer. "I'm not really supposed to be up here, 'cause they're keeping it locked down tight." I wanted so much to fall into witty banter the way we normally would, but my breathing was so difficult that I needed to prep my lungs for anything I said. If I moved too quickly, I'd start a painful coughing fit.

"It's good to see you," I managed carefully and weakly. His eyes were taking me in and I could see him struggling to maintain his bedside manner.

"Listen," he switched to doctor voice. "I just wanted to check in and get a look at you. Like I said, I'm not supposed to be here, so I just want you to know that I might have to jet out at any moment." He put a hand on my foot through the blanket and the warmth of human touch spread up my body like a wind in the leaves. My chest dropped as I let out an emotional breath involuntarily, and then wrangled the coming coughs into the curl of my body with a wheeze to keep them small and rumbling rather than let them spill over into the full cascades of body wracking explosions. There was a delicate art to working around my swollen and infected lungs. It was like surfing in a slowly growing storm, but with no land in sight.

"How are you feeling? Are you able to get up and around? Use the bathroom?" I was looking into his eyes intently. They were the first eyes I'd seen that weren't covered by face-shields in days, and they were so clear and alive. I felt the skin of his hand as he sympathetically took hold of mine. The touch brought back a thousand distant human interactions like a rising sun - so light and easy, but so far away. It shone into my darkness as relief but also laid bare the rocky isolation of my fight, setting off a flow of tears. They were immediately echoed in Josh's eyes. I could see the fear there as he took me in. I was twenty pounds underweight and could barely form words. To have my friend see me suffer burned hot. It drew my failure to heal into sharp clarity.

"You're so strong, and I know you're going to be home and back to teaching classes before you know it." I could feel how hard he was working to be solid for me. "I'm going to need to slip out, but I just wanted you to know that I love you, and we're all here rooting for you, and making sure everything is right where you left it. I think it's my and Ash's turn to bring some food over to Mel and the boys tonight." He let go of my hand and started to put all of his gear back on. I couldn't really say goodbye. I just hurt with exhaustion. I didn't register whatever he said last, muffled by another mask and a face-shield. It didn't really matter. He had been there to touch my hand and show me my reflection in his eyes. I turned again to the lonely fight with a fresh wave of admonished determination.

Sitting behind my house in the crisp winter air, a cold tear pushed to the edge of my eye as I saw his anxious frame slip up the wooden steps. He moved carefully, as if my fragility was something he needed to be careful not to step on.

"Hey, brother," he said, touching my shoulder lightly as he brushed through the unmarked danger zone to sit in the other chair on the porch. The dance of instinctively wanting to draw close, but then hovering back to respect protocol was familiar if still blunt. We went over numbers, my pulse and blood oxygen, my weight, stools, energy level, until the caregiver side of him was satisfied, and then we started to talk more lightly.

I sensed that he was circling something that made him a little anxious. I didn't have the energy to probe, so I waited in the sun and the breeze while he shared the novel stories that had become so oddly normal about kids trying to have college without class-rooms, or friends trying to do jobs that were turned upside down by remote working or collapsing industries and supply lines. Soon enough came the long pause followed by the bullet-biting "so."

"I've booked myself into this crazy retreat in a couple months that should be pretty wild."

I knew Josh to keep things close to the chest for as long as possible and then start to get anxious about them as they approached before finally being ready to talk about it. It could be a surgery for a problem I didn't know he had, or maybe he was hiking a section of the Appalachian Trail that was going to be a challenge. This seemed heavier. He was tapping into a larger than normal vein of resolve to move forward with whatever this was, and it sounded like he was talking himself into it daily.

After a thoughtful pause, he continued. "It's to take a halluci-nogenic medicine called Ayahuasca. It's like a Peruvian traditional practice. It's supposed to be good for anxiety and all sorts of stuff."

I opened my eyes and tilted my head to look at him and saw that his brow was tense and he was looking at the planks of the deck. "I've heard about it on a couple of podcasts where people talk about how it miraculously healed them. I watched a show on Netflix that gets into it in more detail and even shows the place where I booked the retreat. It's this place called Soul Quest"

Josh had no doubt researched it exhaustively. If he was telling me about it, he'd already pulled any medical journals that discussed the effects and risks. He'd have searched far and wide for any addi-tional information to help make sure that it was safe and effective. More than that, I could feel that he was marching towards a lonely struggle with the hope of healing. Soul Quest sounded pretty hokey as a name, and images of gurus and feather fans floated through my head. On the other side of all of that was my friend, straining for relief.

I said, "I'll go with you." I could feel his hand on mine in the hospital and the terrible, lonely struggle that came afterwards flashed in my mind like a spectre. We were connected still, and as weak as I was, I didn't feel any fear. All I could feel was my friend afraid of casting himself into the unknown alone.

"Even though the drug is illegal in the U.S., it's legal if you belong to their particular church since it's part of their tradition. So I'd just have to join their religion on paper. It's not any kind of weird stuff. It seems to make space for all other religious beliefs within it."

My voice was pretty weak so maybe he hadn't heard me. Secondary doubts pushed at my hobbled mind before I spoke again. Will I be able to walk? Will the dojo still keep running without me there? For how long? Am I strong enough for a mind-bending jungle medicine? How's my heart doing? None of my thoughts were enough of a direct threat to derail the words still intent on coming out of my mouth.

"I'll go with you."

"Seriously?" Now he heard me. He locked eyes with me and straightened his back as tension fell from his shoulders, "Oh man, that would be amazing! The room I booked is big enough for you to stay in. Are you serious?" The door to the house opened and Melanie walked out onto the cold porch from the kitchen, shuddering before the door was fully open and pulling her coat and hat tighter around her.

"Hey, Mel," Josh said. "I was just telling Tanner that I'm going to go on an Ayahuasca retreat in April. It's this South American healing medicine." She looked over at me with her tired, bright eyes.

"You should go with him." Only now, weeks after I returned from the hospital, was she letting herself relax into the world of "Tanner is going to be alright." The hospital had been hard on me, but it had ravaged her with another kind of isolation, trying to imagine her world without me. She had hovered for days on the edge, only able to talk to nurses who offered progressively more dire reports. The image of herself as an only parent had started to form. She was certainly recovering from that stress, but was also now the only functioning adult in a house with two teen boys that were struggling hard with adolescence and pandemic lockdown.

In that moment, despite our collective doubts and weariness, we all heard that still, quiet voice whisper *"now"* and put all of our sensible reservations aside.

Chapter 2

Dieta

Signing up on the retreat's website was a three-step process. Before booking the trip, I had to read and sign off on their spiritual mission statement and join their church, making the taking of the medicine legal as the sacrament of their religious practice. It was a loose concept of a church compared to those I had experienced growing up, without orientations, or classes, or rituals. It was a statement of agreement about the healing properties of the medicine, about tolerance for belief systems, and about a bunch of other stuff that I found benign and spiritually friendly.

I imagined my grandfather rolling over in his grave at even a transactional deviation from "The Church." As I thought about it, I had to admit that even twenty something years after he died I couldn't tell you exactly which Protestant sect he belonged to, just what the room looked like where the services were held. I mostly remembered that he didn't want anyone to sit in the pew that his father had donated, and he didn't want to stay and talk to anyone after the service was over like Granny did.

The second step was a thorough report of my medical status, prescriptions, vitamins, prior conditions, mental state, etc. It could be deadly to take Ayahuasca if you had psychosis or were prone to disassociate from reality already. The medicine itself wouldn't harm you, but the vivid and personal hallucinations could trigger a susceptible mind to have a strong break with reality. I was pretty sure I was in good shape there, though it's a fun exercise to decide if you're firmly rooted in reality or not. We would have to stop taking all medications before arriving. For mood-altering medications, you had to stop six weeks early. Most things just had to be stopped a week or so before, but a few things, like blood pressure medication could wait until just a couple of days before. Drinking Ayahuasca raises the blood pressure, so they didn't want anyone to stop earlier and have elevated blood pressure levels when they arrived.

The third step was booking the retreat. Josh wanted to help pay for the room and the flight, but I paid about a thousand dollars to book the weekend. Once I was signed up, they listed a third session in the daytime between the two night sessions that cost about $250 extra. It felt like it was arranged to upsell me which put me a little on edge. It highlighted to me that this was, like a dojo, a place that was about community and healing, but also a business. You had to follow safety protocols because it improved the experience, but also because injuries and lawsuits could mean the end of your business. You had to cover costs and compensate your employees, but since a thousand dollars already seems like a lot of money to people, you started with a lower price and added things on once people were committed. Businesses that curate human development have to manicure a non-threatening introduction so that a customer can encounter the transformation before they overthink the cost.

Once I had booked the retreat, there were additional instructions. I talked to their medic on the phone about the prescriptions I was on and what I needed each one for. She then gave me a schedule for when to stop taking each one, including vitamins. The medication restrictions also came with a strict physical and mental diet (or "dieta"). There was to be no meat, nothing fried or fatty, nothing processed, even many spices were off the menu. We were also to abstain from sex or masturbation for the two weeks prior, and to avoid TV, movies, books, games, or anything else that would take up space in our consciousness. We were cleaning our minds, bodies, and spirits to prepare. I'd spent a lot of time over the years working on focus and meditation, so this intense singularity of purpose was appealing, but as the day approached, I realized that I wasn't bringing an actual intention into the retreat.

When I attended the orientation zoom meetings leading up to the weekend, I got the sense that this experience was going to be overwhelming. There would almost certainly be vomiting, and maybe diarrhea. People would be weeping and wailing and facing visions of their own deaths, and one of the keys to doing it well seemed to be having a clear intention to guide you through the experience. What trauma was I undoing, though? Life is full of challenges and I've struggled plenty, but things were good. My parents were loving, my marriage was getting better every year, my kids were healthy, and I had built a business where I could spend my days on my hobbies.

I'd just been through this rough time in the hospital, and though I was recovering much more slowly than I'd anticipated, I was getting a little better every week. I doubted that any jungle medicine I drank was going to speed that up. The other people on the zoom call were a spectrum from quiet faces asking a few quick logistical questions to people that wanted to talk a lot about their spiritual matters. One common thread was that they all knew they needed healing and why. I was starting to feel like an outsider who had shown up to class without the syllabus or my homework.

I watched the Netflix episode that Josh pointed me to that showed Soul Quest, and talked about people doing Ayahuasca. It was a bit darker than I had anticipated. They talked about a European guy who went to South America and ended up killing the shaman that guided him and then being lynched by the town.

Even at Soul Quest, a person had died years earlier when they had hidden themselves away and kept drinking more and more water. The night that the documentary was filmed, a woman had a seizure and was taken to the hospital. For a one hour show, there was a lot to raise my eyebrows at, but despite all of that, there were people healing and having massive breakthroughs. Something sacred shone through. The dark parts loomed, but the overall message was that it was safe and powerfully, if strangely, effective.

By April, when I was getting packed up to go on the retreat, I had been able to walk around the block multiple times in a row and had started driving and going to work to do administrative things. I still couldn't handle staying on my feet long enough to teach a class. I certainly couldn't exercise enough to sweat. If I gauged my level of exertion from one to ten, with one representing the lowest amount of energy like standing up straight or focusing my atten- tion on a conversation, and ten being minutes of full-out sprinting, or wrestling a bear, then I could currently handle about a three. Walking was fine for a few minutes, close to ten minutes if the terrain was slow and level. I was using the treadmill at the dojo to keep an accurate record of how fast and how long I could walk so that I could see the small improvements. I had used rewards points with my bank to get a watch that could tell my heart rate and blood oxygen all the time, so I could collect even more data on where my limits were.

There was this strange new kind of weariness that I was encoun- tering. It wasn't the exhaustion that came from working my muscles and lungs to create sweat, heavy breathing, and muscle fatigue. This new barrier pulled me out of action with dizziness and asphyx- iation, but without the gruelling work that I normally went through. Feeling my body give up while still relatively relaxed was like having a faulty wire buried deep in my system. It was definitely around my breath, so I bought a breath restriction mask with different levels of resistance and began isolating the work of my lungs.

One day I pushed my limits on the treadmill and decided to just keep walking even after I got to the wall of dizziness where I would normally back off. It's a mindset that I've developed over decades of martial arts training to push past where my body thinks it can go and stretch it towards growth. If I can push past the perceived limit then my mind will reset its expectations. I managed to make it another twenty percent through the swooning dizzy spells and wrote down in my journal that I could push a lot harder than it felt like I could. A few hours later an electric pain started in my legs and hips. It was like every nerve from my navel down to my toes began wailing in waves, and I had a sleepless night writhing in pain that ibuprofen couldn't touch. The next day I called the doctor and he prescribed some pain medication but advised me not to push so hard. He'd had two other patients who were recovering from Covid report a similar response after pushing their recovery. One woman had told him it was more painful than childbirth. O.K., so, ~~I could push a lot harder than it felt like I could~~.

I stopped drinking coffee two weeks out and made giant bowls of quinoa with spinach and beans to parse out for lunch and dinner each day so that I could stay within the bounds of the dieta. I spent hours in meditation looking for an intention to carry into the weekend, but was only finding very generic concepts about healing and peace. It would have to do. Who knew what this medicine wanted to show me.

I decided to just say "here I am. *Let's go.*"

Chapter 3

White Robes and Astroturf

Josh and I met at the airport early on a Friday morning in early April. We had our clear Covid tests in hand from the day before and wore our masks into a jungle of masked airline travelers, all seeming a little too close. My employees had now been able to get their vaccines since we were all licensed child-care workers as part of being able to run summer camps at the dojo. I was asked to wait for 90 days after leaving the hospital, though, because of a supposed shortage of vaccines. As it turned out, there were piles of vaccines lying around since so few Arkansans wanted to be vaccinated. The two facts together didn't make me feel safe in the airport, but by the time I reached the crowded security line with its meager attempts to keep people at a distance, I realized that I had to let it go. Hopefully I still had enough antibodies to resist reinfection, but I was almost certainly in contact with the virus at that moment, not to mention once we crammed into the human sausage grinder that was the plane.

We had a light-hearted if achy trip to Orlando, where the retreat would be held. Josh is one of the most casually funny people I know, and since we were both avoiding thinking too much about what awaited us that night, we just talked and laughed the whole time. I'm big enough at six-foot-two that flying is always uncomfortable. My knees are jammed into the seat in front of me and I'm shoulder-to-shoulder with anyone next to me. It feels like I'm crushed against every surface. Sitting next to Josh with the aisle on my left made it less claustrophobic. My recovery since the hospital was now about eight weeks along. I could stand, sit, or walk without any real trouble. Being in an uncomfortable position, though, meant that I was clenching muscles and suffering a growing discomfort in my hips and back.

On the ground in Orlando we found the curb where a driver from the retreat would pick us up. There was another passenger there named Pete who was waiting for the same ride. I was exhausted from sitting uncomfortably and sank into a dirty stone bench near the pick-up zone.

Josh threw out some small talk. "Man, what do you think about those dietary restrictions?" Pete popped up, eager to talk, just waiting for an introduction.

"Dude, I tried but I can't eat like that. Man, I screwed my girl-friend and had a cheeseburger this morning!" My head tilted up, pulled by a questioning eyebrow.

Was Pete the norm, or was he an oddball? It hadn't occurred to me that anyone would just ignore the rules that we were given. Josh and I had discussed certain things that were negotiable in order to retain family harmony, but we'd both assumed that we had to follow the rules. They said it wouldn't work as well if we didn't, and I had been feeling healthier since starting the strict diet. I was worried about going off of the antacids that I've needed since my early twenties, but following the food restrictions of the dieta I didn't need them at all. The sex restriction was tougher. Melanie and I had to meet halfway on that one and settled on one week instead of two. Staying away from all books and media had made my thoughts very clear and present which was focusing. Hearing Pete toss all the preparations aside made me wonder what was really necessary for the medicine, and what was just a life suggestion for health and clarity. Everything about it was a void of unknowns.

I imagined a van or a light commercial vehicle that could hold six or eight people, so I was surprised when Tom pulled up in his Prius. Tom was over six feet like me, and the four of us were jammed more than tight in the small car. Tom was soft-spoken and kind. He really wanted to give us some tips about drinking Ayahuasca for the first time. He definitely wanted us to know that no two experiences were the same, that we should turn towards troubling visions to go through them, and that it was important to take part in the integration sessions before, during, and especially after. It was clearly a long, ongoing process for him that he'd participated in many times. I wasn't sure what to think about that. I was still imagining this weekend as the main event, and didn't have any idea what to expect. I was just staying open to whatever it was I was about to experience. It hadn't occurred to me, though, that someone might need to do this many times to get results, or that it might be an ongoing therapy.

My legs and hips were starting to scream from the double insult of the cramped car after the tight plane when we finally pulled into the drive of a mid-sized house in a suburban Orlando neighborhood. It had the Floridian qualities of bleak, sandy ground, sun-bleached surfaces of fencing, houses, and trees, and the terminal flatness that felt so odd to me having always lived among hills. We passed the house as we drove down the gravel driveway and started to get a sense of the expanse behind it where we'd be spending our weekend. Nervous looking people walked slowly around, carrying different amounts of tension in their shoulders and hands. Among them were people dressed all in loose, white clothing who floated lightly about, never passing each other without hugging. In some of what I'd seen in shows or read in articles, they mentioned that the facilitators wear all white and that the participants shouldn't. In the zoom integrations they shooed that aside and said it was casual and you should wear whatever you want. Here now, the facilitators were not only all in white, but in flowing skirts, dresses, shirts, and pants that definitely sent out some cultish vibes. Finally to the back of the property, the door of the cramped car opened and I squirted out onto wobbly legs to stretch them and probe their range of motion.

We first went through a Covid screening and basic medical check under a wide-open sun tarp near the parking lot before we could enter the grounds. They checked our temperature, blood pressure, and the clear Covid tests from the clinic and then put us into a golf cart with one of the people in white driving. He said his name was Andrew and then didn't say anything else. He was fit and pretty and didn't make much eye contact. Somehow his lack of chattiness coalesced in my mind into judgment. I wondered if he was just young and self-centered, or if he was looking down on us. What about us wasn't fitting his idea of the "right kind" of Ayahuasca journeyer? I had a surge of that feeling that I was an outsider that didn't belong. What was with the white clothes and lovey dovey staff? It seemed like a bit much to be genuine, and didn't seem to include me and Josh more than superficially. Andrew drove us about 100 feet over rough gravel to where the fake grass that wouldn't sting his bare feet began. Here was where we began walking through the assembling participants and the rectangular lodges where we would take the medicine. In the cart we had passed a yard with two square white buildings and a small field with a couple of backpacking tents set up next to a small pond about twenty feet across. From where we got out of the cart, we followed the plastic grass between a large circular lodge called the maloca, and the house.

The house was shaped like a big "L" forming two sides of a square with two more small square lodges on the third side and a fence making the fourth side of a courtyard the size of a small backyard. It looked to my building brain like this is where the whole thing had started, and the small lodges and everything farther back had been built after as the gatherings grew. The maloca looked like their prize structure, tall and round and unique, and I wondered if they built it early, or after they were more established. It seemed important, so I guessed it was part of the original vision or the first expansion. Behind it were some outdoor showers that looked newly constructed.

We were clearly entering the thick of it now as we passed onto the covered porch of the house to the very center of this cluster of buildings. There were psychedelic wall hangings of colorful animals and celestial beings, tiny and large altars covered with nick-nacks nodding to a variety of traditions, and many more people sitting in the shade or the sun in chairs or on the ground. It seemed like about forty people, but I learned later that there were more than eighty people in attendance that weekend. Everyone was cordial, but there were emotional walls up all around. I could feel it in the way people held themselves, the clothes they wore, and the way they spoke. Some were very reserved, while some were determined to reach out. I understood the reservation but those that were making a show of their comfort made me nervous. I didn't have enough experience to safely distinguish a guru from a madman.

Next we had to speak to the medic. She went over my medications and when I had stopped taking each, took my blood pressure, asked a lot of the questions from the intake form again, and let me know that she'd be there all weekend looking out for me, but that I was healthy and I'd be fine. She didn't seem worried about my weakness from the hospitalization. I was a little doubtful about her. She seemed both competent and knowledgeable, but she was so comfortable with my health and what I was about to do that I became suspicious. Why would she be okay with this? Why would she casually wave someone in my condition through? I expected some limitation to be imposed on me to account for my weakness.

Josh waited for me to be ready and then we followed a staff member in white through a maze of home remodeling to the room Josh had booked. It oddly seemed like the only such room in the place. It was small but dominated by a very comfortable king-sized bed and its own bathroom. Throughout the rest of the facility the bathrooms and showers were outdoor stalls or port-a-potties or in covered areas with curtains instead of doors. The private bathroom with the shower was a major luxury in this place. It turned out that the other bathrooms were less private because people would be escorted to them mid-journey and it would be important to be able to go in and get them out. Someone in mid-journey locking themselves in a bathroom or shower could be a real problem as I'd seen in the Netflix show, and I wondered how much of this layout was a direct result of that incident. We could sleep and rest here, but this room and its bathroom would be off limits during the ceremonies.

We shut ourselves away from all the others in the dark, comfortable room for an hour as the ceremony time ticked closer. Now there was no nervous chatter. The anxious creep of seconds and minutes multiplied by the void of our uncertainty was heavy enough that conversation felt like an obvious avoidance tactic. I tried to clear my head, to search again for a clear intention, but the sound of a gong outside shook me to action, and we hopped off the bed, exchanged a quick fist bump, and joined the uncertain herd, walking slightly slower than my comfortable gait towards the maloca.

Chapter 4

A Knock at the Door

The maloca door was colorful and worn, and the perfect height for my eyes to tell me I would make it under the lintel, but for the crown of my head to catch the frame with a wooden "chok." I slunk into the room rubbing my head to a few worried looks, but most of the people inside seemed too caught up in their own anxiety to notice. The wide circular building angled up like a cone to a high ring of daylight capped with a final circle of roof. Hanging from the center was a gigantic fan that slowly stirred the air. On the outer wall of the maloca were psychedelic tapestries with all kinds of vivid imagery of humanoid figures and animals mixed with cosmic swirls and stars. Thick sleeping pads spoked toward the middle with the pillows up against the tapestry walls.

Just inside the ring of mats were two large concentric circles of chairs that we began scanning, probing the social mathematics of front row versus back row, of giving people space or sliding into a tight spot. The circles of chairs were only broken by the entrance, and opposite it, a straight row of slightly larger chairs with the back row on an elevated stage. In the center of the chair circles there was a pit about three feet deep where a festooned table waited. There was an array of seemingly random ritual elements arranged purposefully across the top, from candles, to bundles of sage, to a piece of driftwood with talismans dangling from it. It reminded me of the decorations Melanie liked to discover out in the world for our house: whimsical suggestions of foreign spirituality about which we know only the sparest nibbles, but felt comforted by their benevolent suggestions.

The straight line of chairs with the riser was already filled with people in all or mostly white clothing who grinned broadly and whispered to each other with an easy intimacy and excitement as they sized up this new group of nervous wrecks. There were instruments and speakers set up behind them on the low stage edged by the raised second row of chairs, but they were out of the way and seemed like they were for later. It looked like the rings of chairs would fill up, so Josh and I tucked in next to a smallish man so that our shoulders wouldn't be cramped and exchanged names and the prevailing question between the guests, "Is it your first time?"

The room had filled to capacity with another dozen people in white that gathered in the central pit, when a woman from the group by the stage rose, microphone in hand, and introduced herself as Verena, one of the founders. After her introduction there was a lengthy program where a dozen staff members listed off the rules and passed the microphone around, each offering their story and advice to us. From the sea of information and encouragement a few things stood out. We couldn't leave once the ceremony started. We couldn't call people or have any electronic devices nearby. Never trust an Ayahuasca fart. Keep your clothes on. Don't jump in the pond.

There were many variations of the reassurance that the facilitators and volunteers and medical staff would be there to help us no matter what we needed. Also, if you lied about your medications or said you stopped taking them but didn't, you could die. Most everything about this place felt safe, but death still had a place at the little table in the middle.

From various mentions in videos and zoom sessions, Josh and I had developed a lingering fear of shitting our pants. They had just brought it up again with the "Ayahuasca farts" comment, which brought it back to the tops of our minds. It got mentioned in shows and articles, and addressed in the integration meetings, but was always tossed aside as no big deal. They said they would clean you up lovingly, and that it was all part of healing. I really didn't want to shit my pants. Josh really, really didn't want to shit his pants. I was worried that I wouldn't be able to focus on the journey if I was worrying about clothes and smells, but Josh's anxiety had taken this worry to a whole different level that I could see he was barely holding back. We had eaten light, highly digestible foods during the first half of the day, and nothing for the last eight hours. We'd each spent some time in his private bathroom making sure our guts were completely empty, but there was still this lingering fear of surprise incontinence. I did my best to stuff it down and clear my head.

Between a few of the facilitators wearing a matching logo on their shirts, a couple of the comments, and some flyers I had seen around the office, I was putting together that this place did special work with veterans suffering from PTSD. One of the detailed accounts in the Netflix show had been a veteran talking about how the medicine helped him, and they seemed to have a secondary organization within, or adjacent to, this group that did veteran's only ceremonies.

I wondered if my dad would consider something like this. As he approached eighty, his flashbacks and nightmares had been increasing. Throughout my life he'd held a diminished sense of his value that seemed to come from the Vietnam war. Between what he'd seen, the stresses of his life there, and the inequity of surviving when others didn't, his life had always carried a weight. I wondered if he might find healing here. What happened for me this weekend would probably be a deciding factor for him. If I could find healing through this door, he would probably follow me through.

After about an hour, the meeting broke up and then it was time to find our mats. Many people left the maloca to go to the separate, smaller lodges for the ceremony, but Josh and I were assigned to take our medicine in the maloca, so we just needed to claim one of the mats up against the walls and stay there. I thought it would be better to have some distance from Josh so that we wouldn't distract each other. It was possible that whoever was next to me would be just as distracting, but hopefully not knowing them would help to keep an emotional distance. *Distance for what?* To relax? None of it sounded relaxing, but there was this sense that it was private and easily interrupted. Then why were we all in a big room together? A man named Carlos with a thick Hispanic accent stood up and addressed about thirty of us that remained there. He split us into two groups each led by a facilitator where we were to begin telling our stories.

I still didn't know what to share about my intentions so I decided to talk about my sickness and being in the hospital. I said I was looking for healing, but even I could hear in my voice that I had no idea what that would look like, or how a hallucinogenic drug could mend a physical problem. The stories of the other people in the room were chilling. There was so much abuse, suicide, and violence that these people were carrying.

One man was a sniper whose targets all came to torment him each night. A woman broke down when she listed her third rape, and trailed off sobbing, unable to finish a list that seemed to go on and on. One was a firefighter who told a story of standing helpless and screaming next to the father of a teen he'd just saved, as a doctor killed the boy because he wouldn't listen to the firefighter's experience. Hearing how father's wail of anguish still torments him struck me deep, where the love for my children holds its explosive power. One woman was a veteran coming to address her traumas in the service, but then her son had taken his own life the week before, and now she was lost in that storm. Many thought of killing themselves every day. I wept several times hearing their stories, including the young veteran, Andrew, who had driven us in the cart a few hours earlier.

I was so ashamed to have put any shallow or base thoughts into my first impression of him when he suffered daily and was volunteering here because he had found such healing. I relived our 100 foot ride in the cart seeing how none of his heavy countenance had anything to do with us. But me, what had I ever suffered? I've never been to war, been raped, abused, or watched friends die in front of me. My kids are healthy. My marriage is great. My job is my dream, and every day students and their parents thank me for doing it and making their lives and families better, filling my heart.

I felt very out of place in this sanctuary of healing with only my exhaustion from my bout with Covid plaguing me. My ears rang when Carlos said, "Many of you have brought great hurt here to be healed tonight. Lean in to even the darkest things you see because healing is on the other side and the medicine wants you to find it. For those of you who are just here to see what this Ayahuasca thing is all about, *buckle up*!"

There it was. I was just along for the ride with no idea what I was doing, and this roller-coaster was slowly ticking towards the top of the first big drop. I looked over at Josh to see him nervously full of hope for healing and wondered if this was a big mistake. *Click. Click. Click.* We walked outside to the courtyard by the house to have sage smoke puffed all around our bodies ceremonially. Then they blessed the bowls holding the medicine and the white porcelain cups by spitting puffs of smoke all around them and into them, this time drawn from a dark, rolled cigar-like wrap. We walked slowly back to the maloca and the staff members carrying trays of the medicine for our group followed us in. A round tray piled with precariously balanced layers of cups around an urn of inky brown liquid in the middle. We lined up to receive our doses and took turns telling them how much we wanted. As a first timer, I was supposed to have one tablespoon since there was no way to know before taking it how much was the correct dose for me. There would be a gong a few hours into the ceremony, and if I was aware of it and my journey hadn't really kicked off, I was to go ask for more. *Click. Click. Click.*

When he poured the single tablespoon into the cup, it sloshed around thick like paint. It was heavy and oily and smelled strongly of mulch and coco. I carried the little white cup to my mat and sat waiting. All I had brought from the room was my water bottle, which I kept rearranging along with the lightweight white trash bucket that I was supposed to vomit in. They instructed us to wait to drink so we could all do it together. *Click. Click. Click.* Everyone moved so slowly and had such quiet conversations about dosage when they got to the front of the line. Internally I yearned for it to be time already, just so I could finally know something. It seemed that the next thing was to drink but the time kept ticking more and more slowly. The last person sat down. Everyone was settled and without any more fanfare the moment to drink rushed to fill my world with a tingling last gasp from my nerves.

I had heard that the taste was so awful that no one would ever use this medicine recreationally, but the chocolaty, earthy mix wasn't too bad. Definitely not tasty, but I wouldn't have any trouble keeping it down. As I settled into the post-nerves glow of commitment, soothing music began to play. Guitars, more exotic strings, and accented voices stirred along. The music was a strange variation on something you might hear during a massage, but with more deliberate strings that had a central american folk feel with asian influence. The words were sometimes in languages I didn't know that seemed to include some portuguese, hindi, and aboriginal languages, alternating with english and the little bit of spanish that I recognized. When I could understand what they were saying, it had the quality of church music. Sweet, straightforward repetitions about being made of love, and Patchamama (the Andean earth goddess), and about the familiar Christian God and Mary, and about Ayahuasca specifically. Some sounded like it was included for its tone and aligned message, but some was clearly a category of "Ayahuasca music" that I'd never heard before.

They had said that it would take thirty to forty minutes for the medicine to kick in and that we should sit up to be sure that it was all settling down in our stomachs. We weren't to drink much water since it would likely be coming up in a few minutes. Some was necessary to wash all the sticky medicine out of the cup and then to get the taste out of my mouth. My urgency for everything to start abated despite the new phase of waiting. Now I was alone with the agent of change instead of its intermediaries, watching and waiting for mystical signs, and a hopeful curiosity set in. I sat cross legged with my eyes closed and my hands resting on my legs. I turned my thoughts inward and focused on letting go of my own lack of intention and the inadequacy of my suffering. I came to a weary gratitude through the back door.

It began with a feeling of unease and movement. I had switched from sitting up cross-legged to lying on my mat as my back had grown tired. Now there was a sense of something shifting in my stomach. I pulled myself back to sitting and made sure I knew where the bucket was. Something definitely felt off. I looked around to see if I was beginning to hallucinate, but besides the trippy tapestries, nothing seemed out of place. The music was definitely becoming more energetic and mystical, with tribal South American drumming taking the place of gentler flutes and strings. The lyrics spoke about healing, rising, mother Aya. Was I just reacting to the buildup of the music? I didn't like the idea that this experience was just being curated by groovy jungle music and the waving, psychedelic tapestries, but I was also feeling drawn in by them. It all sounded and looked hokey, but was also scratching at something deep down.

It was hard to tell how much time had passed. Maybe thirty minutes? I stayed seated to see if my stomach would feel more comfortable, but something was definitely going on that wasn't just vibrations in the music. It developed into a buzzing in my torso and a squirming in my jaw. Was it time to throw up? It really wasn't clear to me. No one else in the room had thrown up, so I spent a minute watching everyone else to see if they seemed to be under the effect. Some were rocking back and forth, and a few were tossing on the mats.

More time passed and sounds of vomiting convulsions began breaking the surging upward movement of the music. Was the music timed to get louder so that it would drown out some of the sounds? It was mostly the sounds of heaving and spitting since nobody had any food in their stomachs. I wondered again if my body was just taking cues from the sounds and the tapestries rather than actually needing to throw up. The churning feeling in my torso wasn't clearly one thing or another. Lying back down and closing my eyes I tried to quiet my body and breathe.

Things were definitely happening now. I was seeing swirling shapes that I couldn't make out. I would open my eyes to see if I was really hallucinating and everything would be as it had been. If it was only when my eyes were closed, was it hallucination or just imagination? As the churning discomfort lodged itself closer to my stomach, I finally decided to try and throw up. Hopefully that would ease some of the distractions in my body and let me focus on what

I was seeing. Dragging myself up was harder than it should have been. It wasn't unlike the helplessness of having a bad fever, but I didn't have any heat discomfort. I was feeling less connected to my body and the mechanics of movement felt far away. I willed myself up by remembering that moving isn't hard for me and leaning into my body's memory of how to do it. The movements were wavy and foreign but I trusted them to move me.

Perched over the white bucket on my hands and knees, I felt like a silverback gorilla. My knuckles curled into the mat and my lower back stretched long and powerful. I let that strong feeling pass through me and liked it. I tried to clench my stomach muscles to throw up, but nothing came. Nothing except that good strong ape feeling. I felt like flexing my torso to connect more with that feeling and began huffing at the bucket, feeling my apeness. It was hard to tell how long I had been flexing and huffing that way when one of the volunteers laid a hand on my shoulder with the lightest touch and whispered in my ear.

"Don't try so hard. Just let it happen." I relaxed my body and just felt the unease moving through me. Then my body heaved on its own. This feeling I knew. It was definitely coming up. I don't throw up quietly. I don't mean to make a lot of noise, but when I retch, it's like I am yelling through each heave. There's such a broad volume of me to contract that all the air is coming out with it and it takes a side trip past my vocal cords.

The tremendous heaves brought back the tablespoon of medicine and the few sips of water but little else. The light hummus and lettuce wraps from the office, which were the only food I had eaten since our equally light lunch, had long since digested. Looking onto the bucket at the little splatters of brown, they seemed to swirl and crawl like ants around the bucket. Ok, so I was definitely hallucinating a little. I lay back down, feeling much more comfortable with the nausea spent and gone, and waited for visions. Time twirled by. There was a lot more swirling. Maybe there was a serpent or dragon sifting in the darkness. It seemed like a cool and powerful thing to see, but I could feel myself interpreting and searching for meaning in it. Could I be seeing it just because I was searching for it?

Something was definitely churning around in the dark of my eyelids, but any time I opened my eyes it all went away and there was just the room. People were writhing and moaning. Tapestries surged and shifted. Sometimes there seemed to be live musicians playing the rhythmic jungle music and other times it was clearly playing from a stereo. I felt out of touch with my body. From time to time I wondered if I had shit myself. Had I? *How would I know?* It was really hard to feel clear signals from my hands to distinguish soiled shorts from clean, but I didn't smell anything. When my eyes were open, I regularly saw one of the volunteers in white walk slowly by. He was a powerful man with long, shaggy hair and beard, and bright, caring eyes. He looked over us all with a kind, heavy gaze that showered me with quiet peace.

When the gong sounded and the music paused, the effects were noticeably waning. I tested my ability to sit up and stand, and I made it to my wobbly but working feet. They had said before that if I could stand up then I wasn't fully in the journey and should have more medicine. I made my way to the much smaller line waiting for another cup. I was tired and felt off kilter, but nothing really noteworthy had happened besides a lot of confusing cross-talk and swirls in my head. All around people were moaning, writhing, and talking to things that weren't there. The man with the cups and medicine looked at me expectantly.

"I'm not really getting there," I said wearily.

"How much did you have?" he said very gently with wide,

probing eyes.

"Just one. It's my first time."

"Let's do one more and see where that gets you," he said clinically.

I returned to my mat with the cup and repeated the earthy drinking, rinsing, and washing down. As I sat and waited again I could feel that the first dose had mostly worn off, leaving weariness but no more movement or hallucinations. The next thirty minutes followed the pattern of the first round with the vibrations in my body picking back up. When the uneasiness built to the point where I felt throwing up was the way out of the twisting discomfort, I did so, remembering to relax and let gravity and my body carry me to the noisy vomiting. Over the next hour or so, more cloudy visions came to my mind. There was a great heart made of metal encased in metal bands. The swirling, serpentine shape danced at the edge of my perception but never became clear. I wanted to draw lines of meaning between the animals I was seeing and feeling and the metal heart. It really seemed to have something to do with me, but I was just guessing into the wind and the effect was fading again, leaving a bitingly painful headache in its wake.

When I decided that nothing more was going to happen, I looked around and saw that about half of the people had left, others were sitting up, and some were asleep on their mats. I remembered a second gong a little while earlier and put together that it had signaled the closing of the ceremony. I got up carefully on still wobbly legs and picked up my water bottle. The man with the shaggy beard appeared at my side as if he'd been behind me the whole time. Standing, I was surprised to find that I was taller than him.

"How 'ya doin' there, brother?" he whispered close to my face as his hands hovered near my back and arm like an aura of support.

"Thanks for looking over me." I said, nodding slowly. "You were a real guardian angel."

"It's my true pleasure. Are you good to walk?" he asked as I took a few steps. They felt shaky but if I didn't think too much about them, I was pretty sure I'd get back to our room alright. He didn't seem to think so because he stayed with me all the way, and guided me instead to the office, where there were some light snacks of carrot sticks and veggie chips. We'd have no more than this quickly digestible fare since we were going to take more medicine in the morning. Anything that we ate had to be completely out of our systems by then. After snacking and leaning on the wall of the kitchen where I felt very closed in by the low ceiling and hallway, I walked back out into the openness of night on steadier legs. There was a large fire in the middle of the courtyard. People were staring at it, walking slowly in all directions, and sitting in chairs talking. I wove through them and past the porch to the room Josh and I were sharing, drinking the remainder of my water bottle. I opened the door quietly, but it was empty. I visited the bathroom with little result besides confirming that my underwear was clean. I brushed my teeth before climbing into the comfortable bed. I was tired, but my mind still swirled with questions about what I'd felt and seen. It was like there were connections to be made but I didn't have all the information to pull the parts together. They were a few scattered links from a very long chain.

Josh came in a while later but I pretended to be asleep. I was afraid that talking would wake me all the way back up and I desperately needed to sleep. I was painfully weary but my mind just wouldn't let go of me. It wasn't a tyranny of thoughts or questions, but a mental tossing and turning like a fever had a hold of me. Josh climbed quietly into bed and turned on his noise machine. Surely the white noise would push me past my busy, turning mind, past the headache, past the soreness in my neck and back from all the contorting and vomiting, but it was a long night of mental squirming with a few brief naps mixed in.

Chapter 5

New Life

In the morning, lying half awake, I saw Josh stirring and lifted myself up so he could see I wasn't sleeping. He didn't look rested either. He looked over at me and said, "Man, I did not sleep at all last night."

"What? I thought you were out. I was trying not to wake you. I don't think I slept more than an hour." His face lit up and his weariness scattered, replaced by solidarity.

"Oh, man! We should've just stayed up talking. How long do we have before we're supposed to do it again?"

"I think a couple of hours. There's a yoga session first that I want to do. My muscles are not happy after all that."

We tried to relate to each other what had happened the night before, but for both of us the experience was cloudy and incomplete. There were little details that we could stretch to draw meaning out of, but it felt like making up new constellations of stars and assigning them purposes. Arbitrary connections between abstract observations. I did have the feeling that going back in might bring me back into the experience where I left off and bring some answers. Taking two tablespoons two hours apart seemed to bring me to the edge, then back out, then to the edge again without getting in. *In where?* Where was I supposed to be getting? I hadn't heard any voices. No great guiding vision had appeared. Just a lot of weird animal feelings probably suggested by the music and tapestries.

We walked together back out into the open air of the court-yard, where similarly taxed and weary people sat, or talked quietly, or walked slowly to no particular place. It was like watching people re-emerging into the rubble strewn streets after a massive earth-quake, but all the devastation was internal. We crossed out of the main house area, past the maloca and across the gravel driveway into the trees, following a coalescence of people heading tenderly that way. I was carrying my water bottle but wasn't wearing shoes. The gravel under my feet was painful, but my feet were hardened from decades of martial arts training so I just tried to move smoothly. Josh did the gravel dance to the other side of the driveway where the rocks yielded to sand. He hammed it up a bit when he saw I was trying to walk normally. He tossed out some good natured ribbing about being a hard-ass martial artist, but his reflexive comedy felt like it was coming from a little farther off than normal.

Yoga was good. My body really needed to stretch. The inverted poses brought some relief to my head and neck. The class was held in a grove of live oaks with branches that swirled overhead and craned down to the ground all around. At the end they said that if we were doing the daytime ceremony we could stay since it would be held there. I liked the sound of that. The twisting trees had a lot to say, and I liked the idea of trying the ceremony again in their presence.

The group ambled in over the next half hour. I found that I was in a relaxed state of weariness without the anxious anticipation of the night before. I picked a woven carpet on fairly level ground, sorting the surface out the way I would the ground cloth for my tent. There were roots and debris here and there, so I cleaned up a level spot and sat with my weary half-thoughts. As sleep deprived participants shuffled in and looked for mats and spots among the trees and clearing, volunteers and staff in white set up a line of chairs behind a table where they gently placed the cups and medicine. They sifted through the gathered participants, giving each other hugs, and finishing the setup.

"Hello, friends," came Carlos' steady, playful voice. "Last night, you met Mama for the first time. This afternoon, you'll take her on a date." As I looked around, I could see people taking this introduction in a variety of ways. Some smiled and nodded, some sat looking between their feet at the mat, while some had animated reactions and whoops that struck me as a bit performative. Carlos seemed to suggest that we had been through a concrete experience last night and this would be the evolution and somehow more intimate. I couldn't figure out what that meant for my experience. I was really hoping that our "date" would involve some clarification.

"Since you've all felt the medicine work inside you now, you can take as much as you like. There won't be a booster, but remember that the medicine you drank last night is still at work in you, so you won't need as much for the same effect." I had been planning on having two tablespoons to see if that would take me across the line, but the idea of last night's doses lingering in me made me less sure. The effects had seemed to fade after a few hours so the thought of them still having a measurable effect called for some recalculation. We lined up as before and waited for our turn to receive a cup. As I waited I bounced back and forth in my mind about how much I should have. At the front of the line as I was bathed in sage smoke, I could hear that people were talking out their dosage plans when they got to the front of the line, so I availed myself of the facilitator's experience.

"I did one last night and didn't get there, so I did one more as a booster and just got close again."

The very young woman in all white who was waiting with a cup for me said, "What do you think about one and a half? It's already in your system, so that would probably be like taking two together last night."

"That sounds right," I agreed. She turned to the bowl of brown murk and spooned a smaller scoop three times into the cup. She turned back to me and closed her eyes, silently blessing the medicine.

"Safe journey, friend." She kept her eyes patiently on mine until I committed to turning away and going back to my mat. The gentle stringy music was already playing. I sat for a few minutes as everyone negotiated doses and blessings, thinking about what was to come and how different this bright, open, natural setting was from the dark cavern of the night before.

We all drank together. I waited through the slightly familiar territory of the earthy drink, the sitting, and waiting for the unease. I focused on trying to bring back the imagery of the night before so that I could pick up where I left off and try to make sense of what I had seen. The breeze and the trees and the sprinkles of sunlight through the expansive depths of the live oaks was a peaceful under-layment for my weary waiting.

The sensation built and shifted, and I became hyper-aware of the texture of the sandy soil, the tiny gnats that swirled about and touched down on my skin from time to time. I had to ask myself if I wanted to be bothered by those bits of nature reaching out to me. I could start waving and brushing them away if I wanted to, but it felt like surrendering to a state of frustration and negativity. I remembered sitting on the Appalachian Trail months into the hike. I was taking a break and noticing that the flies and ants and dirt felt at home on my flesh. How comfortable I felt on the earth, being part of nature. I decided that I would be one with the gnats and sand among the lazy branches of the live oak, and I was.

The inner movements came on stronger when they finally came.

It felt like this time maybe I wouldn't throw up. Like I was meant to keep it with me to make sure enough of it got into my — no, never mind. Here it came. I got up to my hands and knees quickly and positioned myself over the bucket. Opening my eyes and navigating the space of the world outside of my thoughts brought me into an awareness of the other people, the music driving towards some primal crescendo, people in white moving umbrellas to shade journeyers from the migrating sun and spritzing people with cool scented water. I didn't notice anyone else throwing up yet but it was definitely my time. Again I loudly heaved the inky brown muck into the clean white bucket. It looked so foul there, full of swirling darkness, and mucous, and sparks, and fire. It felt good to have something so ugly out of my body. I swallowed several mouthfuls of water. First to get the bilious taste from my mouth, and then to enjoy the sharp clarity of the water's primal refreshment. An intimate breeze tickled the sweat on my face and neck, and I felt my skin take a deep breath.

Falling back to the mat with a feeling of great accomplishment, I wondered if it was over. The work of purging the darkness had a feeling of completion to it. I felt waves of peace and love flow over me and drifted in its current, feeling my stomach and chest with my fingers. As I relaxed, the space around me started to change. There was a bright white and pink expanse emerging in every direction. It glowed with warmth and swirled with love. I floated in that pulsing, loving energy, just feeling grateful and held. Waves of vibration flowed around me and through me, and I could shape it like dust motes with my hands. I could match the vibration by humming, and different tones warmed and pulsed in different parts of my body and in the space around me.

I became aware of another being in the space with me. I knew that I was on the ground between trees surrounded by dozens of people, but this feeling, these vibrations, this other being, were not "out there" with the world. They were in another space with me. If I opened my eyes I saw gentle people dressed in white among tangled tree branches chasing the sunlight. When my eyes closed I was in a world of pink and white and red, love and vibration and magical energy, and there was someone else there. There was something raw and unformed about the other. I was reluctant to look right at it but I could also feel a great responsibility around it, and eventually pulled myself from the free-flowing wash of love to see who it was that was there with me.

It was hard to understand, all blurry and bulbous, with swirling currents of loving energy and possibility dancing around it like swarms of splendor flies. As I drew closer, the swirling energies seemed afraid of me and backed away, attaching and grasping at the figure, but staying on the side opposite me. It dawned on me that the figure was an embryo, but massive, nearly filling the space. I looked back around in a wash of realization as I recognized my chamber as the inside of a womb, netted with red veins coursing with living blood. Warm light shone through the skin and there was movement outside as life went on for the mother.

I investigated the embryo more closely and the energies that swirled around it. There were no recognizable features to make out on its face. I looked more closely at the swirling possibilities, and by reaching out to them, I could call them and feel them in my hands. They had softened towards me, and no longer hid from me, though their focus was on the embryo. They contained the joys and pains of a life to come. Most were healthy formative troubles and joys, but some were hurtful, or dangerous, or malforming. I began to see individuals wrapped up in these energetic futures, and in a flash, knew where I was and who this was. It was Chris and Ming's baby! They had been trying for a baby for a while and had just recently told people that they were pregnant after Melanie had lent them her Chinese fertility scroll. I was in Ming's womb. It all became clear to me, how I could move the energy with my hands and my voice and what that meant here. I already knew that I would be a part of this kid's life someday, but there was important work to do here and now, preparing the way for him and giving him the best possible chance in life by arranging these energies as best I could.

For the next few hours, I rebuilt the energy around this youngest member of my community. I fought and absorbed everything that would hurt him in ways that would break his health or his mind or his spirit. I arranged the hard things so that they would be in balance with the joys. I could feel his unformed consciousness beginning to relax in my commitment. I whispered to him about those hard things, and how I needed to leave them in place because of how they would make him know himself. I whispered to him about joy and how I'd connected it to love and gratitude so that he could find those things more easily when they were near. I made his reality balanced and stable and protected, and then I danced around him as I felt the music around me, and then the trees came back, and then the bright space was only a memory and I looked up at my hands from where I was lying on the ground. I was still able to channel some energy in the sunlight between the live oaks, so I played with the music as it flowed through my fingers, and gradually the world came into hardened focus, and I was just humming and feeling the vibration of my lungs travel through my body to my hands. I was sweaty and a little sunburned. My arms and legs were specked with sandy soil and crushed leaves.

One by one my limbs and senses checked in and seemed to be working, though I still felt wrung out and the signals weren't connecting smoothly enough to move my legs in a coordinated way. "What the hell was that about?" I thought as I dropped my arms back down to the mat. I hadn't been thinking about their baby or pregnancy at all. What happened to Mama Ayahuasca picking up the exploration from last night? What kind of date was that? I felt powerfully good, though. Warm. Loving. Mighty. Hungry. I hadn't had more than a couple of bites for more than a day now and had thrown up three times. We were going to be allowed brothy stew for lunch and I wrangled my misaligned limbs and misfiring senses to reach my feet. I took a few breaths, making sure I was steady, my movement drawing the attention of a slender girl in white with elf ears on. Like the man last night, she floated around me protectively until she was sure I wasn't going to walk into a tree.

"What were you doing back there with your hands?" She asked playfully, but without jest.

"Baby magic," I said, leaving her to wonder at what that was. Maybe she already knew. It might be standard Ayahuasca fare.

I drifted lightly through the ceremonial grounds. My weariness was compounded by a second journey following a night without sleep. My already weakened body was further drained and pained, but my heart was very light and unfettered. Through the trees and across the gravel road I saw my guardian from the night before. He was still smaller than my image of him, but his eyes were just as bright. He realized I was heading over to him before I did and looked up at me with loving anticipation like a father waiting to hear if I'd passed my driving test.

"How was your journey, brother?" he said with genuine interest, putting down his clipboard and turning to face me fully. Without thinking, I kept walking and reached out to hug him, and his arms scooped under mine in an immediate, heartfelt hug.

"I'm real good." I said. I could feel his broad smile break out against my neck through his bushy beard. "What's your name?" I asked sleepily as I pulled away.

"I'm Brandon."

"I like you a lot, man." I said, leaving one hand on his shoulder. "The goodness in you shines real bright."

"I <u>love</u> you, brother," he said, making direct and deep eye contact. It occurred to some part of me that these were strong words and a lot of intimacy with a man I'd barely met. Normally there would be so many swirling thoughts about expectations, and his perception, and norms. I couldn't feel any of that now. All I felt was the need to express a truth to a human and to share some of the love I felt with him. I could sense no hesitation or static in him, either.

Interesting.

Chapter 6

A Still Turning Road

The brothy vegetable soup tasted like life. It danced and evolved in my mouth with complex flavor and texture, though part of my mind felt like reminding me that it was just a decent veggie soup magnified by hunger and exhaustion. My throat was raw from the vomiting, and the muscles of my neck and back were strained. I sat with Josh and the guy Pete who'd shared the car from the airport with us. Everyone looked exhausted, but also their eyes were easy and unguarded. Women who had been sharp-dressed and made-up in the office yesterday afternoon as we waited for our checkups, now had natural morning faces as they curled in chairs with sweat pants and wrinkled t-shirts.

As we gently checked on each other, there was so little fear about judgment. It wasn't just that we were all too tired to care. Walls were crumbling and we felt much more safe and human in the bald truth of our stories. Pete hadn't had sex with his girlfriend before getting on the plane. He was a gay man and he and his partner were fighting and separated. The need for the protective story shields was breaking down. That interaction at the airport the day before didn't feel like a lie to me. It was part of his story and part of his journey, no less necessary than the other rungs on the ladder towards healing.

In addition to a warm, shared openness about our personal truths, I found myself highly attuned to movement in the hearts of those around me. I normally sense people's feelings as a faint signal past their words and body language. Now I felt like I was climbing inside each person I spoke to with all of my attention. I didn't need to have a solution, just to hold something heavy with them for a while. Even more unusual was the number of people who were open and willing to accept help on such a personal level. As the son of a combat veteran, I spoke to a combat veteran who was in danger of losing his son and family. I was able to share about growing up with a suffering veteran father, and he was able to hear in a way that wouldn't have been possible the day before.

After a couple of hours we were called back to the maloca for integration. I had heard facilitators say that the work starts on the mat but really gets implemented during integration. It was a light therapy session with everyone that had shared their stories in my group the day before. Now as each person shared what the first sessions with the medicine had yielded, we looked into where everyone's journey was carrying them next. Each person's suffering was creeping out past the story they thought they could tell, and into the open. For many, what they'd encountered had been painful and difficult, traumas they knew well and were taking the next steps to push through. Some shared stories of relief and healing from some part of what troubled them. It seemed like it was generally hard to contain what they'd experienced in words, but a common theme was that they received the message that they were loved and important in a way they hadn't been able to hear before.

I shared my realization that I was just along for the ride and the wild vision of the womb that came from out of nowhere. The facilitator was challenging us to dig a little deeper as we worked to integrate what we were learning and make actionable items out of our new perspective. He said it was like going to the top of a skyscraper and seeing everything clearly laid out before you, then getting brought back down to street level and trying to hold on to that higher view. He asked me a few probing questions about my illness to see if there was a connection to the womb, but settled with "We'll see where She wants to take you tonight."

I was listening to the other participants' stories and wondering at what was possible. I didn't know these people, but I didn't doubt that they were searching and truthful. One woman told how the whole first night, Aya had shown her that she was a beautiful queen and showed all the people and lands stretched out before her. It sounded corny and self-aggrandizing, but she wept with joy and relief as she talked about it. What sounded silly rang with the sacred, her tears reframing my vision. As she recounted the second session a terrified look came over her as she told us that Aya had shown her the queen vision again but had made her turn around to see that there was a great war, and as queen, it was her responsibility to lead. She seemed genuinely overwhelmed.

Almost everyone spoke of their experience of the medicine as an encounter with something feminine. Besides the femininity of a womb, I hadn't really experienced something clearly male or female. Almost everyone else referred to Ayahuasca as "She" or "Mama." As the integration closed, there was about an hour until the last time we would drink this weekend. I wasn't sure where Josh was, so I sat on a swing by the pond and thought about the weekend. My experience during the daytime ceremony was nice, and supposedly the medicine was building up in my system, so I thought I'd try one tablespoon again. It was the same as the amount that didn't do it for me the night before, but maybe now it would be like taking one and a half and I could have another interesting journey like at the daytime ceremony. Maybe I would experience something about myself and my own healing this time.

Josh found me as I was going towards the courtyard for the smoke cleanse. He was getting the color of his wristband changed. I approached him and waited for him to speak.

"I've decided that I'm not going to drink tonight. This has all been good, but I'm wiped out and that way I can actually get a night of sleep and help you on the flight back." Our flight left in the morning so we'd actually have to slip out before all of the closing ceremonies were done. I nodded as Josh reached out and we shared a warm hug. "How are you holding up?"

"I'm pretty tired," I said, "but actually really clear in my mind. It's hard to explain. I hope I can get more sleep tonight, too."

The line-up for the smoke cleanse and the thirty minutes of quiet ritual that led up to the final session of the weekend had begun. I walked through the process with a weary body and a focused mind. I got my cup with one tablespoon. They checked in to be sure if that would be enough and I explained my thinking. There would be another chance for a booster after two hours if one didn't do it. I sat on the edge of my mat with the cup and my water bottle nearby. I wouldn't need the bucket for a while.

An hour later when the medicine started to take hold, I got the uneasiness, some buzzing, eventually vomiting, but this time I didn't launch off on any mystical journey. The room shifted, people writhed, but I was only an uncomfortable guy on a mat. Swirls worked their way through my mind, but when my eyes were open I was just in a room with groovy tribal music. I knew the time for the booster was approaching, but I was exhausted and didn't want a repeat of the first night. My head was hurting, probably from the strain in my neck and back from all the vomiting. I was so exhausted. I just wanted to sleep. When the bell came, I let it go by, watching those that wanted to go deeper line up for more.

I spent an uncomfortable span of hours on the mat since we couldn't leave before the ritual ended. I tried to relax and rest, focusing on breathing into the muscles in my neck to make them let go. I drifted in and out of the dreamlike waking that had gone on the whole night before until the gong sounded again and we could finally leave the space. I pulled myself up to my much more sturdy feet and carried my water bottle back to Josh's room. He stirred when I came in and asked how I was doing. When I told him about my headache, he offered me some pain killers and some melatonin to help me sleep. It was still a difficult night, but I got a little sleep here and there.

In the morning there was a breakfast of pancakes, fruit, cereal, and granola. I shoveled the filling foods into my stomach and went back for more. Since Josh had opted out of the last ceremony, he'd been able to eat a real dinner the night before and was refreshed, but this was the first substantial meal I'd had in two days. I was stumbling through a fog of exhaustion. Everyone gathered in the maloca for a final ceremony. I was open and raw. The music moved me emotionally, but my mind couldn't really hang on to which emotions were moving. After a few minutes, Josh said the Uber was almost there and we needed to go out front to meet it. We slipped out quietly and were on our way to the airport without any good-byes or blessings. I wanted to sleep in the car but couldn't. Storm clouds gathered along the drive. Josh dragged me through security lines, walkways, and trams to the concourse where we would wait for our flight.

When we got word of the delay for the storm, I was too tired to care, but the delay turned out to be five hours. All morning and into the afternoon, exhausted kids and their families kept piling into the Orlando airport wearing all of their Disney and Star Wars and Harry Potter outfits with Covid masks on top. They were heavily laden with merchandise from theme parks and the weariness of a week of making memories and spending money. The air got thicker and thicker with the rained on, masked, wailing children and their scolding parents. Their despair smelled like wet mouse ears and stale butterbeer. The space kept compressing as seats ran out and all the standing room dried up. More would come in but none would get out. I was absolutely miserable, listing side to side. Waves of pain and exhaustion pushed to take me anywhere else. Josh was comforting, but even his humor and positivity wasn't enough to counter my unanswerable fatigue.

By the time I got home to my comfortable bed and the familiar smells of home and family late that night, I could only give Melanie five minutes of recap before draining into the arms of sleep. It had been interesting, but I didn't think I'd ever want to do it again.

Chapter 7

How Now?

After catching up on sleep, I definitely felt much better. Tasting coffee and non-dieta food again made my stomach and mind surge. The heartburn was back, but so were my routines. There was a certain amount of afterglow from the weekend which must have been chemical, since, aside from the visit with Chris and Ming's Baby, I couldn't make much sense of anything I'd seen or felt. Josh felt enormous relief from his anxiety. In the following weeks he was speaking up in uncomfortable situations more easily, and feeling far less weight on his shoulders day to day. He started to talk about another trip but I was not feeling the need to go through all of that again. While I felt oddly refreshed, it felt more to me like the relief of getting out of a chokehold. The weekend was hard and it was a relief to be done.

Some of our friends were interested in trying it after seeing how much less anxious Josh had become. Darrick, who was going through a hard divorce wanted to seek some relief there, and my father was curious but hesitant. I'd learned more and talked to him about the non-profit that would pay for veterans with PTSD to come for a veterans-only ceremony. They highlighted that the medicine was particularly potent in treating PTSD in veterans and as soon as I asked, were eager to help him fly down. My father's lifelong struggle with his PTSD from the Vietnam war had been a constant feature of my life with him. It had seemed to lessen as I grew older, perhaps because it became less raw, perhaps because my life stood up on its own and I was no longer in tune with it. In either case, it had been resurfacing over the last few years. My friend Lewis, who was a psychiatrist for the VA had told me that veterans lose some of their ability to keep that trauma at bay as they age.

Josh and Darrick planned on going again in July, and I decided to push my dad to go with them since one of the veteran's-only events was that weekend. I still wasn't feeling any changes personally, but I was impressed by the change in Josh, and by how many veterans there seemed to find relief. Their choice of the end of July gave me a definite excuse not to go, or even entertain the possibility when I could tell my dad would be more comfortable if I was there. That was when Chris and Ming's baby was due, and I wanted him to be able to take time off for it, so I had to be on call to cover for him at the dojo.

I had mentioned to Chris on a phone call that I'd had a vision of being in his wife's womb with the baby. When I saw her next in the dojo, heading onto the mat for a workout, she met me with a dramatically raised eyebrow.

"So? How's my womb looking on the inside?" She said with her signature sarcasm.

"Glorious!" I replied, and tried to give her a quick recap of the vision. I expected her to just respond, "Cool!" but she wanted me to come over and tell her and Chris all about it. At their house later, I told them everything I could remember and had written down. They wanted to know exactly what time it was so they could see if the shapes I was seeing on the outside matched where they were. They'd been at a park, which matched the warm lights and sounds I remembered, but there wasn't much to prove. I could feel them wanting to connect to this vivid experience I'd had, but it swirled about them rather than staying still so that they could grab it. She wanted to remember a strange feeling from while I was in my vision, but nothing in particular had stood out for her. We all just wondered at how the baby might respond to me, and if we'd be particularly close, or if he'd ever remember anything about my visitation.

I continued my work with physical recovery. Weekly there was more progress on the treadmill, but if I pushed too hard, I would have another painful episode with my nerves. By May I was able to teach some of my martial arts classes again, but would get dizzy and short of breath if I did too much. My feet were starting to ache all the time and the treadmill was getting harder to keep up with. Hitting the punching bags was no better. Every way I pushed to regain my fitness left me injured or incapacitated in some fashion. Then my recovery would backslide even more while waiting to heal from a training injury. Everything about me was fragile in a way that my body normally was not.

One day in June, Melanie offered me her weekly swimming lesson to try. I was reluctant to go to another location to exercise since I was surrounded by exercise at work. I had also never learned the formal techniques of swimming. I was still a dog-paddler. When I tried it, though, it was a perfect fit. Coach Juliana was a tiny, loud, Brazilian woman who had a great sense for how hard she could push me. I was concerned about the possibility of drowning since exertion made me dizzy and taking deep breaths was tough even out of the water. After being pushed to my limit each session, though, none of my joints or extremities were in pain. I was exhausted and worked-out, but it was all just muscular exertion without the impact of my heavy body on any surface. I was also able to push my limits without triggering a nerve pain attack. I couldn't be sure what the difference was, but it was working and I was making new progress.

There had been news stories about people having heart attacks in the months after leaving the hospital with Covid, so before continuing to push hard to recover my fitness, I had my heart checked out. It turned out to be in great shape, so with the confidence that it wouldn't give out from being pushed, I did just that. I started many laps by telling myself, "Push like it's ok to die on this lap," trusting that I could do more than it felt like I could. I built a routine of swimming three times a week and measuring progress, and the numbers kept getting better. It was taking months instead of weeks to recover, but it was steady, and it looked like I might be half way back to normal.

Chapter 8

Quynh

My teacher Quynh would call from Florida to check on me every couple of months. Ever since I'd moved to Arkansas twelve years earlier, he'd made a point to come visit each year. Quynh Ngo had been the leader of Cuong Nhu (our martial art style) ever since his father, the style's founder, Dong Ngo, had passed away in 2000. Our style was not a well known, sprawling martial art with hundreds of schools. There were just a few dozen schools around the world with only a handful teaching more than a hundred students. Moving to a new town and taking out a loan to start a Cuong Nhu school from scratch as my livelihood was an uncommon feat to attempt, and Quynh began to give a lot of attention to me and my school as our success or failure could color how others thought about taking risks to spread the style in the future. Each year when he visited he would re-energize me, help us with vital improvement, lift up my students, and get to know them all as family.

As my school began to succeed, testing me for higher ranks to encourage others to start schools became a new priority. He wanted to test me publicly at our annual international gathering since I was still young enough to be at the peak of my physical abilities and put on a show. He had most recently asked me to test in 2019 for fifth degree black belt, but since I was working non-stop to remodel our new building, we agreed I would have time to put on a much better show if we waited until the next year. He had been flying out to work with me on a special demonstration every few months since then, and we had been ready to put on an eye-popping show for our fellow stylists in 2020 before everything shut down.

He knew the pandemic was a huge strain and a threat to the existence of our school. My getting sick seemed to him like a bump in the road, easily moved past. He was looking for a time to come out to Arkansas and get me fired up and back up to speed for my test. He was ever optimistic and undeterred by the risks of pandemic travel. He mostly wanted for me to keep my spirits up and get back on track for our big show. I had to tell him I was still far from being able to work on it.

"How about your forms?" he probed over the phone. "How do you feel after doing Bo 6?" The thought of the athletic staff fighting form that he'd created in his youth as a demonstration made my lungs constrict and I had a little chuckle at the thought.

"Man, I couldn't even come close to finishing Bo 6."

"Seriously? What about Empi." I imagined running through the shorter but still athletic form, and saw myself collapsing after a few of the big leaps. The name didn't translate to "Flying Swallow" for no reason.

"No. If I do more than walk through any form, I hit a wall and have to sit down."

"Daaaamn. Man, I might have to get that vaccine. That sounds rough."

"You haven't got it yet? Man, please do. It's no joke. That was one of the worst things I've been through." I could sense him wrestling with it.

"I know a lot of people who've gotten the virus, and nobody's gotten really sick except you and a couple of really old people." It stung to group me with the feeble, but that had been my thought before I got sick as well. I also knew Quynh thought he was invincible. I'd called to check on him when a big hurricane hit Florida, and he answered from outside in his back yard that he wasn't afraid of hurricanes since he knew rising block. He was only half kidding that he would stop a falling branch with his arm using a karate technique. Maybe not even half.

"Yeah, one of my cousins had to go to the hospital for a couple days, but most people I know just had it like a flu."

"So why do you think it hit you so hard?" This was not the way he liked to talk about things. I could hear him stretching his lips and nose in a grimace. Normally we only talked about what we would do and how we could do it. Any time we had to talk about why things couldn't be done was a break from our rhythm.

"Man, I wish I knew."

"Can you eat ok?" He often brought things back to food.

"Yeah, I'm eating fine. I lost about twenty pounds in the hospital, but my appetite is back now." I had returned to cooking and even held to some aspects of the dieta for a while, but my eating habits had mostly returned to normal.

"That's good man! You keep that weight off and it's like a jump start. If you're eating then I know you're gonna' be fine." My weight had returned to normal within the first month of getting out of the hospital, but I just went back to talking about my progress.

"I'm getting stronger every week. Hopefully by the Fall I'll be ready to have you out and I can get back up to speed."

I could tell he was disappointed. I hated that, since he had been so excited for me to put on a show for all of Cuong Nhu the year before. He had been my biggest cheerleader and wanted me to show the gathered martial art style something it had never seen before at our annual gathering. Now I was miles from attempting the challenge he had put before me; a test that I had been so ready for a year earlier.

63

I kept pushing to recover my strength. I was such a beginner at swimming that it was easy to see improvement. Every week I could swim farther without stopping. I could go faster. I could swim longer. I was a long way from being strong, but I was in motion with direction. It was helping me come back to train, too. I was pushing to finish the athletic forms at more than walking speed. I was pushing to spar with my students. Everyone was helpful and encouraging but there was still so far to go.

As July ended and kids were about to go back to school for the first time in a year and a half, I got a call from Robert. Robert and Elizabeth were two married masters in Cuong Nhu living in North Carolina and had been my closest mentors over the last twenty years, even before I moved to Little Rock. Robert's voice was softer and pained. It felt like he was carrying a weight too fragile to drop.

"Hey, man. You know more about being sick with Covid than anybody I know. I got a buddy who doesn't want to go into the hospital and I don't know how serious it is. A few months ago when you were telling me about being sick, what was your blood oxygen level when you said the doctor told you to check-in to the hospital?"

"It was at 91. They said that normally they'd wait until it was below 90, but since I'm athletic, they thought 91 was concerning enough. How low is your friend's?"

"It's at 65."

"Man, they need to be there as soon as they can. I can't imagine it being so low. Are they otherwise healthy? How old?" I asked, but I could already feel what he was talking his way around to saying. I could hear him aching through the words as they finally came.

"It's Quynh. Man, this could be really bad." I felt a chill as the words broke from a guess to reality.

"Did he get vaccinated?"

"I don't think so. I don't know."

"After I told him about my fight with the virus, he said he was going to get it!"

"Yeah, but his sister got the virus, and as much as she struggles with her health, she didn't even have symptoms. He said something to me about his super-genes."

"Well either way, he needs to be in the hospital right now."

When he was taken in, they put him on a ventilator as soon as they could. He was a powerful man with a healthy body and an indomitable spirit, and he lasted 45 days. When his brother called me to tell me he was gone, I was on my way back to the dojo from the pool. When I arrived, the dojo was empty and dark, and I began calling all my black belts one by one to tell them. One of the things I most valued about Quynh was that he had made my people his people. He had touched all of their lives and left his mark and I needed them to hear about his loss from me before they heard it any other way.

In the middle of phone calls and commiserate weeping, I cut a length of black ribbon to sew onto the hem of my uniform. It is Cuong Nhu's symbol of mourning, left on for one year when losing someone close to us. I had worn one for his father, the founder of our style, when he passed in 2000. I wore one for Master Mary Davis, the head of the school I grew up in when she died suddenly in '06. The last time had been for Luis, a beloved student that died just before his black belt test.

I hunted through the dojo and found a needle thick enough to get through the heavy hem of my uniform. I couldn't find a thimble, though. My hands were sweaty and my face was wet with tears and I couldn't push the needle without one. I looked and looked and then decided to find something else to use. The plastic cap of the narrow tube the needle had been in would fit over my finger and had a ridge so that the needle wouldn't slip. I lined the needle up and pushed hard. I felt it give and then a sharp pain. Turning my hand over, I saw the needle had pushed through the plastic lid and under my fingernail all the way to the root of the nail. I pulled it out cursing and began the much harder and bloodier process of pushing it through with the pinch of my throbbing fingers.

I didn't know what to do with my pain. It crouched right in front of my months of work to recover and whispered, "you're too late." Quynh would never come and help me get back to what I could do before. If I managed to do it on my own, he wouldn't get to see it. But, really, he already saw it in his mind. He wanted us to show it to everyone else. That's what I had to do. I had to take all my pain and use it to recover so that I could show everyone his dream. I sat down to write a letter to everyone in Cuong Nhu. I hoped I could capture that swell of optimism and share it with all my fellows around the world, just now finding out that he was gone.

In Memory of Grandmaster Quynh Ngo

The path of the Hero goes like this – Once upon a time, there was a young child whose family was enslaved by an evil sorcerer, whose people fled their home as it was destroyed by fire, who was hunted by wolves, who was narrowly saved from the pharaoh in the hands of a stranger. As the child grew, they discovered that their father was the true king lost to his people, the keeper of the lost artifact of power, or the dark sorcerer who hunted them and only they had the power to redeem. The child took their first step down the path of the hero when they realized that they were the one. They had the spark, the gift, the prophecy, the inherited doom to be the only one that could save the world.

At first it was hard. There were many lessons to learn that caused pain and a bruised ego. They learned from childhood friends how to be true to their inner voice. They learned from wise and wily sages they met along the way that there were new mysteries to master. Then in a moment of terrible challenge, the child who was no longer a child, had to see that the past would combine with the present to unlock a new, untrodden path. Fatal flaws were not only overcome, but found to be a part of the true gift. The Hero emerged to fight, to sacrifice, to come to the edge of disaster and return, scarred but holding the light. There was a great celebration, the medal was given, the crown was placed, the people were saved and the land could rest as the hero protected and nurtured the people. The triumphant theme song rang powerfully into eternity.

You may have known Quynh Ngo as the GrandMaster who gave those wild speeches at the beginning of training camp that swerved from detailed and forceful instruction, to startling metaphor, to food review, and wound their way finally to profound and heartfelt inspiration. Maybe you also took his classes and were swept up in his boundless energy. Maybe he looked right through your mistakes and uncooperative body to the desire inside of you to be more, and grabbed hold of it, shouting its praise to everyone that could hear. For more of you than seems possible, he came to you again and again. He knew your name, your family, your life, and he made a special place in his own life to think about yours.

If you got your black belt, you knew GrandMaster Quynh the leader. You were in Black Belt meetings at Training Camp. You had a look inside the task of administrating schools spread all over the country and the world. If you've had it for a long time, you saw how he envisioned a new being for the style, a way to bring his gifts to bear on his father's bustling, living creation. You saw that it did not always go smoothly, that it required brazen courage, and that the willingness to make mistakes in the ongoing pursuit of progress was a noisy and constant battle.

While I knew him from a distance before, when I made the decision to make Cuong Nhu the vehicle for my life's work, I suddenly felt his gaze like never before. Immediately I was an adopted son. There were conversations like never before as my family became an extension of my training. Focus on my form was no different than focus on my parenting. The fitness of my body was no different than the fitness of my marriage. As my school grew, that extended to my students as well.

Each year when he would visit was like a family reunion as he met new students and built on the relationships he had with the old. Each year was a wake-up call as he looked with laser vision at the dojo and how it was preparing students and gave us course-correcting critique. Each year was a recharge as he took my weariness and infused it with inspiration to great purpose. Now, after an already daunting stretch of physical isolation from the style as a whole, and him in particular, I face the reality that what he gave me of his life is all I will get. The lesson concluded abruptly when I thought we were just taking a water break.

I suspect many of you that will read this are in the midst of a similar reconciliation. He nurtured you like a growing tree, shaping, tending and feeding you, and now it feels like you might starve. The living teaching is now a remembered teaching. He had you reaching for a new height and when you look to see how close you are, his hand isn't there to measure. I hurt. We hurt. Let's try to be together for that so that we can share the anger, the tears, and also the laughter, and the hope.

But here's the thing... Are you ready? If not, then feel free to put this down for a while. I'll wait right here.

Ok.

The child I referred to at the beginning was definitely Quynh, but it's also you. Do you remember when he chose you? It's because you're <u>the one</u>. Watching Quynh Ngo turn into Grand Master Quynh decades ago was an intimidating transformation, but imagine how it felt to him! Do you think he felt ready? The hand that guided him forward, that inspired and measured his progress was removed from view, and he had to put aside much of who he was to become the hero we needed. No one is ever ready. The question is, will you take the heroic step forward? Do you see the land in darkness? Can you hear the gathering of evil forces? Are the tribes scattered to the wind, yearning to be united? This is the time of heroes, and in you was planted the hope of us all. The gardener has left the garden, but the gloves are right there, and as you think back, you can see how he showed you the way.

You may take the step up to inspire the school that you lead, the class that you teach, the class that you train in, your family, your friend, even just yourself. The step up is not the step to get back up on your feet and be great at what you do, but the next step above that, where you see the desire to grow in people around you and lift them up. It is the step where you don't wait for the next instruction, but reach out to find the secrets that will combine with your special gift to create a new reality. It requires leaving your comfort zone, letting your ego be bruised, and reaching for something greater. It also requires you to fail in pursuit of the cause and to get back up, time and time again, to take what failure taught you and use it to win.

You may wonder, "where will the strength come from?" I remember when my dojo was new and there were no other senseis to teach with me. There were days when I didn't have the energy left to teach. I discovered in those moments one of the most powerful truths of leadership: What you give is magnified back to you. No matter how I felt, I would start strong and energetic, and the response back from my class, kids and adults alike, would charge my battery back up a bit. I would pour that energy back into the class, and they would multiply it right back to me. By the end of the day I was invincible, and then I would collapse into sleep.

You know how to light people up, how to inspire, how to lead the way even into darkness. You've been shown. You know how to try, and learn, and try again until you make a breakthrough. You've been shown. You know what it takes to raise the bar for yourself, your classmates, your school, your region. You've been shown. Will there be more leadership in the future? Yes. Could you sit back and wait to be told what's next? Yes. But if Quynh Ngo ever looked into your heart and lit it on fire, I challenge you to stand up and spread that light to those around you. Feel it reflected back on you and multiplied.

He stands behind you, fist raised high.

Chapter 9

There's a Curtain?

Quynh had been the leader of our style for more than twenty years and we'd all assumed things would stay that way for another twenty. In addition, the other children of the founder had stepped away, and for the first time the leadership of Cuong Nhu left the hands of the family that created it. We still had a hierarchy of ranks, and the highest living rank and now new Grand Master, John Burns, was ready and willing to step in. We had all been used to the Ngo family standing above our ranks. I remember the sense that we could reach a certain rank, and the Ngo siblings and their children were moving through those ranks as well, but that being a Ngo was always worth a few more degrees.

To have the Ngo siblings all out of the equation with no signs that the remaining three had any interest in stepping in after Quynh's death was a jarring reality shift. It felt even more distant since we hadn't seen each other for more than a year and were feeling isolated in a world turned upside down by pandemic, partisan strife, and raging protests. We were all struggling to survive as individual schools with the fresh reminder that holding a class carelessly could cost loved ones their lives. Having lost Quynh, we knew that the virus could kill even the strongest of us.

In the midst of this uncertainty, I had hit a plateau in my recovery. Despite months of gradual progress, there was a wall that I couldn't find my way over. This block had capped my ability not only to recover, but to prepare for my delayed rank test. I felt called to step up and do my part offering leadership in Cuong Nhu as the isolation of the pandemic and the loss of whole schools and leaders echoed in the ranks, but it had to be less physical. I had done my best to organize online events to connect us through our isolation, but they paled in comparison to meeting in person. My spirit was willing, but progress with my body was grinding against an infuriating block.

Josh and I had grown much closer during this time, spending many Friday evenings talking about our experience, our progress, and his continually eased mind. In late October he came to me with a proposal. In the summer he'd gone back to take Ayahuasca again with Darrick and my father, who had his flight and retreat covered by the non-profit that I'd looked into when I was there. Ming had gone into labor and had given birth to a healthy son that same weekend.

While my father's report had been hesitant, Josh was still excited about the continuing positive effects on his life and how the depths of his anxiety grew shallower each time he went. Darrick was tight-lipped, except to say that it was helpful and he wanted to go back. From my father's description, it sounded like he never took enough to get anywhere. It sounded like the first and third ceremonies I had experienced: uncomfortable and disorienting. In the weeks that followed, though, he'd started opening up about some experiences in the war. He'd always been very reluctant to share about the events that had so battered his mind, but some of it was flowing out with an ease that I'd never experienced. He didn't notice the change, but to those who knew him, there was a clear, if small, release of tension around this trauma.

Josh was planning to go back in January, and wanted me to come. He was sweetening the deal this time to avoid the traumatic return journey by getting us tickets to Universal studios for a couple of days and a massage the day after the retreat. That way we could decompress for a couple of days instead of ejecting into the airport straight from the ceremony.

I really didn't feel like the first trip had done a lot for me, but as he confided in me over drinks on a Friday night about what he'd seen during his summer journey, Josh had told me something that stuck in my mind. He'd tried taking a much larger dose and had experienced a terrifying loss of self. He'd found himself in a place where an overwhelming sentience had spoken to him through an infinite array of tiny pulsing lozenge shapes. He described it as going past the curtain of what humans are meant to see. They laughed at him in his terror and said, "we think it's hilarious that you think any of this matters."

While I could see how this might be unsettling, this was more like what I had been looking for the first time. I wanted to be in a conversation with that sentience. I wanted to see past that curtain. I also had some real roadblocks to try and clear up now. Quynh's death and my stalled recovery both had me ready to ask for help but unsure what that help could look like. I decided that I needed to cast a wider net in my attempts to recharge and agreed to the second trip.

As the time approached, my depression deepened. In November I went to one of the first regional Cuong Nhu get-to-gethers at the fortieth anniversary celebration of my home school in Atlanta. I tried to perform my test forms for review by a group of peers and higher ranks and was dizzy and winded a short way into them, having to take breaks to catch my breath before continuing. I could see how the sight of my weakness affected the teachers watching me. They'd never seen me struggle like this and were clearly taken aback. They gave me general feedback on movements to correct, and stylistic help about taking it slower intentionally to show control and keep from getting winded. They were trying to put a positive spin on having to slow down, but I didn't like planning to embrace my weakness. I didn't want to adapt. I wanted to return, retrain for my test like before, and show Cuong Nhu what Quynh and I had created for them before the pandemic took it all away.

As I prepared for my second Ayahuasca retreat, I had definite intentions now. I could safely sit on the mat and say what I wanted out of the ceremony. I had to find healing to break this injury's hold on my body, and inspiration to carry me past all of these barriers to my former strength.

Part 2
Fire in the Water

Chapter 10

Guides to the Heart

I began the focused preparations for the second journey a few weeks before leaving. It had been one year since the hospital and several months since I'd made any physical gains in endurance or energy. As I began a strict regimen of dieting and meditation to prepare myself for taking the Ayahuasca again, I was laser focused. I rejoined the zoom calls for a couple of online integration sessions in the weeks leading up to the retreat. These weekly online meetings were encouraged to help reinforce lessons learned and to continue the work as it encountered life outside of the loving setting of the retreat. As the date approached there were meetings to prepare people for the upcoming journey.

On these group video-conferences I listened for clues to help have a more productive weekend this time around, but had a hard time listening due to a particular thread of the conversation. Amidst all the people working on healing was a constant chorus of what felt like spiritual narcissism. While the facilitator tried to provide insight and guidance, interjected comments and a constant chorus from the chat bar would keep spitting out magnanimous sounding pearls of new-age sorcery. "Here's a link to a crystal pendant that will cure that problem." "You need to eat my cousin's special thyme leaves." Magnets, horoscopes, bells, and on, and on, and on. One of the things I tell my upcoming martial artists as their skills increase and they start trying to offer their advice to others is that unless someone has asked you personally for help, unsolicited advice never lands right.

My frustration with these spiritual barkers made it easy for me to be too busy to make it to the meetings. I could feel that those people were hurting and asking for a dose of soothing validation, but outside of the glow of the retreat, my patience for that sort of thing was low. I had, however, gathered a couple of pearls of wisdom from the actual discussions in these meetings that I hoped to use on this second weekend retreat. First was to not open my eyes. What was going on was internal, but since I was totally conscious, the sight of the waking world would pull me out of the work and then I'd have to reorient myself again. I had definitely been opening my eyes a lot the first time around to see if the hallucinations carried out past my closed eyes.

The second tip was to have a guide that related to our intention. No one was specific about whether they needed to be religious icons or ancestors or animals, but they needed to symbolize for me what my goals were. In the weeks leading up to the retreat, I'd chosen two guides for my two intentions. For my healing intention, I chose my grandmother. For inspiration, I chose Quynh.

My grandmother and I were very close. Though I was the fifth of twenty-five grandchildren, I felt like an outsider in many ways. All of my cousins had two to five siblings. All of them were vocally interested in church above all else. Most of the men cared a lot about sports and the military, and most of the women aspired to be housewives and mothers. My father had run from the church, didn't follow sports, cringed from the military because of his experience in the war, and my mother had been our stable income. I was also the only cousin with no siblings, and the only one with divorced parents. My cousins were more than kind to me, but I was always looking in from the outside.

Granny was different. She looked into me in a way that no one else could. Even parts of me that didn't make sense to her, she was able to perceive, love, and nourish. When I was seven she took me to the book store and bought me the blue box Basic set of Dungeons & Dragons. Any other member of my family would've strongly cautioned me to stay away from something that was gradually being vilified by the church community, but Granny connected the dots between my story-telling and love of fantasy and trusted her instincts over public opinion. She was a churchgoing housewife of another age, but her love had no dogma or prejudice of any kind.

I chose her for my healing guide because in addition to our close bond, she was the only person I'd ever watched miraculously heal someone. When I was seventeen and living at my aunt's house, I heard the phone ring and then a commotion and my cousin crying from another part of the house. Her boyfriend from college had been shot in a hunting accident and the doctors didn't think he was going to live. Over the next hour, family that lived in town gathered in my aunt's kitchen. We stood in a circle praying and holding hands for hours while my cousin continued choking back tears. I remember getting restless as the time rolled by and looking across the circle at Granny, only to see her glowing with an orange-gold light. I blinked and shifted my gaze to see if it was something in my eye or a kitchen light near her. The effect came and went, but never stopped. No one else in the circle glowed like that, and I became transfixed.

The hospital would call with updates from the surgery every half hour or so. They thought he might make it, but would never walk. They thought he might walk, but not for months and he'd need a colostomy bag. After a few hours they reported that he would miraculously be fine, though he'd be picking buck-shot out of his skin for decades and his bladder had been stitched up to the size of a walnut. I was convinced I'd seen her heal him from hundreds of miles away, and now I was hoping to channel her spirit towards my own healing.

Quynh was an easy choice. He would fill my energetic tank every time he'd come to visit. If anyone could pick up my spirits and help me move forward, he could. Also I missed him. I'd talked to Robert and Elizabeth in the weeks leading up to this second journey, and they'd told me that if I did see him, to tell him we all love him and miss him. I wasn't sure if talking to the dead was part of an Ayahuasca ceremony, but Robert and Elizabeth had gotten me thinking. If I'm taking chemicals that stimulate the memory and visual centers, everything that happens is in my own mind. Josh had experienced something that seemed like it was an external entity, but that was still likely a construct of his own mind manifesting his anxiety. When you dig deep enough, though, it's very hard to prove that anything is going on outside of your own mind.

Everything we perceive is an interpretation by our brain in order to navigate reality. Colors, shapes, surfaces, and even time and space are interpretations by the conscious mind in order to help the world make sense to us. How much can we say that God, other people, our past selves, a tree or a rock exist outside of us? The question really came down to how much the inside of my own mind was connected to the energies outside of it rather than just interpreting them in isolation. My past experience told me "not that much," but a new curiosity was growing. I had definitely felt connected to other people, but was that an internal reaction to a positive encounter or an energetic bridge to the other that actually connected us in a meaningful way? Was I really connected to anything or anyone, or was it all in my head? If Granny had been connecting to my cousin's boyfriend, did it matter that he was far away? If I was connected to someone, did it matter if they were alive or dead?

In January as we prepared to go, Josh told me that Darrick was coming also, and the three of us would share the room. I had some concerns about bringing Darrick. He was still having a really hard time with his divorce, and I was worried that talking to him and rooming with him was going to bend my thoughts away from the work I wanted to do. He and his son were both long time students of mine, and I loved him dearly, but I needed to focus on my healing and not his that weekend. I felt wrapped up in the struggle that surrounded him and worried that my normal job as a counsel to my students would jar my intentions away from my own task. I didn't know if I could shoulder his grief while trying to escape my own.

On the plane, my hips started throbbing. It felt a lot like the nerve pain from overdoing my recovery, just localized to my hips. On our layover, Josh showed me a yoga stretch to help and took me to an airport chiropractor for a quick adjustment. It all helped in the moment, but after another plane ride and then squeezing into Tom's little Prius again for the ride to the retreat, I was in agony. It was better once we got out and I could stand up, but I had to keep moving my legs and stretching for a while, and they still didn't feel great.

There was no outdoor covid screening tent this time, and we wound through the grounds on foot taking in subtle changes. A few were changes or upgrades to the facilities, but what stood out to me now that I had experienced it all the way through once, was how the peaceful, rooted energy of the staff and volunteers balanced out the lapping waves of anxiety from all the first timers. Now when I saw the staff embracing each other and looking over the group with the knowing smiles that had set me on edge ten months before, I could see that they were all giddy in the knowledge that all of this tension was about to get washed away in tears and sweat and retching, leaving everyone open and raw for healing.

I didn't have nearly the anxiety I had the first time, but it was still there. I knew I was going to go deeper and had no idea what I would see there. I also knew how much work, sleepless exhaustion, discomfort, and vomiting was ahead. Now as I talked to first-timers, I was sharing my limited experience from the first retreat and talking about what I was trying to do this weekend. When I talked to people with more experience, I had really specific questions related to my goals for healing, going deep, and using my guides. Most people's advice came down to "She'll show you what you need to see. You just need to stay focused and be open to it." A woman named Grace offered a really helpful tip.

"It's good that you have clear intentions, but try to treat them like the reins on a powerful horse. You can use them to coax the horse towards where you want to go, but if the horse is determined to go somewhere else, you need to use them to hold on for the ride instead of trying to control it." That made a lot of sense to me and I tucked it into my preparations.

With less anxiety about the coming ritual, the time passed more quickly. It was a chilly January day in Florida and would get cold at night, but there were space heaters around the yard and in the open buildings, so I wasn't too worried. I was in one of the square lodges by the courtyard instead of the maloca this time, but Josh had again booked the one private room to use as our home base with the big comfy bed, though fitting all three of us in it would be a tight squeeze. The opening ceremony and introduction with everyone together in the maloca was just like before. The same introductions, advice, and rules. Keep your clothes on. Don't jump in the pond. Don't trust an Ayahuasca fart. Sitting in the chair through the lengthy introduction was getting to my hips again.

Next came the meeting with my lodge so I filed out of the maloca and walked through the yard to the first of two rectangular lodges by the fence with a row of mats against the inside of each side wall. We all talked about what we were trying to do and what issues we were bringing to the medicine. I was perfectly clear in my intentions this time and knew for certain what I was trying to do. My story was still not a traumatic heartbreaking one but my pain was a real pain that I wanted to soothe, and I had no trouble sharing that struggle. My plan was to take two tablespoons that night. It was the same amount I'd taken the first night last time, but all at once instead of separated by two hours. If that didn't do it, I'd take even more at the daytime ceremony, and more the next night until I finally broke through the curtain.

Chapter 11

Out of Frame

The sun was setting and it was cold when we went out for the smoke cleanse. The guides blessed the medicine and then it was time to line up and take our cups. I expected to have to explain why I wanted more than the minimum to the man in loose white clothing spooning out the syrupy brown drink, but I asked for two and he just asked if it was my first time. When I said, "No," he scooped a second large spoonful into the cup, looked at me kindly and nodded, "Safe journey."

I carried the cup carefully back to my mat and sat cross-legged, arranging my cup and my water bottle at the foot of the mat and placing my bucket to the side since I wouldn't need it for a while. As the last light of the sun disappeared, we all drank together. It tasted a lot worse this time. The ground bark and cocoa tastes were there, but this time it was harder to get down. I'd tried to swallow it all in a quick shot, but a lot was left in the cup, and as I put water in it and used my finger to get it all out, some got on my lips. I tried to wash the taste down but the aftertaste and the smell from my lips and finger were nauseating, and I wondered what would happen if I threw it up right now. I guess I'd get another cup, but I was having to focus to keep this one down.

After a few minutes, my stomach stopped arguing actively with me about the medicine and settled to a basic nausea. Then came the waiting. As I gathered all my thoughts around my focus and my guides, I became more and more uncomfortable sitting. My hips were starting to ache again, and sitting up was making the pain increase. I finally moved back to the wall and positioned my pillow so that I could recline about halfway, and waited for the medicine to kick in.

After about thirty minutes, there was something happening in my torso. A buzzing like electric butterflies growing stronger and stronger. I remembered something like it from my first journey and held on tighter to my guides, reciting to myself that I had come for healing and energy, Granny and Quynh. The vibration extended up my spine and grew stronger in my stomach. I could feel my mind trying to jump around with wonder, to look around in curiosity, but I wanted to stay right there in the middle of that feeling and see where it would take me. I wondered if it was time to throw up, but I didn't feel any particular need to. The vibration was spreading through my hips and shoulders and head and growing even stronger. It felt so warm in the cold night and I realized that my hips didn't hurt at all anymore. Neither did my head or any other part of me. Actually, I wasn't feeling anything from my body. I held on to the vibration, as it had become the core of my sensation.

Then the vibrations reached a crescendo so powerful that I couldn't maintain my hold on my body, and I fell backwards between my atoms and out of the physical world.

Chapter 12

What Can't Be Touched

My new reality was dark and vast like the emptiness of space, but instead of feeling it as a cold and lonely expanse, I was surrounded by powerful energy that surged upward in waves of vibration. It would be inaccurate to say the waves had colors, but I could tell the difference between different kinds of waves. The idea of color was a bit arbitrary and I could choose to acknowledge them as any color or none. Something deeper than my eyes was "seeing" what was around me, and it was challenging to get my bearings in all of that surging energy. I became aware of my body in the vicinity of my consciousness, but I was looking at it from the "inside" or maybe "interside." It was spread out like a constellation of warm, swirling points of light, with vibrating energy pulsing through the length of the spine forward out of the front of the body. I couldn't see my skin or features, just the constellation of energetic patterns that make up my body. I was aware of my physical self, and was still connected to the idea of being inside of it, but it was separate from me. I could move it with effort, stretching and shifting, but it was unwieldy and distant, and there was so much going on around me that I wanted to see and understand.

I watched the energy pouring through my body in awe at how much there was and how beautiful it felt. There was a clear loving intention inside of every wave, and I could see how I was bathed in an endless geyser of loving power that erupted from my center into the world. As I watched, I began to see the energy in motion after it left me. It gained structure and sought people. I couldn't really understand what the structures were. They resembled fractal, serpentine grapevines. What they were doing was clear, though. They were empowering other people. I watched this process for a long time. Energy would build up in my body and then form a tower that would reach out to another person and make them more powerful. I was being shown how these loving energetic constructs had worked on people around me throughout my life.

I began to wonder about people that I hadn't been able to help, and the vision shifted to show me how I needed to be closer for the power to work. Sometimes closeness wasn't about distance, but about time, attention, emotional availability, and conversation. It was a cosmic human closeness that had its own vector. After seeing dozens of examples from my life, I remembered that I was here to heal myself, and I hoped that this energy that could empower others might do that for me.

I brought my consciousness into alignment with my body and then willed all of that surging energy to turn inward to my own body. It felt like a cup being filled with steaming tea. The powerful, loving vibrations filled me up instead of projecting forward from my spine. So much power surely had the ability to heal me. The energy built up and built up, and the vibration felt like holding on to a rocket as it was lifting off. Without any conscious direction, it sprung out of me and to a stranger on a nearby mat. I allowed myself to open an eye and risk losing this deep connection, but the man my energy went to was really there, unknown, writhing on his mat. I closed my eyes again and gave it another try, but again the energy arced to a nearby fellow journeyer.

Frustrated, I returned to watching the flow of energy again. It didn't take long in the coursing flow of loving energy to forget my disappointment and just enjoy existing there. It occurred to me that all of this energy that was pouring out of me in the front must come from somewhere behind me. Throughout the experience I had kept my consciousness oriented to my body's position lying on my back, looking up. Since my body couldn't turn and I wasn't using it anyway, I experimented with turning my awareness around to see where the energy was coming from. I needed to embrace that it was not my eyes that were seeing and that there was no body to turn, only the focus of my consciousness.

I relaxed my hold on the idea of my body in space and eased my conscious perception towards the source. What I saw once I turned is difficult to describe, but experiencing it changed me forever. My body, and specifically my spine, was an aperture between the physical world and the entirety of divine loving energy "behind" everything. While we manifest as separate in the physical world, we are not only from the same place, but are constantly connected by it. All of us are apertures to this energy, and death is simply the relaxing of the pressure that pushes our consciousness into the world. It is difficult work to be in the world, but it's the work of reality. Unless we make these painful, stumbling journeys into reality, love won't enter into the cold calculus of the physical world.

I remembered Robert and Elizabeth's request about finding Quynh and tested to see if I could push past the aperture into the source to look around. It wasn't particularly hard to do, moving my consciousness down the energy that connected me to the source, but it was very hard to take in all I saw. Part of the difficulty comes from the extra-dimensional nature of that place. The "shapes" of things were not just in motion, but in many places at once. To look at a thing was to see it from all sides and the inside and also at all moments of its existence.

It was like a waterfall that went on forever, made up of energies that rippled like the bark of a tree but with as much depth as width, which could all be perceived energetically, but not "seen" the way we see the surfaces of objects. Within those textures were patterns that, like my own self at the aperture, contained the mechanics of selves with their own unique way of channeling the energy into the world. Their infinity merged effortlessly into massive patterns that defied simple individuality. Branching out from it in a million directions were long coursing twines of energetic pattern, still connected to the source, but bridging the difficult expanse to reality. I was one of those strands, but still part of the whole.

I knew Quynh's energy and felt my connection to it, so I followed that feeling to the surface of this infinity of energies and along the top which surged like an ocean. Passing a sea of formed and unformed shapes, I followed our connection to where his unique signature merged with the larger pattern. I approached him slowly, seeing that he was completely engaged. There was no face or body to tell me that this was my teacher but his energetic self was unmistakable. I had felt it so many times before. I was seeing with my heart and it "looked" like the feeling you have when you first reconnect with someone after a long time apart. His soul was searching, working, taking in and sending out energy. I could sense that he was busily reaching for his children, his wife, and his loved ones in a way that was much more intense and hurried than the more vague and placid souls around him.

I didn't have a hand to reach out with or a mouth to speak with, so I sent on the message of love to him energetically like a puff of air. Only the tiniest part of his attention became aware of me there. He seemed lovingly amused to accept me and my gift, and I realized that I was bringing a thimble of water to a waterfall as an offering. He was fully engaged in the immeasurable surging source of all love, and the uniqueness of my love or Robert and Elizabeth's love in the rush of the waterfall was a sweet little whisper.

Awed, but out of place, I pulled myself as steadily as I could back to "reality." I had delved very deep into the energetic world to find Quynh, and I had a slight worry that it might not be possible to re-enter my body. I had wandered far from the strand that connected me to the physical world. My connection to my physical form stood out to me as a bright, sturdy aperture at the surface of reality where my energy swirled into the world in a spiraling geyser. Reaching steadily closer and then pressing through it, I reoriented my consciousness around my body, carrying a transforming picture of where I come from, a place to which I am always connected and will someday fully return.

Getting my bearings reorganized back to the area of my body, I saw that I was not alone in the constellation of myself. Sitting to the "left" of my perception was my grandmother with her head down and her signature puff of white hair. I remembered how she'd sat by me like that with her head down, silently praying when I got sick while I was visiting her and Paw over the summer as a child. I knew that she prayed this way for me even when I was far away. It was just like in my aunt's kitchen when she was wrapped in light.

It wasn't necessary to run to her or exclaim with joy at seeing her after the almost twenty years since my cousins and I carried her casket to where it would be planted, joking and laughing with our loving memories of her all the way. I was in the absolute fullness of her presence, and it felt clear then that I was able to see what I was seeing and explore the energetic space away from my body because she was helping to show it to me. When I was seeing how my energy worked and asking about times that it didn't, it was her that was directing my instruction.

I knew without words that she wanted me to see how I worked in the world and what my effect on others was as I interacted with them. Seeing her again reminded me of my desire for healing, and encouraged by her presence, I tried again. I felt sure that with her blessing and my new perception, I would finally be able to keep the energy within myself and be healed. I folded all of the waves of radiating energy back into my energetic body, and again felt the warm, loving surge of all of that power filling every part of me and doubling, and doubling, and doubling, and then it was gone again. It had branched off to a mat near me, filling the man lying there with loving power to move forward.

I felt frustration and rejection swelling in me, and then, as abruptly as a slamming door, all the vibration stopped. I had accepted the powerful waves of energy pulsing through my energetic and physical self as my new reality, and to have them stop so suddenly made the space around me feel small and quiet. Granny was looking right at me and I was in my body. Her left eye had that droop from Bell's palsy that I so missed seeing.

"What are you doing, Tanner?" Her face had all the love and energy of her life's fullness with none of the diminished confusion that dampened her last years into a pained vigil.

"I want to be strong again. I'm trying... I'm trying to heal myself with the energy. It makes people..."

"It doesn't work like that," she interrupted. "I've been showing you how it works. You bring so much power into the world, but it's not for you." It felt like a hammer to my gut. "I'm not teaching you to how cast spells or how to grow or use your power. I just want you to see how it already works. I want you to understand what you're already doing every day and how important it is."

"But I'm not here to understand the past! I want to heal so I can move forward. I'm still so far behind." I couldn't believe that Granny was telling me that there would be no healing. It had been my one hope to move forward with my recovery. A deep ache grasped at me that I would never be able to live up to any of what I had been able to do just a year before. "This power builds and heals. Surely it can go both ways?" Granny was standing now, and I was aware of every bit of her. All of her body's scars stood out to me. Her fingers were bent and gnarled, her left eye wouldn't open all the way, her back was bent, and her bones and joints and spirit held a thousand grievances. She was showing them proudly.

"These are my badges from a life lived serving and healing others. Sometimes I had to take their suffering into myself because it was too hard for them to let it go on their own." She was radiant in her cloak of badges. "You build and heal and it takes a toll on you. You know this and it's exactly what you wanted." I could see my life's joy in all the moments she was talking about, but she still didn't understand that all of that would end if I couldn't get back to my old self.

"I see that, and I do love it, but I've been trying for a year to get back on my feet from this sickness, and I've stopped improving. How can I do what needs to be done if I'm always less than what I need to be?"

"Oh, child. You really don't understand." She paused and let a few torturous moments pass before calling up the words that would crack me open to my core.

"You have to stop acting like you're a person who's trying to recover from Covid. *You died of Covid.*"

Chapter 13

I Am

Panic spread all over me and I looked for a way out, but there was no way around Granny's loving face. "You died there in the hospital, and Josh was the only one who got to stand over you at your funeral." The space around me became the hospital and I was looking up at Josh. His glove was off and his hand was touching mine. His closed eyes were swollen and steaming with tears.

"It's not the way any of us wanted, but that was it." I could sense Melanie and the boys at home imagining a world without me, and my family and friends wondering why I would get sick when so many less healthy people did not. "The person that came out of the hospital wasn't the Tanner you're torturing yourself to get back to. You're a whole new person. You fought hard to be born again and when you won, you took your first breath."

I was taken back to that night after Josh left. The painkillers only tipped their hats to the pain from throwing my neck and back out with coughing fits. Doubled over and trying to cradle my chest against the inferno of inflammation holding court in my lungs, I heard the nurse tell me that if I couldn't beat it tonight, the next step was the gurney down to a ventilator. "There's nothing more we can do for you up here." I saw her looking at the oxygen tubes and my numbers glowing on the wall and monitor behind my bed. "If you've got anything left to fight with," she said with an exhausted bleakness, "now's the time."

For the next six hours, already exhausted, weak, injured, and sleep-deprived, I fought tooth and nail with the virus. I would try to breathe, move to another position to try again, get kicked around by explosive coughs that felt like body punches with my inflamed lungs and pain-wracked torso. I used every breathing exercise I'd ever trained through martial arts and meditation to control the flow of air, diffuse my experience of pain, and calm my rising panic. In the midst of it, unable to breathe and writhing in pain, I fell over the edge of the cliff. There wasn't enough air to maintain the fight. I flipped myself to my knees as smoothly as I could muster in my panic, and assumed the kneeling inverted position that I had practiced to shift the fluid in my lungs and create space. No relief came, and a wave of agonizing coughs tore through me like a gang kicking me as I huddled on my knees. I could feel myself dying.

I looked over at the emergency call button with desperation. But if I pushed it, would there be relief or would they just take me to the ventilator? Death in the bed, or death in the call for help. As the coughs lashed my face against the bed, I chose to grab the sliver of hope that they might be able to give me one last bit of relief. I groped for the button through the tears running down my contorted face. Death was closing in, whether from the prongs of pain driven through my chest and stopping my air, or from helping hands taking my mind offline as they gave my life to the machines.

I fought for breath and begged for relief from the fire, from the pressure, from the exhausted blackness that closed around my vision. I pushed back with everything and prayed for gloved hands to appear and take the fight from me, but they never came. Violent minutes of beating that felt like hours kept passing under the crush of death as I realized there would be no help. Only the fight. *There's no one here but me and you. Only one of us gets out of here alive.* Seconds, to minutes, to hours. Tears upon tears, snot upon spit, bile upon blood. And then a breath came that was just a fraction of a percent easier. Then the next and the next were easier still. And then I slept.

"You were born from that bed like a new baby from the womb. You had to learn to stand again, to walk, to run." I saw all of the months of slowly building my strength after coming home. "You learned to swim and grew even stronger. In every place that you ran into obstacles, you came up with new ways around them that helped you climb even higher."

"You're an entirely new person, and you need to start being proud of every way that you grow and skill that you learn. But first you need to mourn the old Tanner and let him go." The tears started to flow immediately. It was so much all at once. It was the loss of an identity that was the center of my every goal and action. It was the death of every plan for the future that balanced on my old self and his capabilities. It was anger at dying in my prime from a virus that seemed to target the weak and unhealthy. It was more tears about Quynh. I wept and wept and felt cleansing fires burning everything down around me.

I was somewhat aware of my body and used the paper towels in my bucket to wipe tears and mucus from my face. I realized that I'd never vomited and lifted myself over the bucket to purge the anger and sadness from myself, but while I retched and contracted, and could feel a dredge pulling at the deepest corners of my self to clean them out, all that went into the bucket were tears and mucus and spit. Instead of purging the physical contents of my stomach, I felt my aching desperation spilling out of my soul.

I fell back down on the mat and felt, in the fire's wake, an expanse of fertile, charcoal-pocked soil, ripe for new growth. I sat warmly in the middle of her words; *you should be proud*.

"You're a new person, Tanner. Don't ever compare yourself to the old versions of yourself. Remember his stories and use everything he learned that serves you, but you're not bound by his expectations. You get to try new things and find new ways." She was fading now, and the chill of the air around me was becoming real. My body was becoming the house of my consciousness. I laughed to myself wearily, wept in spurts, still drenching the paper towels wadded in my hand. I raised my hand barely above my head and one of the volunteers in white smoothly descended on me.

"Can I have some paper towels and a pencil and paper?" He already had a roll of paper towels and as he lowered the roll to the ground in an unusual way, I realized he was missing an arm. He gently held the roll with his foot and removed squares one at a time from the roll with his one hand. I was mesmerized by how little his impairment troubled or slowed him as he used what he had to meet my need with elegant wholeness. Next he walked silently to get me a piece of paper and stub of pencil, and I began to write everything Granny had shown me while it was fresh on my mind. My hand was unsteady, and my writing looked like the scrawl of my elementary school composition books.

The ceremony had ended and it was ok to get up and go, but my body was remarkably weary and it was still a challenge to move my limbs. Many mats around me were empty and some hosted sleeping people, while some were still clearly in the thick of their journeys. I rested more, wrote more, considered sleeping there on my mat and then realized that as tired as I was, my mind was not going to stop spinning with all that I'd just seen. I remembered the sleepless nights of my first retreat, and gathered myself up and rose to my feet. Help in white was again by my side, but after a few steps, I had my heavy legs under control.

I carefully stepped through the courtyard where people stared at the fire pit in the middle and huddled in dim corners with their new visions and broken walls. I had a light snack of vegetables and hummus in the kitchen, unable to put everything I'd seen together enough to say more than that "it was really perfect" to anyone else there that asked how my journey went. Then I filled up a fresh water bottle and quietly probed the door to Josh's private room in case he was sleeping. The room was dark, and I waited for my eyes to adjust, not sure if Josh and Darrick were already spread out over the precious expanse of that perfect mattress. After a moment, though, I realized it was empty.

I flipped on the light and sorted through my suitcase aimlessly. Actually, I wanted to go to the bathroom. I closed myself in the private room and was caught by my reflection in the mirror. Somehow I looked like a new person. I couldn't pick out what exactly was different, but what I saw in the mirror looked healthier and more promising than what I'd seen during the day. Also, I needed to throw up.

Finally the black, sticky ooze found its way out of my belly, and I heaved for several sessions, losing my snacks and water and some other mysterious debris in the process. Having the medicine all out made me feel even more possessed of my body, and I treated myself to a long shower and a change of clothes before climbing into that heavenly bed and making a cocoon out of extra pillows and the heavy, warm comforter. Now with a light, I looked over what I'd written in the dark of the hut and clarified phrases that were hard to read but fresh on my mind.

Josh came in looking ragged and followed my lead with the shower. We debriefed for a bit in the bed before he went out to look for Darrick among the firelight and shuffling pilgrims. Before long they'd returned and we all piled into the expanse of duvet and welcoming mattress. We talked some about our journeys, but so much of it was still processing. It was hard to put my weight behind words like "I died and was reborn. You were there, Josh, and we'll always be deeply connected by that experience." I felt so light and positive but the experience swirled around my mind like a still burning fire. I wanted to share but there was an uncertainty about talking without processing the information. What was certain was that we were all lighter in our souls, relieved of painful shackles, and ready to laugh and spin the threads of friendship lightly into the late night.

Chapter 14

The Medicine

I managed a few scattered naps in the dark morning hours after Darrick decided to return to his mat and Josh turned the noise machine on and the light off. My mind was still so busy with what I'd experienced. So much of it defied my everyday senses. Normally I perceive a three-dimensional world as a two-dimensional image on my retina that stays in sync with the moment that I'm experiencing. I hear vibrations that send signals via my ears into my brain instead of just receiving words and concepts instantly in my heart. Many things I'd seen the night before felt like I was experiencing them in four dimensions and were not limited to the moment of my existence or my body's location. My mind wanted to process and record it all, but it had to collapse what I'd seen down to flattened storybook images and then turn those into words.

When Josh and I were finally willing to admit that we were getting up, I started to shift my attention to the daytime ceremony and found that I was nauseated and gagging at just the thought of drinking more of the earthy brew. I thought it would pass, but the more I imagined it, the more I was certain that I wouldn't even be able to hold the drink near my face without retching, much less put it in my mouth.

I wasn't sure what to do. I'd only been to one of the three sessions set for this weekend and had gotten so much healing and revelation out of it. Was I really not going to be able to go to the other two? In truth, I was more than happy with what I'd learned the night before and would be pleased if that was the totality of my weekend progress, but it also didn't seem right to quit just after starting. I wrestled with it for a while before seeking out one of the facilitators.

I found Brandon packing chewing tobacco into his lip near the trees. I felt a moment of dissonance to see this angelic being doing something I found distasteful, but it passed like a flutter, his chewing becoming just another aspect of the wholeness of a human being. His eyes eagerly sought mine out as they did when I'd come to him almost a year earlier.

"Hey, Brandon."

"How was your night, brother?" They were almost the same words he'd said to me before, but he was no less interested and one hundred percent in the moment with me.

"It was actually a massive, healing revelation," I said, wondering how much he wanted to know. It felt like he'd be happy to hear every detail, but the daytime ceremony was approaching and I needed to get this figured out. "The weird thing, now, is that even thinking about drinking again makes me gag. I don't know what's going on. I don't know if She wants me not to drink, or if I'm scared, or if my body just can't handle it." It felt oddly natural in this moment to speak of the medicine as a revered "She" the way I'd heard the guides do it.

"Your body can totally handle it, brother. Here's the question you have to find the answer to: Is this message coming from your heart or from your ego? See, your ego hates this medicine, because it tears it apart every time you drink it. Your heart, though, your heart is how mother Aya talks to you. If she doesn't want you to drink, then there's something else she wants you to see." He had a wild-eyed certainty that hinted at many stories stacked behind his words.

"Hm. Thanks. That's actually really helpful."

We shared a wordless, enveloping hug, and I walked over to the swing by the pond, searching my feelings. Was there some part of me that was hiding from further revelation? What I'd seen and heard the night before had set me free from a year of suffering. It hadn't given me back my body, but it had given me back my heart and shown me how to be proud again. I honestly wanted more, but something inside was telling me not to drink any more. So I went to the office, declared my intention to sit out of the remaining ceremonies, and they switched out my wristband. My new wristband showed that I wasn't going to participate in the ceremonies, so I got to eat with the volunteers and move around the facility when everyone else was confined to the ceremony grounds.

While about a quarter of the participants went to partake in the daytime ceremony, I took a yoga class to work on whatever was happening in my hips that was making them ache so sharply. When the ceremony ended I ate lunch with the weary travelers, opening my ear to what they wanted to share and watching as their walls were further breached with some jealousy. I considered taking a nap, but I wanted to sleep through the night so I just let my weariness compound. Darrick had taken twice the dose that I took the night before and stayed for a couple of hours longer under the effects of the medicine, so we'd lost touch with him as he looked for food and a quiet place to process what must've been an intense journey. Josh and I were curious about what that journey was like, but Darrick didn't want to talk yet, so we left him to rest in the room.

There was a demonstration of something called "shadow integration" in the afternoon, and Josh and I sat wearily in a circle of chairs in the maloca to see what that meant. Once people had gathered, an energetic man named Steven explained how broken he was and how difficult his life and childhood were. My eyelids were drooping, and I wondered if I'd be able to stay awake. After explaining that the "shadow" was our childhood self that had created walls and shields in our consciousness to protect us from trauma, and how reconnecting with this self would help us recover from the trauma, Steven asked for a volunteer. A man's hand shot up quickly.

"Oh. So quick to volunteer!" Stephen said, with an air of bravado. The man with his hand up looked comfortable and laughed at the affront. "Ok. What's your deal?"

"I have anger issues" the eager man said "most recently I started yelling because my wife really doesn't understand why I come here and won't open her mind to it." Immediately a little flag shot up in my sleepy mind. My gut told me this guy knew he was in a place where everyone was on board with coming here and that he'd get a slap on the wrist about losing his temper, but the conversation would turn to better arguments to win over his wife about this place. A safe admission to gain status with an approving group. That is not what happened. I was in no danger of falling asleep.

I saw a change in Steven's demeanor like a hunting dog picking up a scent. He went right for the throat of the man's hidden motivations behind the anger, his relationship, and his willingness to volunteer, and would not let him out of the corner no matter how hard he back-pedaled. Steven opened up the motivations to reveal responses to childhood trauma and wouldn't back down until the man was willing to confront that trauma. The next half hour was a loud and fast deep-dive into the man's fears about abandonment going back to his single mother's string of boyfriends. They dug to the source of the fear, found the place where the anger lived, shined light into the darkness, and pulled out the malnourished child that had been trapped there for decades. We were all weeping by the time it was done, and the eager man was laid painfully bare, but cut deftly so as to heal back stronger. I was floored. Steven was an artist of human deconstruction.

We left the maloca where the shadow integration had taken place and still had a little while to sit and chat before the last ceremony. Josh wasn't able to tell me much about his daytime ceremony. He hinted at healing vision, but didn't have concrete images to tell me about. It seemed that he wasn't getting a coherent experience like I'd had the night before or even a year earlier in the womb, but he mentioned looking around his childhood house, and finding himself in a familiar old place. We both wanted to check on Darrick, but didn't find him. We had trouble being worried about him in the afterglow of the medicine. I had worried before that Darrick's troubles would intrude on my ability to dig deep, but that concern seemed laughable in the flowing energy of the ritual space. Nobody's troubles could obstruct the work that was happening in me, even having not had any of the medicine that day. I felt centered and loved and important.

I went to integration with my group as they prepared for the last journey, sharing what I'd seen and my decision to not drink any more. The volunteer running that group was open to my plan, but a little reluctant to give in to the idea that not drinking the medicine that night would further my progress. The overall feeling seemed to be that more medicine was good and less medicine was less good. I'd done all the thinking about it that I could, though. Brandon's advice seemed to be my clearest guide. I could feel his understanding and experience in his clear breakdown of the ego versus the heart and I had resolved that my ego was not the source of the resistance. I watched the evening ceremony begin from the outside, slow and smoky, giving Josh and the re-emerged Darrick hugs as they went to their mats to dive back into their own depths.

I joined the volunteers to eat a quiet vegetarian dinner which they were grabbing off of a dimly lit table in the house as they came and went between duties. I found a cozy seat to eat in the growing dark and looked forward to a good night of sleep before we began a couple of relaxing days post retreat.

In bed alone, I set myself up for a long night of deep sleep, having had almost no sleep the night before and feeling painfully exhausted. I positioned pillows and blankets to make the perfect cocoon again and waited for the warm, comfortable embrace of sleep. It wasn't coming as quickly as I'd hoped. I ran through the meditations that normally help me drift off, first the tall grass, and then my favorite: receding into water. Not only were they not working, but my hips were starting to ache sharply despite the extreme comfort of the pillowy bed. I fitfully sought out a better position that would quiet them, but the ache was getting worse.

I got out of bed to repeat some of the yoga from the session that day and the stretch that Josh had shown me in the airport. There was some relief, but the persistent ache kept building, and while I could push it away momentarily, it seemed intent on coming back to reassert itself. I thought about looking through Josh's bags for some pain-killers, but a little tickle in the back of my mind remembered the night before when the pain in my hips had melted away when the medicine kicked in and the vibrations took me out of my body.

Following that thought, I positioned my body the way I had on the mat and put my palms to the bed the way I had to the floor the night before. I began breathing deeply and holding those intentions in my mind again. I thought I was tricking myself when the vibrations began. I had started humming with the out breaths and at first I guessed that I was just recreating the feeling with my vocal cords. It was an aggressive hum, like a breathy moan changing pitches to direct vibration to different parts of my torso, but the vibrations were building outside of my humming and developing outside of my guidance. They had filled my belly and now my chest and were starting to stretch into my neck and head, bringing the euphoric feeling of transformation that I had experienced the night before and washing away my pain in a warm, loving wave.

As the vibration built past my ability to encompass it, there was a slip, and I was again shaken through the spaces between the molecules of my physical self and out into the waves of energy where I could observe the workings of my body from the other side. The pain in my hips was gone. I didn't really have hips to feel pain in. I watched the fountains of energy that passed through me at points along my spine and then radiated in spirals out through the front of my body. It was so much to take in that some time passed in observation before I grasped fully that this was happening without drinking the medicine, and that Granny was again sitting and waiting for me. She was filled with love and patience, but I sensed an urgency in the space.

Chapter 15

A Still, Small Voice

"There are only two kinds of acts that are true," she said, snaring my full attention away from my swirling wonder. "First are acts that allow you to understand how loved you are and how lucky you are to experience the vast beauty of the world in each moment that you are alive."

She bombarded my consciousness with a series of moments from my life when a sight, or a story, or an interaction consumed me so completely that there was no past or future and I was entirely caught up in that moment. I gathered from her examples that she was talking about gratitude and about intentional acts that build joy in the presence of the moment. I saw the moments when there was no way to look away like the moments when I took my sons from Melanie's belly; the moment I asked her to marry me; or the top of Katahdin at the end of the appalachian trail. I also saw intentional moments when I was fully present; riding bareback on a horse; breaking out into a dewy meadow with the smell of honeysuckle in my nose; chasing fireflies on a summer night; or reclining on my porch just realizing how grateful I was to be present in that place at that time.

"The second kind of true act is anything that helps share that love with another person," and again, a wide review of examples from my life where I reached out to another to lift them up or deepen a connection flashed through my senses. It was clear that these acts were passing out an energetic resource that was built up by the experience of gratitude and love. These moments were startling in their clarity and the degree to which both I and the other were wholly present.

I could see the value of these things but my thoughts started to cast a wider net, testing Granny's maxim against a broader range of experiences. "You can tell that an opportunity for the second kind of truth is present in two ways," she continued, re-targeting my probing thoughts. "The first is that there is always risk, and the second is the presence of the still, small voice." That rung a bell from far distant churches that made me think of the voice of God, but I couldn't place the story it came from. This was the first time Granny had mentioned anything even vaguely related to Christianity in these discussions.

The Church was the cornerstone of her spiritual life, but she rarely discussed it with me in her life and didn't seem to be angling for a discussion of Christianity now. In fact, her voice seemed different now. She was speaking in sweeping philosophical terms that would have been unusual coming from my reserved, unassuming grandmother. I sensed that she had learned or tapped into a vast knowledge since her death. There was also a quality of urgency that wasn't there the night before, like she needed to teach this lesson, and didn't have time to let it slowly reveal itself. She had lost some of her patient, familiar tone.

"There is always risk when you hear the voice, and only by acting in that moment in spite of the risk can you experience the truth or share it with another." The concept was getting more focused. The risk and the still, small voice were key, but there were so many things that happened in safety that also seemed true.

"The rest is illusion," she challenged in answer to my thought. "We feel the passing of opportunities to experience the truth that were lost to our fear of risk. We fixate on the possibility of that passed moment, and instead of letting them go and being present in the next moment, we become determined to recreate the lost moment in a way that gives us control and removes the risk. Then we build and build and drown in illusion, deaf to the still, small voice and blind to the sacred risk of the present moment."

"We lay out all of our plans and work and plot the risk out of them. Years later when we finally succeed in making our perfect, risk-free simulation of that lost moment, we bathe ourselves in success only to find it fleeting. Our deflation leads to doubt and we might decide that there is no truth after all, and that our own memories of that lost moment are part of the illusion. Living in the past we are again lost in illusion and deaf to the still, small voice and the sacred risk of the moment."

It was a lot to take in, but as before, she showed me example after example in rapid succession to be sure I understood completely. We make money to have a place to live, a safe bed to sleep in, and food to eat. The food is stocked for days, with many choices about what to eat on a given day. This should free us to have more meaningful experiences, but how much more in the moment we are when we gather our food each day based on what is happening around us. Even more so, when we are not sure how we'll eat, the source of our food becomes a sacred connection. We can meet it like an injured soul lost in the past, like a fearful soul lost in the future, or like a holy man present in the moment. If we can be fully present, then the adventure, or act of grace, or test of will that arises from it becomes sacred. In the presence of those moments, we can hear the quiet voice which whispers the holy word, "now."

This voice almost always heralds panic, doubt, and questioning. "Surely it's for someone else — My intentions will be misunderstood — I'm sure to fail or be embarrassed — I don't have this figured out." But the voice's message echoes "now." Then the moment passes. The voice is gone. We are left with only our fantasy. Illusion.

"If I miss these moments, will my life just slide by in misery?" I was overwhelmed by how rare it was to hear the voice much less have the courage to act on it.

"No, Tanner. You can be happy or miserable whether you answer the voice or not. The currency of happiness is the truth of love and gratitude. The majestic awe of your time in this life, however, does stand on your answering the voice."

"So I'm squandering the most essential element of life when I miss one? What if I miss them all?" I was stuck on the idea that life was so overrun with busy work that I was missing out on all that matters. There was a change in her tone, as if my growing panic had dissolved the need for urgent teaching. Her loving eyes held mine with a sympathetic frown.

"There's no judgment, sweetheart. It's terrifying, and most people are doing all right to experience the truth three or four times in their life. Maybe in your next life you get twenty or thirty, and that's better, and there's joy in that, but failure to act is no crime."

"How many chances will I get?"

"Maybe a hundred. You never know how long you've got, so the next one is the only one that matters. Stay present. You can feel the urgency but don't let it distract you." There had been this sense of urgency to everything I'd seen. The pulsing energy funneling through my body was imprinted with a call to benefit the lives of as many people as possible. The whisper of the voice was quiet, but held a knowing immediacy. It said "now" and not "here" or "that person" which would both be somewhat less anxiety-inducing.

I saw the ascetic holy man of countless traditions, whose eyes and thoughts and footsteps led only towards the divine. In each I could see how they lived in the small voice, accepting every risk and answering every call, even to their deaths. They couldn't have a job because it would create safety that eliminated risk. They couldn't have family, or possessions, or any other worldly snare if they were to answer every call of the voice. I imagined myself letting go of every connection to be fully in the voice that way.

"Oh, sweetie. Melanie would kill you. You're not doing that to her," and we laughed together at my ego.

"So then is it evil when you hear the voice and sabotage it in an attempt to create control?"

"No. There's no such thing as evil. There's just love and fear."

"So if a person murders for no reason or commits genocide, they're just afraid?"

"Those are very deep and complicated types of fear, but, yes." I felt like this was a big leap, and my mind spun with how to balance that much pain and loss without any evil force. It was like a massive calculus problem where she was telling me that all of the evil in the equation zeroed out but I couldn't comprehend the calculation at that scale, and she had switched back to the less familiar voice that felt harder to question. It was like my Granny was channeling a deeper source of wisdom that she was able to share now that she was free of the bonds of her life. It also felt like the urgency had returned and she wanted to move on.

"So do our souls get punished for fear, or is fear the punishment itself?"

"Only love comes from this side. The fear is all over there. You could call the work of the living world a battle against fear, fueled by risk-filled splashes of the truth. I showed you death and the ability to come back whenever you're ready to try again." I remembered how grand, but serene and elegant it was on the energetic side. It wasn't clear to me that time had any part to play in that process, or that time necessarily moved forward by default in an individual's choice to re-enter reality. It also seemed like the notion of sustained individuality in the process was over-simplistic. "So even for a murderer, the fear and suffering is on the murderer."

"But it makes more fear in the world, so wouldn't that be evil?" I just couldn't get away from it.

"Still not in the way you're thinking. The fear is so much bigger than that. It orchestrated the social net that trapped every actor in that terrible drama with the specific murder as one of a thousand negative effects. The fearful web of illusion strings through everything in the calculating reality of the physical world. All that can break through the web are the two true acts." I would have to think more about evil, but I felt I was understanding the basic formula for truth and repeated it back.

"Anything that makes you realize how loved you are and how lucky you are to be right here right now." I saw moments from my life flicker by like beacons. Each moment had centered me and fueled me. "And anything that shares that truth with someone else."

"And you'll know when you have a chance..." She prompted.

"...when I am present in the moment to hear the still, small voice." I could feel the effect passing. My body was around me again and the room and soft bed were coming back. She said one last thing before leaving me:

"You don't need the medicine. You are the medicine."

I lay there in awe, processing all I'd heard.

My pain was gone.

Chapter 16

The Plastic Temple

In the morning, I was up before the sun. I left the bed where Josh had returned as I slept and wandered to the courtyard where the cool deep blue of the sky lazily washed away the stars. Hearing a "toc, toc, toc" of tapping wood, I went into the house. A volunteer was chopping fruit for breakfast.

"Good morning!" he said with more energy than I expected.

"Can I help?" I offered, just being present to the task of the moment.

"Uh, yeah, I guess." He handed me a big knife and nodded to a pile of cantaloupes. I realized as I began cutting that I wasn't one hundred percent connected to my body and maybe shouldn't be using a sharp knife, but we were talking about life and martial arts, and I resolved to stick with it and just go slow and steady. It felt good to help prepare food for others.

Through breakfast and the morning, I listened to people open up about their healing. I told Josh about my mysterious, medicine-less journey. He said he'd had a rough go of it the night before and I was worried that it would be inopportune to talk about my breakthroughs when he had been through a beat down. Instead it gave him a big lift to hear the story and wonder at the mystery of a recurring journey. He didn't know how to elaborate on what he'd experienced, but he was envious of the clarity of my journey, making me think that he'd been through a much more abstract kind of work.

I hadn't seen a lot of Darrick over the weekend besides the first night when we laughed in the bed. We'd missed him during the shadow integration and he'd kept mostly to himself and his mat since then. He was open to camaraderie, but tight-lipped about what he was seeing on his journeys. I knew enough of Darrick's history to know that he had some serious demons to face, but if he was making any progress against them, he wasn't telling us besides to knit his brow and say "it was good" while nodding intently. It was hard to reconcile the conversant vivid teachings of my visions with what seemed to be muddy and exhausting experiences that my friends were having. They had both been here more times and had several more journeys than me, and reported only positive outcomes in the weeks and months after. I wondered what was different about the way we were interacting with the medicine.

We stayed through the whole closing ceremony this time, and for the integration meetings after that. When I talked to the group from my lodge about what had happened to me the night before, the facilitator told me that the medicine stayed in your system for about a week. It was a relief to hear that this happened all the time, but when I asked more about journeys without the medicine, she said she'd never heard of someone experiencing another vivid journey a day later like I was describing. Normally people just felt the afterglow during that time and were still open to change and healing.

We took an Uber to the hotel and napped a little before going to eat a robust dinner of delights that we'd been missing for two weeks. We had massages and sat in a sauna to talk more and process more as the passing hours helped coalesce our thoughts. We were all glowing and feeling the loving warmth of our combined journeys, though it came out in jokes and silliness more than soulful discussion. Even the hard sessions like Josh's the night before left healing and peace in their wake, and we were riding that wave in love and laughter. There were deep teachings to ponder, but in the moment, the weightlessness of spirit was the gift.

I awoke in the hotel that night in pain again, this time with a biting headache. After some restless shifting, I remembered the night before and placed my hands palm down on the bed beside me, and began to breathe deeply with a sub vocal hum so as not to wake Josh and Darrick in the beds nearby. I held the feeling of the vibrating energy in my mind, but I also had this new awareness that allowed me to perceive through my heart, holding an idea or person in an entirely different way than my mind did. Within minutes I felt the humming get picked up as vibration in my gut and build on its own. I kept breathing deeply and it spread lower into my hips and upward into my diaphragm. I wasn't having any visions, but as the vibration bathed my body, the headache dissolved. Instead of building to an out-of-body teaching experience, the vibration peaked and then abated, but took my headache with it. I wondered how much longer this strange power would continue. Up to a week for the medicine to leave my system, the facilitator had said.

The next day was surreal. Still in the afterglow of the Ayahuasca and with a deep and open love for all people, we went into Universal Studios theme park. Instead of any cynicism or judgment about monetizing childhood fantasy, I was enraptured by the joy and awe of the children themselves, and I jumped into it, opening myself to wonder. We reveled in the uncertainty and sway of anticipation and revelation. Josh's memory of being there before with his family would lead us towards something they'd enjoyed only to find it closed or out of service. By instantly dropping any disappointment tied to the built-up anticipation, we could be present to where we were and see that the effort had led us to something else just as wondrous that would've gone unnoticed if we'd been mired in our attachment to the original goal. All the little moments where one idea met its sudden end just led to other little joys as long as we let go and stayed present to what was actually around us rather than our ideas of what should be. The whole day was a fairytale practice session for living in the moment.

The easy, present bliss of each moment even through discomfort or struggle or rejection brought me back to my months on the Appalachian Trail. Every time it seemed like a plan or an expectation was in jeopardy and we'd let go and find ourselves in something better, I'd exclaim, "We win again!" Our A.T. motto had always been a badge, not of victory in the sense that most would recognize it, but of a state of mind so present to the moment that all of life's ups and downs were sacred victories. There was no way to fail in that mindset except to lose it.

Chapter 17

The Inner Path

During the Monday night after Universal Studios and the Tuesday night after the return trip, there was no energetic journey. I'd actually been so tired both nights that I'd slept right through and hadn't made any attempt. Perhaps the lack of pain waking me in the night had broken the cycle, though I'd been pretty sore after the many miles walked at Universal Studios.

Every Wednesday night is "date night" for me and Melanie. Everyone who knows us knows not to call or expect us to join in any other activity on Wednesday night. It started after ten years of marriage when the pressure of two kids and a new business opened at the start of a recession threatened to tear us apart. We had been to the Pantry a few times over the years. It had opened the same month as we had opened the dojo. We could rarely afford it, but would commiserate with the owner, and hoped that spending our money there might bless our own endeavor. When the dojo first turned a tiny profit but our marriage was in its biggest slump ever, we decided to carve out time in the middle of the week for each other. We've spent each Wednesday night at the Pantry ever since. That Wednesday night ritual is the anchoring practice of our marriage.

That Wednesday after returning from Florida I was especially relaxed. After a weekend of mind-expanding work and a day of childlike play, I didn't have the first part of the week to wind down from. I had a hard session of swimming after working a half day, and then we walked the five blocks to the restaurant as I began trying to explain some of what I'd seen that weekend. Melanie was patient and receptive, but a story like that is a lot to process for anyone who's on the outside. They have to listen patiently, wondering if their partner is about to join a cult, lose their mind, become an addict, or tell them they're leaving because what they've seen is taking them in a new direction.

Soon we moved past it and fell back into our normal five-hour date night conversation as the wine flowed and the hearty Czech food paraded slowly across our table. Tipsy and in love, we wound our way through the familiar neighborhood trees back to the house for massage oil, and candles, and groovy music, and sex that you can only find with someone who's been loving you for decades. Sometimes we'll sleep all the way through the night to find ourselves still entangled in the morning. That night I woke after an hour or so to use the bathroom.

I slipped on some underwear and headed to the bathroom to relieve my bladder, hearing the clicking late-night sounds of my teenagers gaming with their friends. I thought about their difficulties with adolescence and missing years of socialization in school. Pandemic zoom schooling had removed all desire from them to put any effort into school, and we were trapped as parents between enforcing responsibility and acknowledging that they were suffering from an unprecedented disconnection. The games were a distraction drug, and yet, also the only socialization they got as they bantered with friends locally and strangers internationally. At that moment frustration was far from me, and I decided not to come down on them about being up late with their games.

Back in my room, I delighted in the comfort of my own bed and the sight of my naked, sleeping wife. I wondered about the vibrations and whether they were gone for good. In the restrictions from the weeks before, we couldn't eat any of the foods I'd just filled myself with. We couldn't drink or have sex, both of which I'd just done to my fill. Since I hadn't felt them in a few days, I figured the vibrations were gone and the secondary visions and pain relief had wound down and away. All the same, I was curious, so I planted my hands on the bed beside me, palms down, and began to breathe deeply and hum lightly at varying frequencies to feel the buzz of my vocalization in different places along my spine. Focusing the humming vibration on my heart, I tried to hold the heart-image of the energetic world while letting my mind relax.

After a few minutes, I felt like there was something there, but it wasn't quite catching into the full, all-encompassing vibrations from previous days. I tried breathing more deeply for several minutes, and gradually the familiar vibrations came pouring in, much more acutely than they had on Sunday in the hotel. I could feel the full pressure of the spiraling vibrations pouring up from my belly and sternum. My heavy breathing fed and stoked the vibrations, while my humming guided the focus of the vibration to specific areas of my body. I felt the energy flow through me in a loving cascade.

"You're freaking me out a little," came Melanie's voice to my left. I wondered if it would all tumble down if I talked to her.

"It's happening right now. The vibrations I was telling you about. Put your hand on me. I want to see if you can feel it." It had occurred to me that the vibrations were actually some kind of euphoric shivering that could be measured or felt from the outside. She slid her hand over to my chest. I half expected to feel some kind of charged interaction of my energy with hers, but it just carried on uninterrupted.

"Nope. Normal. You breathing hard like that reminds me of the night before I took you to the hospital."

"Oh, no. I'm doing so good right now, baby. I can stop if it's too freaky, though."

"No, as long as you're alright and not too noisy." I went back to breathing but kept it quieter, not trying to stoke the energy higher. Then I wondered about the boys. I knew Wayah at least was up from the sound of his still clacking computer keyboard. We'd talked quite a bit about my weekend before I went, and I'd told him about what had happened when I got back. After years of difficult parenting and rebellion, it had been a note that struck up a genuine and honest conversation.

I wasn't sure if getting out of bed or even sitting up would make it stop, but when I rose to walk to his room, it didn't change a bit. I walked smoothly to his door and pushed it open, seeing the glow in the dark of his game framing his silhouette. I remembered how Granny had shown me how drawing closer to him would help my energy flow to him and so I walked up behind him and put my hands on his chest. My touch startled him a little and he looked up at me in the dark, pulling off his headphones. Normally this was a moment when I would be telling him that he needed to stop, and he braced for chastisement.

"Can you feel that?" I said, humming and focusing on pushing the energy into him. I could feel how it surged forward out of me, but couldn't tell what it was doing from there.

"Um, what's going on, dad?" He said with some trepidation. His shoulders had tensed at my touch and were still holding.

"I've got the vibration I told you about going. I want to see if I can connect it to you. Try humming like this. Hmmmmmmm." I listened and felt for him to pick it up like a radio receiving a signal, but he didn't.

"Uh, Dad? Can we do this another time?" I could see that he was unnerved by this twist.

"Sure, kiddo. Go on to sleep. It's late."

I went back to my bed and returned to my own vibrations. By humming up and down the musical scale, the vibration of the humming would come to match the vibration of locations up and down my spine. I hummed in tune with those locations and settled into each one moving up from the bottom of my gut. When I came to my chest, I could feel that the vibration was more faint, and so I focused on that location with the humming and tried to breathe directly into it. It gradually built up and came to vibrate with the same intensity as the lower areas. With great surprise, like slipping on a puddle in the dark, I fell back out of my body again.

It was less dramatic than the first two times. Instead of my body seeming like a vast constellation, it seemed like my body just spread out around me locally. I was definitely back at a distance looking through. I watched the energies pour through me, tinted with the sounds of my humming. I cast about for a while, trying to turn and look through the source of the energy to speak to the dead again as Melanie's grandmother had recently passed and I thought I might find her. I could see back to the source, but it was like looking through a keyhole at the majesty I had witnessed before. I returned my attention to the space around my own consciousness in the world and the connection between me and Melanie.

I began to see a series of energetic circuits involving the vibrating spirals of the body. The vibration made me think of orgasm and the way the body would quiver deeply, but these energetic vibrations were a higher frequency and apparently not physically shaking my body. Since one of the sources of the vibration was deep in my pelvis, I visualized a circuit that joined two people. It seemed like the act of sex might bring two people so fully into the moment that their energy would spiral together. The pressing of the body together was a way of joining the radiating sources of energy at a moment when people were wholly in the present and could feel the flow.

From there I could see how a good, committed hug also lined up the radiating energies of the spine. I saw a series like a flip book of great hugs in my life, all fully committed to the moment and the exchange of energy. Pulling back even further, I saw more complex circuits of energy. A teacher provides energy to a student in the form of inspiration, which the student converts into struggle and growth, which the teacher reclaims as purpose. Each circuit increased the energy involved instead of just exchanging it. By being fully present, these circuits acted like the second type of truth. I hadn't seen it this way before, how the exchange could sustain its power with a net result of more true energy from the other side entering the world through all of the people involved. To benefit, one had to be present to the circuit and overcome their fears.

Just as I realized this was built on the earlier concept of the two true acts, there was a shift. I saw false circuits that felt controlled and safe, but actually bled energy and robbed it from others to create an illusory gain in one part of the circuit. Another teacher is stuck in their past and expects students to give them energy the way they used to, but fears to invest what remains of their dwindling passion. The students respond with anxiety and do their best to meet the teacher's demands, holding their inspiration back for a better home. This makes the teacher feel hollow inside which they take out on the students by lowering their expectations, believing that this generation has less to offer than the one they remember fondly. The teacher believes that they are standing as an example of something greater, while devouring the empty calories of long dead inspiration.

With the false circuits, people will either try to control the outcome of the energy circuit to benefit themselves or to force others to give the energy to begin the circuit. These would ultimately spend more energy than was gained in total, or give an illusory benefit to one while hurting others. The true circuits always sustain the energy of everyone involved and build in power with each transaction.

I felt my body laugh out loud as I watched the comical ways that we try to be safe and certain while draining ourselves dry: Teenage lovers hemorrhaging anxious energy for fear of giving voice to their desires in the wrong way at the wrong moment, young parents enduring the crush of a hated job rather than risking uncertainty, someone in need of inspiration hiding behind a list of everything they need to do before they take a shot at their dream instead of just starting. Despite the tragedy, I couldn't help but find it all comical, but I reminded myself to stay quiet so as not to wake Melanie again and began to return to my physical self. It would've been tragic if there was only one chance, or a punishment for failure, but it was all just love. It was like watching a sleepy baby refuse to go to bed despite their exhaustion. I could feel myself coming out of it and as I passed through the liminal space around my body, I was aware of Granny watching over me and felt my left eyelid droop like hers did. A little nod from my loving guide. Once back in my body, I fell back into a deep sleep.

Over the next week, I tried to create the vibrations in a number of other ways and other times. I tried the guest room so as not to bother Melanie, but I wasn't able to find the connection. I tried to start the vibration in the basement as part of a morning meditation, but got nothing. The week since I had taken the medicine had passed, so it was probably just out of my system, but the powerful out of body experience on Wednesday after feeling like it was gone had left me hoping.

I had taken psychedelics before. Several times in my life I had eaten Psilocybin mushrooms. The first had been a blissful experience on the Appalachian Trail with close friends laughing and playing in the wilderness. The most recent had been as an adult and parent, becoming very aware of my many overlapping responsibilities from a bird's eye view. There were usually hallucinations, often just flowing distortions of what was around me. There was a sense of being very aware of the space close around me and my internal workings. There was a lot of laughter, with anxiety connected to anything that surprised me by entering the space from the outside.

My Ayahuasca experience was something completely different. The hallucinations that I was experiencing were all-encompassing experiences of another place. In that place, I was fully in tune with my mind and my senses rather than feeling silly and mentally askew. What was the most intriguing was the presence of my grandmother there. Any other time I had hallucinated (even from extreme fever), the voices that would come to me could be easily traced back to the workings of my own mind. Perhaps some creativity was encountered, but it was clearly my own brand of creativity. My mind has a flavor to its workings that I know well. This was something else.

My grandmother was speaking in her voice, but not with the words she used to use. The tone was familiar, but she spoke with a cosmic confidence about things I didn't understand. If it was all coming from inside my head, it would all make sense, right? She was showing me new paradigms, making bold statements, showing me examples, defending against my arguments, and then summing them up clearly and concisely. I was being met by an enlightened form of my beloved Granny that was not coming from my own mind.

The next Friday, exactly two weeks after drinking the medicine, I went to bed with powerful anxiety. I had teachers in town running seminars and students taking tests, which had taken up much of my time just as an acquaintance was trying to put together what looked like an incredible investment opportunity. I'd missed the deadline to file some paperwork because I was in the middle of seminars. I wasn't sure the opportunity was lost, but I was kicking myself for not figuring out a way to secure the deal, and it was keeping me awake. Something in the back of my mind whispered to me about the pains in my hips and my head that had gone away with the altered state of the past weeks.

I decided to try to connect to the energy again. I planted my palms and began breathing and humming. I knew the medicine was all out of my system, but I hoped that the focused practice contained enough of the healing that it might help. I felt a distant buzzing, but it could've all been in my head. I picked up the speed and depth of my breath, humming on the exhalation, and continued for several minutes. Then it was there. The vibration took over my belly and kept up without my heavy breathing to sustain it. I didn't leave my body or have any visions, but the pain of my anxiety not only melted away like warm butter, but showed itself to be no different from the pains in my body. Even without the vivid visions, this felt like a valuable lesson. All of my pains, both mental and physical, pass through my mind as signals from a fearful body, and all can be left behind.

That weekend was long and exhausting with multiple seminars and extra sessions. After everyone left town, we finished Sunday night with a family dinner at my in-laws' house. I got home and crashed hard at around nine-o-clock. I woke at about two in the morning and lay still, wondering if I would get back to sleep. In my forties I had begun sleeping a bit less overall and sometimes if I got five or six good hours of sleep, my body would decide it was enough. It made going to bed early a potential disruption. After being able to "connect" on Friday, as I had begun to call the process of seeking out the vibrations, I was curious to see if I could keep doing it this far out from taking the medicine.

I stepped through the ritual again, palms down, breathing, humming. It seemed that very deep, brisk breaths were key, and I dug into the process, knowing that it would take at least fifteen minutes of deep breathing and humming to connect. When it picked up again and the vibrations began coursing through me, I was again aware of my grandmother showing me how energy works and how we stumble over ourselves in trying to find a safer way around the hard truth. These examples started with intimacy and how we have a basic energetic desire to form energetic connections with others, but the survival and reproduction needs of our bodies, minds, and social structures bend the pure desire out of shape as we wrestle around socially, mentally, and physically appropriate ways to experience pure love and connection.

She showed me why gender can be confusing as it comes from the meeting of the body with the world and not from the energetic self, which is a genderless pattern capable of working through any body at any time. There are traits and actions that we associate with masculinity and femininity as powerful conceptual frameworks, including this overpoweringly feminine energy that was communicating with me, but they don't fit onto people like hats. Each physical body contains its own particular mix of genitals, hormones, memories, and a spectrum of masculinity and femininity like a balance of yin and yang. For that matter, all of the squishy details of this vessel designed to replicate itself and protect the house of our consciousness were volatile and multifaceted. It was a wondrous suit that we used to experience the world, but the adaptability that allowed it to survive also came with potentially befuddling complexity and inconsistency.

I could see how different bodies had great strengths and weaknesses that intermeshed with the signature of the spirit to create a unique person. I saw how important and challenging that work is, and how frustrating it could be. How when choosing to re-enter the world for a new life one might choose to be a dog to enjoy the unbridled canine enthusiasm for a decade, or to spend a hundred years in the elegant balance of being a tree, or spend a span of months following the orchestrated purpose of an ant's life before taking another run at the complexity of humanity.

What on earth was going on? It had been more than two weeks now since I drank the Ayahuasca, but still these vibrations and visions were continuing. I needed to find more guidance. I started with googling "Ayahuasca vibration," which brought up discussions about hummingbirds. I hadn't thought about it before, but the vibration wasn't unlike the buzz of a hummingbird's wing beats. I found a few discussions about recapturing some feelings with integration, but couldn't find anything about replicating the effect weeks after. Surely I wasn't the only person experiencing this. I called a friend named Taran from elementary school who I knew had an analytical mind and a background that I would predict might include either experience with Ayahuasca or at least knowledge about it. When I talked to him I found out that Taran had actually lived in South America for years as part of a tradition that did Ayahuasca as a regular part of their spiritual life.

I told him all about what I had experienced and was continuing to experience, and he told me that he hadn't heard of that particular effect but that all sorts of things were possible in the practice.

"It sounds like you got exactly what we'd want you to get out of your experience with Aya. My only advice is to take a lot of notes and keep doing what you're doing."

The next Friday, now three weeks after taking the medicine, I was snowed in and on a video meeting with a colleague who liked to throw out references to meditation and energy and quantum reality. As our meeting ended, I said, "Hey, Nick. Can you stick around for a minute? I want to ask you a meditation question."

"Absolutely, bro," he said with redoubled attention. I gave him the quick version of the retreat and focused on the vibrations, the locations, and the way they moved. "Dude. You're talking about chakras!" Nick said certainly. "Check out this video. It's a chakra meditation I freakin' love."

I thanked him, but was a little resistant to the idea. I had spent a lot of time learning about the Chinese science of chi meridians in the martial arts as they relate to damage or healing. I'd experienced mixed results, deciding ultimately that the pressure points were about blood flow and the nervous system instead of a mystical chi energy. Whenever I heard someone talk about chakras, it was connected to a group of practices that I had found to be ineffectual and flighty. I'd had people place sacred items on my chakras while trying to do remote acupuncture on me with no effect and many beloved friends that wanted to practice reiki on me. I always felt the presence of their loving intention, and no more. Chakras had been filed away in my mind with all the many iterations of wishful thinking.

I looked up the video that Nick linked to and heard a voice that turned me off immediately. I tilted my head back and to the side. He was speaking in the "Let's meditate, bro" soft, inspirational surfer voice. He wanted us to hum at certain frequencies -*Ok, that's promising*- as we moved through the chakra points on the body along the spine -*Oh no*- As he began, the humming was exactly what I'd intuited on my own. The points were exactly where I'd felt them, even down to the rotation and direction.

"Ok, fine. Screw my preconceived ideas. I'm apparently experiencing my chakras."

Chapter 18

Of Spinning Wheels

If chakras are a real thing that I just wasn't able to experience before, there was a lot of new testing and exploration to be done. I ordered a huge encyclopedic resource about chakras that was very highly reviewed and started reading online blogs and websites. I prioritized the ones that also discussed vibration and frequency since those aspects had been very clear to me in my own out-of-body experience. Many sites talked a lot about chakras having different colors that matched the visual spectrum. I skipped over the ones that relied heavily on color since everything I had "seen" in that space had been through my heart and not my eyes. Pairing what I experienced to colors felt inadequate and overly simplistic to my mind.

It seemed like everything I read touched on aspects of what I'd experienced, then added a lot of other details that were irrelevant in energetic space but made it all feel more fleshed out when you were a physical human person who lived in the world. I had to keep in mind that while my experiences were vivid and filled with revelation, they only represented about ten hours, and this was an idea that was thousands of years old just in its discussion. There were likely worlds and worlds of detail and information left to discover if I could find sources that weren't just making things up to fill in the blanks that the conscious mind needs to make an idea seem credible. It was such a difficult space to navigate. People would always present themselves with a voice of authority, so it was impossible to tell who was speaking from direct experience, and who was just reinterpreting reinterpretations and claiming understanding in an unverifiable echo chamber.

Even so, new revelations were coming through my own ongoing experimentation very quickly. The notes I had heard in the video that connected the humming to each chakra separately were the major scale. This seemed odd since this scale is a very western and relatively recent invention. There are many sets of chakras people discuss, but the most common has seven chakras, starting at the root (or perineum), continuing up to the sacral (below the navel), the solar plexus, the heart, the throat, the third eye, and the crown (on top of the head).

The root chakra was paired with C Major and, from what I read in books and online, connected to family, origins, and feelings of home and comfort. While the humming that I used to activate them wandered about in a droning fashion, holding C Major would hit the root chakra very specifically. I was reminded that Bob Dylan referred to C Major as "the people's key" and began to pick at the guitar, strumming and singing songs in C to feel how my chakras reacted.

This experimentation went on and on. Since the chakras were tied to concepts as well as vibrations, could a song using combinations of sounds that correlated with the chakras that reinforced the subject of the song have greater impact? Would minor tones and seventh chords that brought the listener close to the major chord without reaching it create longing for that principle? I tried playing One by U2, which used an F major 7th chord (close to F, but just a little off) throughout the verses, switching to the complete F major chord only near the end during a heartfelt lyrical plea to see if I felt a longing and culmination from my heart chakra. Logically, it would combine the lyrical concept with the aligned chakra sound frequency vibrating near my heart from the guitar. I felt only my normal emotional reaction to the song, but now wondered if these vibrations were creating the emotion I already felt. It felt like a type of clarity more than an amplification.

The big book of chakras was immense and far better as a reference than something to consume cover to cover. I also found that when I followed anyone else's information over what I'd experienced on my own, I would have a much harder time finding the vibrations when I meditated. It felt like the more I tried to decipher using outside knowledge, the less I was able to experience. I had to let my mind and its expectations get out of the way. By relaxing my desire to understand and just allowing myself to observe, I made a couple of interesting personal discoveries. First was that when I connected, I would first be aware of vibration first from my sacral and solar plexus chakras. These are associated with creativity (or reproduction) and personal power. As my connection to the vibrations grew, my root chakra would become clear in its vibration. Every time I left my body, it would happen as my awareness reached up to the heart chakra and I felt its vibration build.

In my journeys at that point, I was outside my body looking in and everything was clear. During meditation, I could keep walking up the chakras, activating them individually. There was one hitch. The throat chakra felt like a very weak signal. Moving on, the third eye and crown would ring out clearly. The throat is associated with communication, the voice, but also one's "voice," or personal outspoken message. Hm.

During all of this exploration I was steadily training for my fifth degree black belt test in Cuong Nhu. Our annual Memorial Day conference was set to return after missing the last two years due to the pandemic, and my long delayed test was back on. Six of my advanced students worked with me on it several times a week, pushing to see how much we could get my body to do by May. IATC (our International Annual Training Camp) was the only place to take advanced rank tests in Cuong Nhu. This three day gathering of our martial art style each year was our most anticipated event. Not only for advanced testing but because our friends and training partners from around the country and the world were all gathered in one place. Along with days of training, testing, and demonstrations, was a rolling social event that lasted late into each night of the event. We would huddle in college dorm rooms where the event is held to tell old stories, remember long lost friends, and get to know the upcoming generations. There was music, dancing, and a hefty dose of energy that wore my body out, but left my spirit charged up for another year of teaching and training. Testing at IATC meant feeling the gathered love and energy of hundreds of close friends building me up, but it also meant showing everyone all at once that I was still in a weakened body.

Because of my revelations with Granny, I was at peace with whatever I could do, and proud of my progress, but I knew that the test might be a surprising disappointment to others. Most of the masters that would judge my performance hadn't seen my diminished state yet and were used to seeing me at full strength. People throughout the style that had trained with me in the past would see a steep drop in power and endurance from what they'd seen before the pandemic. I didn't think the masters would fail me, as much of what qualified us to test at high rank was based on our leadership, and my development of one of the largest schools in the style from scratch and in a relatively short time still stood as a high achievement. It was the disappointment that nagged at me. I wasn't ready to see the eyes of my peers as I slipped from an inspiration to someone that was promoted based solely on lifetime achievement.

I was making some progress again, boosted by my changed

attitude of pride in my new accomplishments and the feeling of a new start. I was swimming harder and faster, even through the winter, my little coach wrapped in a parka by the pool, barking out challenges and corrections. I often felt as I set off from one edge of the pool that I didn't know where the strength would come from to finish what she was asking of me, but it felt good to throw myself against it. Holding my breath also felt like the most meaningful way to recover from not being able to breathe.

Something in the balance of holding my breath, struggling with my body, and the cold living pressure of the water made me feel close to Quynh when I was pushing my limit. In the muffled sound-darkness under the water, my not breathing gently touched a place of strength. When I was in the hospital it was a deep act of will not to breath into infected lungs that would burst into bone breaking coughs. When Quynh was in the hospital on the respirator, my heart was there where he couldn't breathe in. Under the water, striving to move meter after meter, my heart touched his heart through the will not to breathe, and connected us both to the will to live.

"Ok, Tannar. Ju are going to zwim to one quarter before ju take a bureath," came Juiliana's sharp voice through that thick Portugués accent. Then the rest of the instruction piled like a tall stack of blocks on my head as she described only taking three breaths over the length of the olympic sized pool.

"Aaa." I had never taken anywhere near that few breaths when swimming fifty meters. "I'm gonna give that a try, but if I start to drown, I don't think you're big enough to pull me out, and there's no one else around." I would often get dizzy or faint but had never felt I would completely pass out, just that I suddenly needed to gasp repeatedly for air. It felt like if I pushed for this I might cross a new line.

"Oh, Tannar!" Her shoulders bounced in her robe as she laughed.

"Ju'r not nearly touff enough to drown jorself!"

I grinned broadly in the water and etched the quote on my mind for later.

I had scheduled my next trip to Florida for another Ayahuasca retreat in early July. I planned to finish my test during our annual gathering at IATC at the end of May and then go back to take the next step deeper into this energetic world that Granny had shown me, free from the stress of testing. I was learning all I could about my body and chakras and meditation, but there were blocks that I was eager to see the other side of. I knew there was more to know, but wanted to learn from the source instead of trying to figure out which pieces of knowledge in books would help me. I was comfortable finding my chakras through my breathing meditation but more and more aware that book knowledge of them didn't make them stronger. I hadn't found anyone else who could feel them or the vibration, but people could see how it changed me, sometimes starting at my appearance and saying things like, "What's up with you? You're glowing!"

I was walking through the grocery store thinking about why my throat chakra was always hard to reach when I turned down an aisle and saw my friend Jason. Jason had trained at my dojo some, but his daughter was still a student. We hung out as friends from time to time, but he'd been busy with his struggling massage and reiki practice, and I'd been busy trying to recover myself and the dojo from the pandemic.

As I saw him, a flash came over me. I remembered times in the past when he'd done reiki on me and I'd felt nothing more than his loving presence. What if it wasn't nonsense, but I was just closed off to it? I walked up to him and booked a session for the next day. When I arrived at the small office, he led me into a completely blue room with a standard massage table and a smattering of Hindu symbols and pictures. I'd seen those types of symbols in a lot of my recent reading, but hadn't started memorizing exact symbols in connection to what they meant.

After I told him what I'd seen, and what I'd been experimenting with, he said, "So, what would you like to work on with me today?" I'd really made the appointment on impulse, but I knew what I wanted to see.

"I want to see if what you're doing and what I've been doing are related. I also want to see why my throat chakra seems to be muted."

"Well." He swiveled in his chair slowly back and forth. "You may have noticed that this whole room is blue. Blue is the color of the throat chakra. The symbol behind you" — a single Hindu rune hung framed on the wall — "is the symbol for the throat chakra. This whole room was decorated to help connect to it." He had the matter-of-fact smile that I remembered from the Ayahuasca volunteers who knew we were all headed into the ceremony to be transformed.

"Well, I guess I'm in the right place," I said as I lay on the table. I had thought about trying to connect to my chakras there on the table to see how he responded, but I decided not to help him. I wouldn't do the breathing or the humming. I wanted see what he could do on his own. I didn't have to wait long. He closed his eyes and held his hands a centimeter from my head, moving them around the surface of me but never making contact. The response was startlingly quick. Not since drinking the sacred medicine had I felt the vibrating energy course through me like that. It was exploding from my whole spine and up and down my arms and legs. I could feel it pouring from my hands. For our whole session together I was coursing with energy, and when he stopped, it passed gently away. I grabbed his hand. I was covered with sweat.

"Could you feel that?" I asked, knowing the answer.

"Yup."

I had more sessions with Jason and cast my net out for others that might be able to turn on the vibrations without my assistance. I found a few more people that were able to open up my chakras without my help. It became my litmus test for the whole category of mystical mumbo jumbo that I was trying to make room for in my new reasoning. I thought, "If you can make the lights come on without me doing the work, then I'll listen to your mumbo and try to integrate your jumbo."

Anne was one of the three people I found that was able to flip on all the switches. She met with me several times and was really curious about the details of the experience. She eventually told me about one of her teachers that lived far away in Oregon who wanted to meet with me. I shared some correspondence with her teacher to describe what I was experiencing, paid her considerable fee, and then we met on a video conference. She claimed to be doing remote viewing on me and sensing my energy from thousands of miles away. I was open but skeptical, giving her some trust based on her student's ability to access my energetic self. After getting the basics and scanning me, she said, "Who are you?" That could mean a lot of things.

"As in?"

"What's your training and where are you trying to go with this?" I hadn't really thought about that. I was just exploring a wild new frontier. Training?

"No training. I'm just trying to make sense of this experience," I responded cautiously. Her eyebrows furrowed like she sensed that something was off. I felt like I may have stumbled into a private area without the proper credentials.

"What do you do for work?" She probed, redirecting with a flutter of what felt like frustration.

"I'm a martial arts teacher."

"For how long?" Her eyebrow raised.

"Well I've been studying martial arts for almost forty years but doing it as my work for closer to twenty." She sat back in her chair and dropped her shoulders, seemingly satisfied. Her face relaxed. "So you've been working on controlled breathing, focusing through struggle and pain, acting with grace in the midst of frightening attack, and controlling your body and your energy with great care and precision?" She was giving me the smug look of a professor waiting for you to finish a theorem that they see you can solve. "For forty years," she added after a pause. I nodded, seeing how all of that training would be helpful in navigating a frightening and unbalancing otherworldly dimension. "I think I understand better. So now the question is, do you intend to become a shaman and healer?"

"I'm pretty sure that's not where I'm headed," I brought back quickly. "I'm seeing all of this as refining and augmenting what I do as a teacher."

"Well you need to be very careful with this." She seemed truly concerned. "You've been shown how much power is moving through you, and now you're learning new ways to connect with it. It's easy for that to spill over onto your loved ones and those that support you in your life. It's not uncommon for an irresponsible shaman to be a widower several times over since his wife will take on all of that uncontrolled energy."

I hadn't thought of that at all. We talked more about telling stories and being responsible with what I learn, but what stuck with me was that my relationships could be a pathway for irresponsibly harnessed energy to crush those close to me.

Chapter 19

Ever Turning

Coung Nhu's 2022 annual training camp, and with it my test, got canceled again. The chance of the virus being introduced with so many people getting together from all over the country and the world was still too high, and the university we were meeting at would be forced to quarantine us all for ten days if there was an outbreak. People would miss flights home, wouldn't be able to afford the additional cost of quarantine housing, and so on, and so on. My test couldn't wait another year so I reluctantly started making preparations to have masters and friends travel to me in Little Rock for a local test at the end of the summer.

Not only had my fifth degree test been put off for three years already, but the fatigue of restarting and re-envisioning the test requirements over and over again was wearing on my students as much as myself. Each time the test was delayed, the elaborate, choreographed demonstration had to be re-trained since a different combination of people would be available. It was like rehearsing for a play only to have it put off for a year, and then again, and again.

The version I made with Quynh for the 2020 IATC had twelve people. Only six of those had been able to keep working on it during the pandemic and we'd rewritten it to accommodate the change. Then we'd rebuilt it from scratch when I realized that I wasn't going to heal in time. Three of those that would have helped with my test in May would be traveling or back to college in August so I would have to rework the whole thing from scratch again to match a new, hopefully slightly higher fitness level, and reformat it to be done by only the three advanced adult students who were my core team during the summer. Additionally, everyone was mentally exhausted from years of pandemic and preparing for their own tests now simultaneously instead of being able to just focus on mine. It was going to be a tough summer. It also meant I'd go to Florida before the test instead of after. Instead of being a regrouping experience focused on my new life after the test, my next Ayahuasca journey would take place during the height of my anxious preparation.

I'd hit a broad plateau in my recovery. After months of micro improvements, I'd leveled off and my endurance had stabilized, but well below its previous level. I wasn't able to complete my weapons forms at speed and had built in a lot of dramatic pauses to catch my breath. If I got carried away, though, and really went for it (as I was prone to do when testing), I wouldn't make it to the pauses without getting dizzy and disoriented. "You're not nearly tough enough to drown yourself, Tanner" became my mantra as I pushed through the dizziness and flirted with blackout. The demo, even shortened and stripped to the bare minimum of what I needed to do instead of the epic show of skill that Quynh and I had wanted, was still impossible for me at full speed. It had to be separated into sections, and those sections needed pauses that had to be carefully choreographed so that they would look somewhat natural instead of looking like a guy constantly trying to catch his breath.

I had started using canned oxygen before and during training like high-altitude athletes use. It didn't help me go longer, it just helped me recover a little faster. I had talked to the doctor for a pro sports team about athletes recovering from situations like mine, and she gave me a list of both legal and not-yet-approved supplements they were trying, but nothing had shown itself to be a cure yet and athletic careers were being lost to covid-related respiratory issues.

I had an appointment to see a pulmonologist about my lungs since it felt like they gave out very consistently when I hit about eighty percent exertion. I wondered if there was scar tissue from my painful hospital trials that just reduced the amount of oxygen that came with each breath. The tail end of the pandemic was a tough time to see a pulmonologist, though. They were overworked, overbooked, and exhausted from double-duty. My appointment kept getting rescheduled, and looked like it wouldn't be until the week of the test in early August.

It was in the midst of all of this discovery and uncertainty that I got back on the plane to Florida. This time with Josh, Darrick, and Josh's nineteen year old son, Beck, who had been one of my students from the time he was six years old. My long-time students feel like my own children to me, and I thought I might worry too much about him. I remembered, though, that once I drank the medicine, none of that would be able to reach me.

Part 3
The Hammer of Creation and Destruction

Chapter 20

A Crown of Storms

This time, arriving in Florida, I was optimistic and eager. After the revelations of my last trip had changed my entire world-view, I was ready to dive deeper and continue my progress. The break-down of truth and illusion had become a deep guiding formula. The revelation that I was new and didn't have to compare myself to any other previous lives had released me and led to more growth and peace. The opening of the energetic world and chakras had become a fascinating new experience of my body and my energetic exchange with reality that continued to reveal new facets. Now I was returning to the source to enter the second part and go even deeper. I had no idea where deeper was, but I felt like I had peeked my head into an explosive new view of reality, and after six months of study, I was ready to go see my Granny and find out what was next.

We traveled together by plane and passed the familiar steps of the cramped ride from the airport with Tom, the first check-in with the vitals, and then the medical review of prescriptions and our mental state. I had almost no anxiety, but there was still the noxious knowledge of the purging transition that I had to go through before getting to that place of learning and transformation. It was hard every time. The taste of the tea was so hard last time that I had some concern about being able to drink it at all, and I never liked throwing up or the neck and throat soreness that followed. On the other side of that transition, though, was a deep knowl-edge that came from experiencing mind-altering truth first hand.

If I had heard only the description of what I experienced last time, it would have been interesting or even inspirational, but would not have changed me. I had to see it, question it, have it repeated and shown to me over and over.

Josh wanted his comfortable private room to be a home base for everyone, but with four of us now including his son, I wasn't planning on being there as much. I would make an exception for the shower, though. That private air conditioned bathroom was several levels above the outdoor, semi-private ones that everyone else got to use. I also preferred to leave my bag in the room before going to the small lodge by the fence to pick out a mat. Not because I was worried about theft, but because space was so limited around the mats. Everyone in the mat-filled lodge had the familiar trepidation of every first day. We were headed for something hard, but hopefully also for relief. We didn't know each other yet, but were kind and optimistic. Being on my third retreat put me in the ranks of the experienced, but there were several people with dozens of journeys under their belts. Seeing people on their twenty fifth experience made me wonder how long I was in this for. It felt like I was moving along a path and making clear progress, but was there an end, or was it just intense therapy that would last all my life?

A girl on a mat across from me caught my eye. She was clearly an athlete but had an unusual muscle configuration. She was heavy on leg strength with thick, powerful ankles and feet. Spending as much time with bodies as I do in the martial arts, I have a fascination with puzzling out people's activities by the particular development of their musculature. I was leaning towards running, but a runner's legs were usually leaner. Cyclists didn't have those ankles. I brought myself back to my intention. Staring at young women wasn't why I was there.

Through the rest of the afternoon I did my best to bring together everything I'd learned about chakras and my meditations on how they work through me. I waded in the relief I'd gained from the revelation that I was newborn, and reviewed the breakdown of truth, illusion, and the still quiet voice. I was ready. We had our group introductions, learning about everyone in the lodge. *Aha! The girl across from me said she was a skier!* I hadn't seen skiers while growing up in the south but the musculature matched the activity and checked off the box in my mind.

I shared my goals, though I felt a little out of place talking about trying to build energetic knowledge in the midst of so many people's stories of tragedy and suffering. My primary stress was about my upcoming test, and about how much leadership I should take on in Cuong Nhu with the Ngo family no longer above us and schools struggling from years of not being able to have normal classes and tests. My lungs still weren't allowing me to exert my body on the level expected for my test that was just a few weeks away. I felt fine about my personal progress ever since my last retreat and the lessons from Granny, but I was dreading showing my teachers how weak I was compared to before. I worried that instead of seeing the growth of a new self, they would just see me as less than I had been.

The ceremonies began. We were cleansed with sage smoke and Florida water before everyone slowly, thoughtfully shuffled to their ceremonial areas. Then the medicine was brought out and blessed and we made lines to request our dosage and go back to our lodge to wait with our cups. The now familiar slowness of the process was a meditation in itself. The waving of the sage followed no set schedule but obeyed only a fully present connection between two people in search of healing, each one a poem where no ticking clock could intrude.

I had chosen to take two tablespoons again since that had put me so perfectly in contact with Granny six months earlier. I sat with my cup in silence, listening to the facilitator call out the prayer to protect against evil and lead towards healing. I thought of Granny's words, "There is no such thing as evil. Only love and fear."

We all drank together, and I shuddered from the acrid, woody taste, but the tea stayed down. With a grimace, I rinsed the cup and drank the awful sedimentary dregs and then took several pulls off my water bottle. I had to move the cup far away from me to keep from fighting with the smell of it. Sloshing water in my mouth diluted the taste enough that sitting back on the mat left me with only the bearable traces to manage. It was moving in my stomach, but my fear that I wouldn't be able to keep it down gradually passed. I focused on my chakra work and knowledge. My meditation with its humming probe of my body and spine was very soothing. I considered engaging in the whole process of breathing and lighting up my chakras, but I opted to wait and focus and let the process guide me like holding the reins of the horse. Time drew slowly past as the music gently held the two rows of people carrying all their hopes in their turning stomachs.

It began with a light feeling just below my diaphragm. There was movement that wasn't coming from me. I scanned myself to see if I was nauseous, but aside from the plain distasteful heaviness that started the moment I drank, there was no other discomfort. This was just movement. It spread through my body and into my back and neck and head. I was reminded of the feeling of energetic release I had last time, but this was different. Now there was power coursing through me like vines and bone. My face and body began to stretch as something inside of me pushed against my skin. I could feel my jaw and cheeks opening, my inner body driving for the surface, transforming my physical self into something wildly more powerful and primal.

There was something inside of me that didn't belong, that

polluted this expanding form. It was doubt and unworthiness, and the power wanted it out. I searched my being for it and felt it lingering in the recesses of my mind and body. It needed to come out, but how? I writhed on the mat, not sure how to move in the midst of transformation, but overwhelmed with the urgency. We couldn't move on until I had cleansed myself of this unworthiness. It was a primal fight to lift myself from the mat and move against my own fear and weakness. I was at my bucket on my hands and knees feeling the power of the earth coursing through me and demanding I be rid of this crude and worthless shackle.

As I vomited, I wasn't just throwing up in a bucket. It was the deep inner work of purging myself of fear. With transformed eyes I saw the black, inky filth splattering in the bucket. It swirled and squirmed like spiders that tried to crawl back up and out. I dredged my body for lingering doubt again and again. There seemed to always be a little bit more, and somewhere deep down I could feel that the unworthiness was out of me, but its source was still there like a leaky pipe in my depths, and soon it would fill back up. I rinsed out my mouth and fell back to the mat. A little piece of me thought, "I made it, I'm done. That was good work," and then the coursing movement in me accelerated, pushing me apart with a feeling of panic that quickly gave way to my memory of the other side from before.

It was not my Granny that burst forth from the transforming darkness, but *Her.* She was everything all at once. Even now my mind can remember everything about the experience of being in Her presence, but I could never draw Her because the eyes are not adequate to see. She was the mother, the daughter, the grand-mother (including mine), the lover, pregnant, barren, enduring. She was the teacher that guides you to the truth with loving patience, the stern voice that compels you out of your desire not to let Her down, and the tease that holds back just enough to make you keep to the course instead of skipping ahead. She was also the earth, and the vine, and the grape, and the decay. Time lost its hold as I took in the wonder of Her.

When I gathered my consciousness together and could be aware of myself in Her presence again, I realized this was my moment to show Her all I'd learned. I breathed and hummed and tuned in to my chakras, being aware of them and ready to go deeper into my understanding. I buzzed with excitement about what mysteries must lay behind even those that I'd discovered over the past months.

She held me in Her awareness. Her many pairs of eyes loved me, evaluated me, measured me, tested me.

"Good," She said, and then abruptly whisked all of my new knowledge aside like a movie character dramatically sweeping everything off a desk. I was at a loss. We weren't going to dig into chakras and energy vibrations at all! I could feel Her affirm my work and move on. I had done my homework and it was time for a completely different lesson. There was no vibration here. During my previous journeys and in all of my meditations over the last six months, the experience was centered around powerful vibrations that connected me to the root of my existence. Now I was in a place of stillness and above me was a familiar symbol.

My mother's family migrated relatively recently from Norway. Maybe my great great grandparents on my mother's mother's side had immigrated, but my mother had cousins who were second generation Americans with names like Thorbrand and Haarlan. I'd had almost no contact with that part of my heritage since my mother's family had been estranged from us for many years. I'd met what I thought of as my Viking cousins after I finished the Appalachian Trail. They lived in Maine and we met when they picked me up at the end of the six-and-a-half month hike. Long before that, my mother had given me a necklace that she said all the young Norwegian boys wore. It was a light silver pendant of Mjolnir, the hammer of Thor. It looked like a boat anchor or an upside down "T" with dotted patterns on it.

I had worn the necklace for a few years and even carved the symbol onto my walking stick on the Appalachian Trail. The silver necklace had a very light chain that seemed too fragile and I didn't like jewelry touching my skin in general. I didn't know if it was lost or in a box, but I was very surprised to see its outline floating above me. The last time I'd worn it was in college nearly thirty years earlier, and at the time Thor was something that few people were familiar with unless they read lots of Marvel comics or had a special interest in Norse mythology. Now, the Marvel movies were everywhere you looked, and everyone everywhere knew about Thor, and some even knew the name of his godly hammer Mjolnir. The movie version looked much different than the symbol I knew. It was blocky like in the comic books instead of the traditional boat anchor shape.

"You need to pick up the hammer," She said.

"Really? The hammer of Thor?" I was a bit incredulous.

"No, that's *your* hammer," her voice reverberated around me. I looked at it, but it just didn't seem right. It seemed fake, or wrong, and if it was really what she said it was, then who the hell was I to carry something known in myth to be only for the most worthy among gods and mortals. I looked at it and felt my insides squirm. This all seemed really cheesy and out of place when I was here to seek deeper mysteries. What happened to my grandmother watching over me and showing me who I was in the world?

"It's not right," I said. "It's not for me." I thought of my struggle with rising to take on a stronger leadership role within my martial art style. My body was weak, my mind was foggy, and I was only a shadow of the martial artist I'd been a couple of years ago. I imagined other leaders in the style rejecting the thought of me wielding the Hammer of Thor.

"The Hammer of Tanner," She corrected. In the space of my heart, words and thoughts seemed equally apparent to Her. "No one is trying to pick up that hammer. It's heavy. It's dangerous. It is destruction and creation. The hammer builds up and knocks down with the same motion. People don't want it. They wish that someone else would pick it up for them."

Thoughts swirled in my mind. Doubts, fears, visions of leaders in conflict, and behind it all, the slow creep of unworthiness gathering like water invading a leaky vessel.

"Why me? There are so many good leaders." The whole situation was making me feel exhausted.

"You have two rare powers, and together they make it possible to use the hammer." I wondered if She was talking about the chakras now. Perhaps this would all circle back to what I had been working on.

"No," She responded to my thoughts, "your energy is just how you naturally interact with the world. You have two important powers that serve the people." My thoughts searched my past. Powers? I can kick really quickly for my size, but I'm not the fastest. I'm good at visualizing things? None of what came to mind fell into the category of "powers."

"Tonight I'll teach you about the first, and tomorrow, the second," She said "but first, you need to pick up the Hammer."

I had heard enough. Whatever was going on, wherever this was leading, I wasn't getting anywhere by fighting it. This wasn't the lesson I thought I was learning tonight, but if it was anything like the last one, my life was about to change. I put my hand around the wide handle. It wasn't a contoured shape made to fit the hand. But a hard, angular wedge, tapered to make it more likely to slip out of the grasp than stay. It was hot and incredibly heavy. I quickly added my other hand to the effort and pulled it up above my chest. It took all my focus to keep my grip and keep it up in the air. As I struggled with it, I could also feel it pulsing like a quivering heartbeat.

"Good," She said, "your first power is Calling the Storm." Hm. I didn't quite get that. I do love storms, and in the heat of the long summer in the woods on the Appalachian Trail, I'd repeatedly tried to make it rain and fantasized about surviving a lighting strike.

"You can call on change without fear. The rain feeds and the winds cool, but the storm is wild. The winds can rend and the lightning can kill and burn. Once the change begins, everyone wants to hide from its uncertainty. People are willing to bear the suffering of a rotting life rather than risk the uncertainty of change."

"You think I'm fearless?"

"No. But you're not afraid to stride into the unknown. You were a child raised in a chaos of instability that calloused you to the fear of it." I saw myself living in twenty-four homes before I was twenty years old. Never able to feel the concept of "home" that many of my friends had. The Hammer had come to rest on my chest, and She gestured for me to lift it up again. It took so much to keep it up, but the work wasn't muscular. My shoulders didn't burn from exertion. All of the exhaustion was internal and energetic. It drained me where the flow of life entered my body. I pushed the hammer up off my chest, moaning.

Once it was lifted, She began to show me examples from my life of my use of the storm power. In my early life it had only taken the form of adventure. Traveling to unknown places without a plan and trusting that I'd find my way. Setting out on the Appalachian Trail without any real backpacking experience. Stepping into situations that were uncertain without any more than the vaguest idea how I would succeed. After I was married and had children, the power was really put to the test. Now other people's lives would be affected by the waves of change. Starting a new business when my first child was newborn and my wife wasn't working put us all at risk instead of just me. Moving away and starting a bigger one with a bank loan during the opening bell of the 2008 recession far more so. Now that my community had grown to the hundreds, they were all affected by the changes I might call down.

"They want you to do it," She said. I was feeling overwhelmed with the risk that I put everyone through every time I made changes to things they cared about. How many times had I calculated how many people might be lost to the community when I made changes? How many people's connected energy had been lost in making changes that I thought were necessary for survival and growth?

"They want you to do it," She repeated. She showed me that no one wants to make the hard, uncertain decisions that determine our survival. No one wants to take that responsibility since change contains inevitable loss and pain, but they know that something has to change in order for the group to survive and thrive, and are inspired to be a part of the new possibilities that change brings.

The drain was so strong that I was having trouble paying attention and also keeping the hammer aloft.

"What about my strength? I still can't breathe enough for even my test in a few weeks. That won't inspire people. How am I going to find the energy to keep this hammer up with everything else going on?"

My mind was filled with visions of myself teaching classes in the early days of the dojo when I never had a break or a vacation since there were no other teachers. I saw how tired I would become, and how, showing up exhausted to class and putting out my last bit of energy, the class would reflect it back onto me and charge me right back up just as I'd written in my letter about Quynh. I saw how energy moved back and forth between me and the students like the breath of our fledgling community and how that energy multiplied in a circuit.

"If you want more energy, then give more."

Since my time in the hospital, I had adapted to teaching much less. My most advanced students, already used to teaching, had stepped in to take over for months when I could barely walk, and I had been easing back into teaching gradually. Since my energy was so low, I'd tried to spread it out and keep from exhausting myself all at once. Over time I'd decided that letting them teach more would build them up to be better teachers and elevate them in the eyes of the younger students, so I stayed back. I embraced the role of a senior leader dropping in to reinforce and test, but mostly teaching advanced students. Now She was telling me that my energy wasn't coming back because my teaching wasn't coming back. My mind swam with visions of lifting up the students and shouting their praises while drinking the energy that their work and love poured back into me.

Dropping out of visual memories into my heart-vision, I saw the larger exchange of the schools and teachers in our style passing energy back and forth with students and each other. It was a wide energetic web connected at a million points in the past, present, and future, all surging with life. In the center of it, I saw O'Sensei, Quynh's father, the founder of the style, still sharing energy and radiating love through his creation even as it grew far past him. Twenty years after his death, there was still energy to sustain his attention. Leaning back fully into the web would give me all the energy I needed. I saw all the work of exchange, the pull of leadership and how it lifted and strengthened the web.

As I was watching our style's energetic exchange, I could feel myself beginning to emerge from the medicine. The chill edge of physical sensation was returning. As my window was closing, I wondered at how to navigate this elaborate web as I questioned the place of my leadership within the style.

"There is no physical crown," She said. I immediately remembered one of my teachers telling me that "you don't need a belt to lead." I saw the shape of a crown on a shady figure. "The crown is just a symbol. It's the shape of a leader's head held high." I could see the shape of a crown on a head, but it was just the head itself, lifted higher. I saw in that moment that my throat chakra was blocked because my head was down.

"You don't wait to be anointed. Just make the changes you want to see in the world and when people follow, that's leadership."

I lowered the hammer and relaxed into my mat, spent and sweaty. I felt cold and groped around in the "real" world to cover myself with a blanket. After a few tries I determined that I couldn't understand blankets yet. I raised my hand and a broad-shouldered figure in white quietly flowed to my side out of the dark. Without my asking he wordlessly wrapped my legs and feet with great care and honor. I relaxed fully into his strength and felt my tension scatter.

"And then let them honor you," she added. My mind filled with my test. My teachers and leaders were preparing to drive and fly from all around the country to my school to test me. I had so much fear still about seeing their faces as they realized how much I'd lost. I was entering the first test where I didn't think I could impress them, and I was deeply unhappy about it.

"Do you really think that these people who've watched you

grow for decades don't understand what you're going through?" My mind spread out around my teachers, away from myself and my ego. As I entered their personal spaces, I could see their understanding of everything I was going through. Their desire to come and support me through this ordeal, to mourn what had been lost, and to honor the work I'd done. I felt so small looking back at the cocoon of my ego, and how much it had limited my expectations of these people I'd respected for so long.

"Let them honor you." She bid me rest my soul from this work. She called me to rest my mind from its doubt. She let me sleep.

Chapter 21

A Hand Full of Fire

In the morning I felt optimistic. The night had been simultaneously exhausting and energizing. I was weary, but ready to start the second leg of this internal triathlon. I had actually managed to sleep a bit on my mat and felt solid enough for the next ceremony which would start fairly soon. I wasn't allowed to eat since I'd be purging again soon, but I walked out to check on my friends, and especially Beck, who'd just had his first ceremony last night. I was curious what She'd bring to someone with so many fewer years of life lived. Also, he'd been my student in the martial arts for more than a decade, and I just wanted to put my arms around him, no matter what he'd been through.

The guys were tired but well. Josh had been through a very hard night with it. After he'd come out of the ceremony, he had eaten a few of the veggie chips that were supposed to be light enough to be safe for digestion, but the sugars in the chips had been enough to restart the reaction with the Ayahuasca and it had sent him, unprepared, right back into the experience for several more hours of writhing discomfort. He had gotten the emotional wind knocked out of him and was done for the weekend. Beck had really battled with his own anxiety in order to drink the medicine the night before, and his experience had been that he wasn't really ready for Her teaching, and needed to go and let himself be a child for a while. He was done for the weekend, too. Darrick, was still in for the remaining journeys, but he remained tight-lipped about what he'd been through in the night as he had in the past.

I wanted to tell them about the unexpected teaching about the hammer and knew they'd only be happy for me, but I held back a bit and just said it was "great and empowering." I wanted to see what she'd told me was coming next and have some time to wrap my mind around it all. I was still self-conscious about sharing my perspective-changing revelations when everyone around me seemed to be struggling. It felt like bragging, and sounded like the kind of egotistical statement you'd make just before it all came crashing down on you. So I kept it to myself for the time being. Through all of these journeys, I kept waiting for my friends to have the kind of empowering breakthroughs I was having. I wanted to share that joy and exploration of ideas from the other side. I wanted to hear what life-changing secrets She had in store for them, and gather all of our teachings into a tome of combined knowledge. So far, from what I could gather, they were still reinforcing the core message, "you are a being made of and deserving of love." As tough as many of the sessions were, that reinforcement was still worth coming back again and again for.

As I walked to the new outdoor site for the daytime ceremony, I pondered the balance between suffering and empowerment. So many people around me were in so much pain and I was learning about magical hammers and powers. But the pain and exhaustion of the hammer was a true gauntlet. The suffering of unworthiness was an ordeal. It seemed that all human beings contained exactly one unit of human suffering. Sometimes it was defined externally, and sometimes it would come from inside. Sometimes it was the pressure of responsibility or the weight of exertion from their life's work. For others it was from abuse or persecution. But from the perspective of each person, it was one full measure. There is no way to measure your suffering against another's. At its core it is their entire struggle, all-consuming and tyrannical. We meet it with our whole self and define it and are defined by it, but its measure remains one.

I picked out a blanket spread out on the sandy Florida dirt in the outdoor ceremony ground. I got down and checked for roots that might be poking up through the woven blanket and repositioned it to flatten it out a bit. My skier cabin mate was a couple of mats over, and we nodded to each other, both lost in preparatory thought. I set down my water bottle and waited. Part of me wanted to do some work to focus my mind, but I was so exhausted from exertion and little sleep that I had to settle for peaceful waiting. I knew that She was going to come into my preparation, giggle at my attempt to establish control, and then show me something I could never have expected. So I just got comfortable and enjoyed being on the dirt outdoors. It was warm and humid in Florida in July, but there was also an optimistic breeze that hinted at the idea of cool air in the future. A few gray clouds floated across the morning sky. I missed the twisting trees from the year before and worried that the sun would cook me if the shadows moved away as the sun rose during the hours of the ceremony.

I tuned out of the pep-talk, hearing Carlos' voice again suggestively call the daytime ceremony a "date." I still didn't feel like I was on a date. I felt like I'd found my cosmic teacher and was showing up to train early in the morning, unsure what the lesson would be. I got in line to ask for my two tablespoons again. There was a chance that it would be more intense since I had two in my system from last night, but I didn't feel like I'd come to the edge of my comfort and wasn't worried about it. The time crawled by with my thoughts and the clouds, and then we drank. I relaxed with the music to wait. This was the first time I'd done the daytime ceremony since our first visit and even though I hadn't really connected the first night that time, I'd thought that in the daytime I would continue where I left off searching through shadows in the dark. That hadn't happened at all. My visit to the womb was a complete surprise. She'd told me She would reveal my second power today, but based on my last daytime journey it was just as likely that I'd end up in space or talking to a tree.

Again I probed the idea that this drug was just making me see random things and that none of them related to each other or had anything to do with the world outside of my head. But that really hadn't been my experience so far. The things I'd learned had fundamentally changed the way I interact with the world for the better. The theories I'd learned had applied to my life perfectly and consistently. The chakra attunement had continued to work long after the Ayahuasca had worn off. I could feel it starting again. The movement inside my core that twisted through me and out in all directions. As I felt the oncoming transformation, She demanded that I purge my unworthiness again, and I did so, retching the creeping darkness out into the white bucket, but feeling it continue to creep quietly in behind.

"Pick it up," She said, motioning to the hammer. OK. So we were going back in right where we'd left off. As I grasped the handle with both hands and squeezed, thunder rolled across the Florida sky, and a petrichor breeze washed over me.

"Oh hell yes," I thought, squeezing the handle tighter.

"Your second power is to *Wield the Lightning*." I was done with questioning Her. No, I had never caught lightning in my hand, but I was a willing student, ready to put aside my doubts. What were we talking about here?

"When the storm rages and all the pieces go up in the air, you have the power to arrange them as they come down into something better and new. The lightning that can destroy, you will wield to energize." As the thunder rolled through the sky of the real world and the wind blew over us with welcome puffs of rain, she showed me how I'd done this in the past, and how to do it in the future with everyone I knew. She called it "bringing them lightning," and it involved engaging with each person so that I could sense what was swirling out of place, and guide those wayward pieces to make them whole and re-energize them. It seemed like trouble often came from people trying to hold tight to relationships, jobs, or ideas when their lives had changed so that the connection couldn't hold the way it once did. The pieces were still there but they didn't fit anymore, and suffering swirled through their chaos. It was about helping people realign to changes, even when those changes were long past.

Most of the people She showed me were martial artists, students, and teachers. Some had ceased training so long ago that I didn't think they'd want me "bringing lightning" into their lives. She agreed, but wanted me to see how it would be done. In the midst of people I'd known for years, She inserted the skier girl a couple of mats over, showing me the reformative flavor of re-energizing that she needed. There were no other strangers. Only people already in my life.

As I puzzled at this introduction of an outsider, it caused me to assess the variety of people she'd brought up and stick on a massive omission. I stopped Her and asked, "What about Melanie? You've shown me how to help so many people, but she's the one I've vowed to help most of all." She gestured for me to look behind myself, and I turned my consciousness. Melanie was there in her absolute wholeness. From the infant and little girl through to the college student that I first fell for, the lone traveller, my wife and lover, the mother of my children, but also the parts of her that weren't for me or were in the future. Age, weakness, and death were all there. It took my breath away to see her in complete fullness and bursting with every aspect of life. My lightning and storms fed her, wounded her, tested her, and were absorbed by her. We existed in a harmonious balance, and my storms were beautiful and even inspiring to her, but not what made her whole.

She brought me back to my practice. Call the storm to break up what no longer worked, wield the lightning to build up and energize what was thought lost. She showed me what true armor was, comprised of horizontal bands of metal, each made of the work of a person I had lifted up. It was so light because the accomplishments of these people held it up. It was so strong because they gave it back willingly and supported it. Yes, this was the empowerment I wanted. Not taken but offered in love.

I felt a new uneasiness around my stomach and legs. It was hard to pull back from the teaching, but I took a moment to figure out what was going on with my seemingly far away body. Ah. I needed to pee. How would that happen? Could I wait until this was over? Probably not a good idea. Opening my eyes and slipping out of the energetic world into the world of texture and light and air, I looked at all the people around me writhing in the shelter of the trees or lying still on blankets under the cloudy sky. I could see port-a-potties lined up across the ceremony ground, but I couldn't imagine standing, much less walking in this state. I was in mid-journey only partially connected to my body. I floated around the possibilities for a while before raising my hand to signal one of the volunteers. A small woman in white slid over to me quietly.

"I need to pee," I whispered out of unfamiliar lips. She must've signaled to others because a much larger set of hands helped me to my feet. I was extremely wobbly and the ground didn't seem like a certain thing. I tried to relax and flow with the familiar movements of walking, but the sixty foot walk around the edge of the grounds felt like a mile through a dimly lit and uneven cave. They helped me into the port-a-potty, and I looked down at the little corner-set urinal cone through the green light of the chamber.

"I'm pretty sure I know how all this works," I thought, looking at my pants and the open urinal hole attached to the wall. It seemed like there was a lot that could go wrong. After a few moments I decided to let instinct take over and just moved my hands around my pants, trusting them to do what they knew how to do. Soon there was liquid streaming into the hole and I could feel the pressure in my body subsiding. After spending a little longer wondering at the mysteries of my big, complicated body, I exited the green door and tried to walk back around to my blanket through the sprinkles of rain under the overcast sky. Two men stayed very close and whenever I wavered, gentle hands would sweep in to support me.

Back on my blanket, it took almost no time to return to the work. She wanted to make sure I saw enough examples of how to wield the lightning that I would understand it completely. We puzzled through institutional change, organizational change, but mostly She wanted me to maximize my effect on individual people. As She was demonstrating how I would help a student that I knew had a crush on me, I was brought back to the conundrum of teaching and leading people around the lure of sexuality. We give people inspiration and meaning, remain solid when other relationships in their lives are failing, lift up their kids when a spouse might be letting them down, or stand on the cusp of teacher and parent and friend as their sexuality first begins to form. It is a tale as old as time for a teacher, preacher, politician, or anyone else that motivates a community to get into hot water for allowing that sexual energy to take over. If the leader is inexperienced or has instability in their lives, their fears will make them grab hold of that power and seek out control in the realms of the physical, where fear holds sway.

Internal stability is one of the greatest gifts that a leader can give to a community. I had always thought of the denial of sexual connections as a commitment of honor and willpower that a stable leader made for the good of the community. Now I was seeing the nature of powerful energy exchange, and seeing that in fact the energy was the same energy, just set into different paths and circuits. It wasn't the denial of one energy and the acceptance of another, but the acceptance of a person's pure energy directed into true paths that were not about the physical, fearful world. The fact that the energy was the same power was exactly what made the way challenging when a leader was needy, fearful, or imbalanced. Noticing my own distraction, I wondered if She could clarify these thoughts for me. Maybe it was unrelated to my powers and She would just tell me to get back to work. I decided to risk chastisement and ask Her about it.

"What about guiding someone around their sexual energy?" I felt like I needed to delicately word my question, but as I began to ask it, I knew that She knew everything I had ever experienced, my deepest thoughts, my every concern, and could neither be offended or confused by anything that I said.

"Energy is energy, and action is action," She said lovingly. Your physical body will continue to prod you about sex, just as the people you know will never escape the bodies they wear. Sex is your biological drive to reproduce, so your body will raise it reflexively. As your mind protects the body, your thoughts will serve those purposes as well and multiply them when you are afraid or unstable. Remember how you saw that we all seek a pure exchange of energy, and sex is just one of the many ways that the exchanges and circuits can manifest? Don't deny yourself or these people that you're helping the exchange of energy, just stabilize yourself so that you can create clear intentional circuits that serve the spirit rather than allowing the body to barge in on the conversation. There are so many other brilliant energetic exchanges." I could see it, but just the nearest corner of it. It had the pure ring of truth to it, but I wasn't precisely sure how it would work in the "world." I could also see how it involved the truth of grace by being fearlessly present to the moment. I was nearing the end of my journey, feeling the outer world come into focus, and instead of running me through many test repetitions, She drew my attention over to the skier who was already pulling herself up from the mat to go back to the house for food.

"So you're saying just try it out?"

The storm and the teaching had passed, leaving me weary but empowered on the mat, I stared at the sky and the passing clouds. When I stood, I felt like I was ten feet tall. I'm six feet, two inches, and am used to having most people be below my eye level, but now it felt like I was looking down at the tops of everyone's heads from far above. I floated along to where lunch was being served and soaked up the hearty vegetable smell until I had a full bowl in my hands.

As I turned around, I saw the skier with an empty seat beside her. I lowered myself carefully into it, still feeling a little loose in my body.

"Remind me what your name is," I said. I always have the hardest time with names.

"Caite," she said, with a knowing smile on her lips. I sensed that she was used to guys wanting to remember her name. Ok. Here we go.

"How did you do last night and this morning?"

She rolled it around in a way that told me she hadn't locked in on relief or healing yet. "Last night I took one to start and didn't feel anything, so I took two for the booster and still didn't get much more than nausea and some visuals. So this morning I tried four." Her brow furrowed. "I got somewhere with that, but I still couldn't really get out of my own head."

"Crazy. That's twice as much as I've ever taken. Two is what gets me into the zone."

"Yeah. I guess we're all different." She had the weariness that we all had from the rigors of the ceremony and the added lack of rest, but also a heaviness about it all. I ate quietly for a bit before choosing my words.

"This is an odd thing to say, but during this last ceremony She made a point of talking about how I could help you. She said you need some lightning." She looked at me sideways with a sparkle in her eye and a challenging smile that reminded me of my AT hiker friends.

"Yeah, I could use some lightning," she said adventurously, nodding slowly. She told me about how she had been a skier, and had been in an accident that had shaken her confidence. She was considering switching to a new sport, but wasn't sure if that would be possible. I was still not completely clear about this heavy weight around her getting to ski. I had a couple of friends that loved skiing and went whenever they could, but if they had an accident that made them have to back off a bit, I couldn't imagine it hitting them this hard.

"Do you want to see a video of my accident?" she said with an odd gleefulness.

"Oh, God. Someone was filming you when you crashed?" I imagined another skier recording their kid with Caite crashing in the background.

"The helicopter is always filming when I ski." She looked at me patiently and held up her phone with a video on it. The pieces fell into place as I watched a skier flying down a mountain that was certainly not a ski mountain. This was just a snowy, rocky wall somewhere that no one would risk their life trying to ski down. I realized that if I knew about skiing, I probably would have recognized her already. She was crazy good, a professional skier, and defying death on film was her actual job. It all made sense. Her intense, shock-absorbing legs and feet, why a bad crash would put her mind into a tailspin about who she was, even that fearless adventuring look in her eye.

The pieces swirled together in my mind. I could see how to give her lightning. I could see where to push, what needed to be broken down, and how to start bringing her mind back towards the certainty that had carried her out the doors of helicopters without a parachute and won her fans' adoration. I could also see how there was raw energy in that exchange that could get dragged by our biology into sexual energy, but was available to be molded into many forms. At the root we wanted a pure energetic exchange much deeper than physical drives, but bodies and hormones would ask about sex unless the energetic exchange could be clearly defined another way. In the past I would've said this was a straight-forward thing. Just don't have sex with people you shouldn't be having sex with. Now I was seeing a complex structure to build using this gift She'd shown me. It wasn't plain denial, it was an intentional work of art.

Josh and the guys came by and said they were going to shadow integration and invited me along. I remembered the intense display at our second retreat and definitely wanted to see it again. I invited Caite but when she declined, I told her we'd talk more about lightning after her ceremony in the morning. We'd only had a brief ten-minute talk to begin building the circuit I had in mind, but I felt good about how we'd begun.

Chapter 22

A Date With the Shadow

I had been thoroughly impressed by Steven's shadow integration in January. I was exhausted again, but remembered how the demonstration had been more than enough to keep me attentive and awake. I'd slept a little the night before, but both ceremonies that weekend had been rigorous sessions where She made me hold the hammer up for hours, and I was exhausted. I dropped into a seat next to Beck who was feeling lighter now that he'd overcome his anxieties leading up to the ceremony the night before. I suspected that the medicine had gotten into him in ways that he wouldn't realize for some time, even with a single low dose. Josh and Darrick were nearby. The session started much like the last time, and I wondered who, if anyone, would volunteer this time. When Steven called for people with issues they'd volunteer to dig into, Beck's hand went up. Even as I thought "No, no, no! Not here in front of me and your father. You have no idea how deep this shovel digs," I could see clearly that, although there were several volunteers, he would of course be the one. Josh was squirming in his seat a few chairs away.

The issue he volunteered was anxiety, which he came by honestly from his father. Steven, though, wanted to dig into the mechanism underneath that feeling. The questions came fast and hard about when the panic attacks came, what triggered them, what trail of breadcrumbs could be picked up and followed deeper into the thicket of his mind. Beck handled the questions bravely and honestly. There were many times when he was offered an easy path that wouldn't pierce directly into his personal trauma, but he pushed back and redirected the blade of questioning into his bleeding core. I was so proud of and impressed with him. He stood in the center of a circle of strangers and two of the authority figures in his life and took it all on. The whole circle of onlookers was weeping as we watched him fight. And then that familiar unworthiness. My own unworthiness echoed inside of me and I remembered how I'd had to purge it during both ceremonies that weekend and could feel it filling right back up.

Why was this feeling so relentless? I'd always grappled with the feeling that I deserve less, and I heard it echoed around me over and over in the unworthy feelings of others. Decades before, when I really began to shine as a martial artist and teacher, I became aware of an invisible wall that surrounded me at all times. When an instructor, or master, or onlooker would approach me with corrections or criticism, my mind was fully engaged. I studied. I learned. I improved. Criticism made sense and made me better.

When, however, anyone approached me with praise, compliments, or congratulations, an ugly trap would spring to catch those words before they reached my mind and twist them. An automatic process would dissect the compliment for hidden criticism. If none was obvious, it would analyze what this person hoped to gain by manipulating me with hollow praise. If no motivation was obvious, it would tell me that I'd done so badly that they were complimenting me out of pity to keep me from quitting.

All of this would happen in an instant, before the words even reached my conscious mind, and I would find myself wrestling with anger and rejection while loving people smiled at me, unaware that they'd set off a tempest of anxiety. After creating several awkward situations with my masters by trying clumsily to deflect authentic compliments with humor, I realized that I needed to overcome this absurd reaction. All I'd come up with over the years, though, was to automatically say, "Thanks! That means a lot to me," which gave my mind time to calm down and see through the grotesque filter of unworthiness. But the initial reaction had never abated under the pressure of repeated, reasoned dissection.

The more I was able to open up to others about it, the more I discovered that this feeling seemed to be fairly common. It even plagued this young man who was barely nineteen years old. But as I watched him through his tears and mine, wrestling full on with this demon, I found myself inspired to fight as well. I resolved that as empowered as I felt from the first two journeys of the weekend, tonight it was time to do some honest work. The unworthiness that She'd made me purge at the beginning of both sessions in order to proceed with the Hammer and the Lightning now seemed like a clear signal fire. I wept at the sight of my student being bathed with love and relief, and steeled myself for battle.

Chapter 23

A Night in Armor

As the sun was setting I sat at the edge of my mat looking down at my two tablespoons waiting noxiously in the white porcelain cup. I dug and dug through my mind for the source of the seeping gash of unworthiness at my core. It definitely came from my childhood. I could recall instances from high school when my mind was overthrown with this confusion. I went through many years of depression after my parents' divorce. Could that be the source? Before that, there were years of moving between houses as my family separated and came back together over and over. There was significant loss and instability there.

The divorce had actually been a relief to me, though. After years of fighting, unrest, and sudden moves between apartments, I finally knew it was settled. Dealing with the divorce itself was much easier than the looming fear of the thing. As uncertain as that made some aspects of my life, others felt more stable for the first time. One thing I never doubted was my parents' love for me. Did I feel unworthy because I somehow felt responsible for the end of their relationship? That didn't really make sense, given that their relationship had been a source of stress in my life up until they parted.

I'd been given a scholarship to the private school where my mother worked part time when I was very young and they'd allowed me to stay at the school on scholarship after she moved on to other work. Most of the kids I went to school with were wildly affluent compared to our family. It had occurred to me that constantly watching my friend's families do things we'd never be able to do, and go to camps and on vacations that were far out of reach for me might have grown into a feeling of unworthiness. Whatever the source was, I just couldn't see it clearly. Now it was time to drink and dive beneath the black waters of my mind to see if She could help me.

For the third time that weekend, I drank and managed to keep it down despite the immediate sickly twist in my gut. I swished a couple of sips of water around my mouth to dissolve the taste, and moved the stinking cup far enough away to keep the smell out of my nose. I sat in the music and waited. I kept searching for the root wound, but my thoughts had become circular with no more clues to follow.

When the churning inside me began, I traveled the increasingly familiar path through the search to understand the movement in my body, to embracing the feeling of growing out past myself, to harmonizing with the growing and pulsating power. Then came the need to purge, for the third time this weekend centered around my creeping unworthiness. I wrestled with my own inability to move towards this challenge and then, embracing the knowledge that I was the only one who could, I came up to my hands and knees to scrape out the dregs of unworthiness from the corners of my being and vomit their writhing filth into my white bucket.

Victorious, I fell back on my mat, exhausted. I felt, as I usually did at this point in the journey, like I was done. Visions, power, movement, challenge, work, battle, victory, done. As with the other two journeys this weekend, I was thrown immediately into Her presence. She waited quietly in Her state of all-encompassing femininity and eternity.

"Why do I feel this way?" I asked her under my breath. She didn't speak and continued to wait. It wasn't enough. I had to commit more. "Why do I have this constant and absurd feeling of unworthiness?" I said in a steady voice, looking directly at her.

"Ok," She said with a hint of compassion, "let's go."

I found myself on the playground of my childhood private school. I was in fifth grade and all alone in a panic. No one else was on the playground and it was dark just after lunchtime. Storm clouds spat rain. I had forgotten that it was raining. Of course I knew that day.

"You know, but you don't know," She said. The divorce had been earlier that year, and my weak performance at school had slid into downright neglect of my schoolwork as my parents were unable to keep up with me and my responsibilities. I had lost both the motivation to do schoolwork and the ability to organize my thoughts. My teacher had tried in a dozen ways to motivate me, all to no avail. I was back to living in two apartments with my separated parents, and they both tried their best to capture my attention and affection, less to compete with each other and more to repair the damage they knew I was managing. Most recently they had both bought Betamax video cassette recorders so that we could rent movies to watch at home. Such a brave new world we lived in.

A week earlier, my father had given me a gold ring. His father had given it to him in his youth, and he ceremoniously passed it on to me. In the forty years since, I had forgotten about the ring. It meant so much to me for one week. That's why I was on the playground alone that day. At lunch recess we had been playing tether ball. I gravitated to the game because I was very tall and coordinated for my age, and once I got my hands on the ball, my opponent rarely got to touch it again. It was one of a very few things that made me feel in control. Swinging my hand over and over again, the ring had almost slipped off since it barely fit me, and so I'd taken it off and placed it on the low wall near the tether ball court. When recess ended, I forgot it as I fell into the flow of children back to the classrooms. The rain had just started sprinkling steadily under the darkening sky.

Just before I got to class, I remembered the ring and in a panic, sprinted out of line and back across campus to the playground, but it wasn't on the wall where I'd left it. There was a damp gathering of leaves and sediment slowly mulching into dirt all along the base of the wall, and I pushed it aside carefully all around the area below the spot where I remembered placing the ring, hoping to uncover it. Nothing. The panic was building. The lost and found! Of course someone had turned it in to the office. I sprinted through the growing sprinkle to the darkening brick porch that led into the main building where the administrators worked. The secretary looked up at me quizzically.

"What do you need, Tanner?" She hadn't settled on whether she should use a stern disciplinary voice for a child not where they should be or the compassionate voice to greet a child in obvious distress.

"Did someone turn in a gold ring that they found on the wall of the playground at lunch?"

"No, honey." That couldn't be right, so I offered more.

"It is wide on one side and has a big letter 'C' on it."

"No, no rings today."

"Well it doesn't look exactly like a 'C' since it's all frilly and there are a lot of extra lines."

"Tanner, there aren't any lost rings to choose from. You need to get to your class." I ran out of the office and back to the leaf piles below the wall. Now the rain was fattening from a drizzle to a steady rain that was drenching my back and hair. I sifted through the leaves again and again, tears mixing with the splattering, cold rain.

"Tanner! Peter's looking for you and he's really mad. You were supposed to be there fifteen minutes ago. You'd better run!" My class's co-teacher with her umbrella like a tower in the dark. I ran past her, crying to meet the teacher to whom I'd only been a disappointment this whole year. I splashed across the cracked paving stones where I normally slowed in an obsessive attempt to avoid every crease and line.

When I entered our classroom, it was only me and him. All the other kids had gone to their math classes. Our classroom slept coldly without the pounding energy of the children, and my teacher looked up as if surprised and then pulled on a mask of disappointment, throwing up his hands and letting them fall helplessly on the desk in surrender as he began his most recent attempt to change my course. Now I stood outside of both of them, young Tanner and the fifth-grade teacher. I hovered at the outskirts of the memory, seeing not only the teacher and the student, but the forces at work on both of them in front of the storm darkened windows.

"You know, there are a lot of kids that would give anything to be able to come here for school and will never get the chance." I saw how my ten-year-old soul was lying split open from the trauma of the divorce, from the years of moving from house to house, and freshly raw from betraying my father's trust by losing his family ring.

"You're here on scholarship because you tested well in kindergarten, and you write something clever every few years, but you don't pull your weight." I could see him from the outside, searching for a handle to pull that would wake me, shake me, drive me to break free of my indifference. I could feel the moment bearing down like a roaring wave.

"You don't deserve to be here." *Yes.* "There are kids who could use your scholarship here to really do great things." *There.*

I could feel a great relief in the midst of the crushing words. My ten-year-old self plastered them over the bleeding wounds in his soul. They answered his doubts, formed a wall in his mind to protect him from his own iniquity. When something wasn't fair, it was because he wasn't worthy. When someone else had more, it was because he didn't deserve it like they did. When people told him he wasn't good enough, it wouldn't hurt, because he already knew that. When they lied to him and then laughed with their friends that he believed it, he wouldn't be fooled. *Ever. Again.*

I watched my young self, now armored with unworthiness, re-enter an uncertain life, determined to do what he could despite his lowliness. At the same time I saw the teacher, new to his job, half the age I am now, feeling deep down that his words had fallen too hard. He determined to do better, but that failure had wounded him, too. My life's successes would be in spite of him instead of owing him thanks. My own teaching heart wept to see his hurt. Like rewinding a VCR, I returned my mind to my child self from before that day, before donning the armor of unworthiness, and took that little unarmored boy into myself. I held him and showed him the great things we would do and how sacred our time in this world was and had always been. I felt through him the long lost sensation of unarmored skin. We were worthy.

"Now, rest, Tanner," She whispered. It had all happened in a relatively short time, and I was far from coming out of the influence of the medicine. Energy pulsed around me, and the atoms of my body shifted and surged with the roiling energy pouring off of Her. "That was hard." She bid me let go and feel the pure force of love around me, and I did so. Even in the midst of energetic forces I could barely understand, in the rolling, hallucinating, disorienting pulse of the medicine, I knew that the unworthiness was gone and would never come back. I felt Her loving embrace hold me and surround me in pure mother energy. When my body returned and the feeling of the mat below me substituted itself for the ocean of surging love, I followed my exhausted mind straight to sleep.

I woke to breakfast, food, and friends, feeling lighter than I ever recalled feeling in my adult life. I talked again to Caite, making plans for how to help each other in the coming months as I worked to stay true to what I'd learned and she tried to carve out a new path. I was still a little uncertain about the full flavor of our energetic exchange, until, finishing breakfast together she said, "I didn't get to spend much time with my dad growing up. You've got some solid dad energy that I can get behind."

Those were good words for what I was looking for. It was tricky to label and codify this energy that was all coming out of love but could take so many forms. "Dad energy" felt right. As I carried my backpack to where our ride was waiting, I reflected on how I was leaving Florida with far more than I'd hoped, and none of the things that I had expected. I was empowered, at peace, freed from unworthiness, and clear on how to use my power to help others. If only I could take a full breath.

Part 4
Unity

Chapter 24

The Ghost in My Chest

I returned to the balancing act of preparing for my test. From the grand display I had prepared to show the style more than two years before, I had whittled down in gut-wrenching slices to the jagged bedrock of what I could do now a year and a half out of the hospital. My preparation over the last few months had been about optimistic predictions of what I would be able to do when August came around. My three partners, all dedicated students for more than a decade and talented martial artists, were patient with me and were helping me to look my best for the demonstration, but as we approached the test day, we needed to make some hard decisions about what we could actually expect to be able to do that day.

Board breaking wouldn't be any trouble. My explosive power within a single movement was unchanged. Public speaking, which was required for all advanced testing, was a piece I was looking forward to since it would allow me to tell the story of this test and frame it for those looking on.

For my katas, also called forms, I could still only complete them with long dramatic pauses mixed in. These energetic sequences were sixty to a hundred steps long. They used both traditional weapons and empty hands, and showed power, coordination, precision, and artistry. They weren't really meant to test the endurance of an advanced martial artist, but for me now, each one had become a delicate balance between exertion and pauses to catch my breath. If I lost myself in the performance and stayed at the speed and power that I had been accustomed to for the past forty years, I would reel with dizziness and would need to take a seat, huffing to recover in the middle of the form. I'd done my best to arrange the pauses artistically so that the viewers might not even notice that I was gasping for air.

My swimming coach had given me canned oxygen so that I could fill my lungs with pure oxygen before starting and again when I was done to help with recovery. I didn't notice a big change, but even a few percent was worth carrying the can around.

Sparring, our controlled but continuous fighting, would cut to the heart of my weakness, since under pressure it was impossible to pause and breathe. On the other hand, everyone I would be fighting knew what I was going through and wanted to see me do well. They would push hard when I had energy and hopefully give me space when I needed to recover. I had some concern about passing out in front of everyone, but I chuckled to remember my swimming coach telling me I wasn't nearly tough enough to drown myself.

The demonstration was what I was the most concerned about. While we had choreographed it extensively, it was still a simulation of fighting three armed opponents simultaneously and repeatedly. It was meant to show what I had learned in forty years of training, and showcase the skills I had honed. This was the section that Quynh had traveled to build with me. We had made this masterpiece together, and I'd been forced to amputate piece after piece from it for the last year. Each of the four sections, even after all the changes, were long enough to push me just a little over the edge, and at the end of a long day of testing it would be far more challenging.

We had decided that between the segments I would kneel in the starting position for the next segment and catch my breath while the others cleared the disarmed weapons from the last segment off of the floor and set out the weapons they would use for the next. Then they would kneel with me and wait as long as I needed to catch my breath, and when I was ready and rose to my feet, we would begin again.

In the midst of all the final preparations, I pondered the lessons I'd learned about the hammer and the lighting. The voice of unworthiness had recessed to the back of my mind. I could still hear it, but as a far-off heckler, easy to ignore. It was no longer the primary filter of my experiences with others. Instead of viewing the masters flying in from around the country as stoic figures who would finally see my unworthiness revealed, I saw how we all fed each other with energy and love, and relished the idea of gathering them all around me. I looked forward to hearing the small voice and taking the opportunity to give lightning to those around me who needed it.

Two days before the test I finally got in to see a pulmonologist after seven months of trying. In the waiting room, I got a call from Robert and Elizabeth to wish me well. Because of health concerns, they wouldn't be at my test since they were still not traveling or meeting with groups for fear of getting Covid. After my time in the hospital and Quynh's death, I could completely understand, but still, they were close to my heart, and I wished they would be there. Some of the words in my speech were meant for their ears.

"We know you'll do great and kick ass, and we just wanted to be the first to go ahead and congratulate you on your accomplishment," Robert said. I could imagine him and Elizabeth leaning in over her phone.

"We love you and we'll try to get someone to help us see on Zoom," came Elizabeth's steady voice. I could feel her intent gaze.

"I love you guys, and I'll really miss seeing your faces here. You're a big part of my journey." I tried to pass on my longing without making them feel guilty for taking care of themselves.

"Mister Critz, Tanner?" came a voice from the hall by the waiting room.

"Guys, I need to run," I said while standing and heading towards the door, "but I'll be imagining you both there on Saturday."

After getting weighed and waiting a while longer, a tech joined me in a room full of glass chambers and breathing tubes.

"You're not our normal customer in this department," she told me appraisingly. "Usually I get guys in their seventies after a life-time of smoking. You seem to be breathing fine."

"I am, but when I exert myself, I hit a wall, and exerting myself is critical to my job." She asked a number of details about how and when it happened, and how it felt. "My guess based on past performance is that my lungs are about twenty percent damaged," I posited my months old theory.

"Well if you have eighty percent capacity, there's not a whole lot that we can do for you," she said, putting up her clipboard, "so let's see where you're at."

There were a dozen tests that involved blowing or drawing against a tube as long or as hard as possible. Some were in a chamber that tested pressure and air movement. I felt my lungs had been thoroughly gauged. Finally we were done, and she smiled at me like someone trying on something new.

"Weeyall," she began, drawing on her singsong Arkansas accent, "factoring in your height, age, weight, gender, ethnicity, and background, you've got nearly one hundred forty percent of the lung capacity and oxygen transfer that we would expect. Like I said earlier, I don't think your lungs are a problem." Soon I was back in front of the pulmonologist.

"I told you," he said.

"So why can't I breathe?" I fired at him.

"Well. Covid is still really new and we're learning as we go. One theory is that you may have post-traumatic stress from your time in the hospital." I flashed back to the scene of my "death."

"So has anything been helping with that?"

"I'd recommend trying EMDR. It's a treatment that uses light stimulation in the eyes to help reset neural pathways." He kept describing this treatment, which sounded expensive and long, but I already knew what I was going to try first. If only I'd known that I had PTSD to sort out a month ago! I also wondered why She hadn't brought it up to me. It seemed like something so central to my issue would be first on Her list.

There were definitely things I had to ask for to receive. Maybe it was about being ready to hear them. I suddenly felt strange about my test. I struggled so much to breathe, and knowing that the resistance was all in my mind made me feel like I should be able to just shake it off, but that didn't work. A wound in the mind is not really different from a wound in the body. In a sense, all wounds were in the mind. I was still going to have to take my test that weekend wounded.

Chapter 25

Love and Honor

People were beginning to arrive from both coasts by car and plane. Grand Master John Burns and Master Didi Goodman, another married pair of masters, had flown from California to oversee my test and that of my advanced students. Master Jessica, Quynh's widow and an annual visitor to the dojo, had flown from Florida to give a black belt test to one of my students who was headed for college soon after the test. Teachers and friends from Florida, Georgia, Alabama, and Texas had driven with groups of students to join in the testing and celebration.

I really like to spar when people first arrive. It is a way to reconnect deeply that words can't approach. Once we've been sparring for a few minutes, we fall into the zone, acting and reacting at the speed of our reflexes. We're totally in the moment together, and it's like no time has passed. Now I was really wrestling with my endurance, but it was also a good way to let my peers and teachers see where I was in that struggle, while also seeing that I was whole and in good spirits.

I sparred with Grand Master John, always one of my favorite matches because of his wily skill and agility despite being many years my senior. He could turn up the pace and see me collapse at any moment, but I felt him probing the line and checking on my fitness and ability. I sparred other students and teachers, running into my limits here and there, but it felt good to hit and be hit, to flow with my friends, to feel my body move with its practiced fluidity.

Walking into the back room to put a food donation for the next day's potluck into the fridge, I saw two people who made my mind bend for a moment. Seeing Robert and Elizabeth there made perfect sense since they were on the short list of people that I wanted to have there, but they had also just told me two days before that they couldn't make it, and they lived a thirteen hour drive away. There they were with double masks on, warding off my reflexive huge hug, but giddy as kids on Christmas morning.

"You're here!" I exclaimed.

"When we talked to you on the phone and heard you saying you wished we could be here, we just looked at each other and knew we had to come," Elizabeth said with sparkling eyes that suggested her conspiratorial grin was hiding behind the mask.

"Yeah, man. We just grabbed our stuff and hit the road right then!" Robert jumped in with a grasping hand gesture. "We got a few hours down the road and were like, 'We should probably tell someone we left so they don't think we're dead!'" Robert absolutely loves a good story, and was getting animated now. "So I call Thu, and I'm like 'Thu! We're going to Little Rock to be there for Tanner's test!' And she goes, 'I know, I already told Christina you were going,' and I'm like, 'What? We just decided and jumped in the car an hour ago!' and she says, 'I knew you wouldn't miss it.'"

All the business of organizing and visitors left me, and I floated in the full knowledge that I had brought my people here to give them my message, to introduce them to this new me, and all was as it should be. The next day, not only I and the other candidates, masters, and testers assembled for a long day of testing, but hundreds of students and families were there to watch. I was as ready as I could be, and all that was left was to begin.

The test was exactly the gauntlet I had prepared for. Board breaking passed easily for me. The katas were mostly good, with the dramatic pauses built in to catch my breath. The longest kata, Bo 6, which Quynh had created, was a real challenge since I was reflexively bucking to go all out, and having to constantly reign it back in. Near the end I let loose and then got dizzy, leaving out a move, but few knew the kata well enough to catch it.

I sucked on the canned oxygen before and after each performance, trying to shorten the recovery before the next section. Grand Master John let me choose the order in which I would perform the katas so that I could optimize my output. He and Master Didi wanted to test what I could do, but they were ready to curate the test to be sure I could give it all I had. I kept trying to reconcile that my inability to breathe was in my mind. How could my mind hold me back from a resource that I wanted, and therefore it wanted, so badly? It was holding itself back against its own will!

The demonstration came just before the end. After that was just my speech. We marched onto the floor, bowed to each other, the masters, and the audience, and performed the first section. Pretty good. I was definitely feeling some minor exhaustion from a day of testing, but it went relatively well. I knelt to catch my breath as my crew set up the weapons for the next segment. It took me about five deep breaths before I was ready to stand up, signaling my students to attack. Weapons clashed and redirected to counterstrike, disarm, and take-down my attackers. I was in the flow with my students but as we neared the end of the second section I could feel the tension in my chest as my oxygen got thinner by the second and the muscles around my lungs started to panic.

I knelt for the third section. Five breaths, six, seven. I looked around at my students, all kneeling with an eye on me to see when I rose. I couldn't wait too long. I got up even though I wanted a few more breaths. A three sectional staff from Chris hurled through the air at my head, and I batted it away with my tonfa* in a daze. Dodge, strike, block, counterstrike. I wove in and out, throwing them to the ground, rolling, leaping, and finally back down to my knee.

As my students positioned themselves and the weapons for the final segment, I couldn't see straight. This was the hardest section and I really needed to get my breath if I was going to have any chance of finishing it. Seven breaths, eight, it was taking too long. I heard someone in the audience take in the sharp exhalation that told me they were crying. A wash of peace came over me. There was a time before my journeys when I would've interpreted that sob as my absolute failure. People were crying because they were so sorry to see me fail. Now I glanced over to see people who loved me, who were deeply moved by my struggle, who were inspired to see me fight back with everything. I still couldn't take a full breath, but in my peace, I heard the voice say "Now."

I stood, and we began. Sticks and blades, duck and weave, striking and throwing. Everything was spinning, and I flowed with it, staying just out of reach of the dark ring in my vision that would close into a full blackout. My heart pounded against my lungs and filled my ears as Chris and I rolled back into the final strike where I took his weapon and drove it down on top of him. It was finally done and I rose carefully on unsteady legs, knowing that all of the struggle with my lungs was done for the day. All that was left was to share my heart and my new knowledge with my people. I had the whole speech written down, but in that exhaustion, I could see the words in my mind plain as day, and instead of leaving the floor to get the notes, I called on a student to bring me my water bottle, and began without any intermission.

"My name is Tanner Critz. If you don't know who I am, I want to

---

* a traditional Okinawan weapon like a blocky nightstick.

welcome you to Unity." I looked around at all the people gathered in the mat side of the dojo (we call it the Mojo for short). "And to all my friends that have traveled through months, years, or decades of training, and come in planes, cars, and vans, whether you told me or not that you were coming, I'm so glad you're here. It means the world to me."

"My father always said my wealth is in my friends." I felt my voice catch in my throat as the waves of my heart crashed against the levy of my chest, spilling over before receding. "I always thought that was a consolation prize for being poor, but he really is right. My wealth is in my friends." I took a deep pull from my water and an equally deep breath.

"If you're familiar with these tests, they take about a year of intense preparation, even after the point where we think somebody's ready to do it. Then you go for it, and go for it for a year, and get it done. That's not how this went at all." I took another gasp and a long draw on my water. My heart rate was slowing, but even just projecting my voice was an exertion.

"When I was asked to test, everything was in full flower. We had just gathered as a community to buy this building, paint, and remodel it into our home. Gaylan had just come back to work for me. Chris, who I had sent away after love, had come back and brought a new family. Everything was amazing, and Quynh was so excited about it, he flew up here, intent on multiplying my vision of what I was going to do with my test into a culmination of his dreams and his father's dreams. I was so fired up about showing it to you guys at training camp that year." I pulled at the back of my neck and looked down. "There were almost ninety of us ready to go to Raleigh, which would have been our record, when training camp got canceled. And then suddenly we were just trying to survive. We were trying to have classes when we couldn't come in here, and trying to have community when we couldn't meet each other, and trying to train when we couldn't touch each other."

"Quynh was really trying hard to keep the fire lit about my test, and trying to keep me motivated, but we wanted to wait until everyone could see it, because the whole point was to share the fire, you know? We were still navigating the hurdle of trying to keep up our training with masks, distance, and quarantines when the virus took me down hard." I was back in the hospital for a moment, staring into the void that somehow still sat in my chest blocking my breath.

"For months, my great goal was to sit up straight, to stand up long enough to take a shower, to walk around the block." I had to pace my words to keep from choking up as my heart surged again and again. "To walk up a flight of stairs. But I got to learn in that time that this dojo could stand up on its own, and that it could help me far more than I have ever been able to help it."

"And then the virus took Quynh." I paused to take a deep breath and made teary eyed contact with Jessica. "I was so weak at the time. All I could imagine was that I had to get all of my strength back. I have to rebuild everything so I can show everybody what we came up with. I've got to share this dream. So I started the hardest year of training I've ever done in my life. About six months in I realized that this test was coming up, and I can't do any of it. I can't do any of the things Quynh and I worked on to show you. So I made the really, really hard decision that I had to rebuild it. I had to start from scratch and trade that vision for practicality. I had to have something I could actually do with this body. I had to store that dream away for the next generation." I looked around past squirming kids, to some of my teen students clustered in the front.

"Starting with that realization, that I had to rebuild the whole thing, I began to dread this day. It had become in my mind the day

I had to show you guys that I was weaker, that I was lesser, that I had been forced to compromise. It's just not what I wanted to do. Even as my friends and teachers bought plane tickets and made reservations, it felt like stones piling on top of my dread. I wished there was some quiet way to do this. Could we just do it in secret? Nobody needed to see what I was doing."

"Then I had a vision. If you want that whole story you'll need to give me several hours and several drinks. But I was able to pull back far enough to see my life clearly, far enough that the cobwebs of my illusions were ripped from their anchors and fell away. And since that day, I've been so glad that you guys were coming." Loving tears overwhelmed me but no longer stopped my throat.

"So here's what I saw: My wealth is in my friends. My armor and my shield is my friends. My strength, which has never been in this big, heavy body, is in you guys. The power that I wield to change this world around me has never come from my hands and feet, but has always come from you. And what's more, I cannot help but honor the dreams of my teachers, and their teachers, from the moment we all join our striving together in Unity. And my weakness, this illness that I may carry for another day, or another decade, or for the rest of my life, is <u>sacred</u>, because it draws me closer to everyone that steps in to steady me."

"And so I want to thank you all for carrying me to this place, and for allowing me, in my season, whether that was the past, the present, or the future, to carry you." I bowed to them all, and it was done. There was a lot of bowing, hugging, and tears. The image that flashed in my mind a month earlier when She said, "let them honor you" appeared before me exactly as I'd seen it.

The energy of the moment began to dissipate. The hugs and photos were all taken. The students and visitors all acknowledged until the doors were finally locked. Then we went home for a shower, only to return a couple of hours later for one of our great parties. Dodgeball in the matted dojo, music and dance in the hardwood dojo, and food and camaraderie in the central lounge. I could finally relax with my friends, and peers, and teachers, after years of work and heaps of dread. There were many people at the party that Aya had told me how to bring lightning to, and I made my way around to them, giving them a hint of the story, and asking if they wanted some lightning. I would've thought that fewer people would say yes to my asking them this odd question, but the healing power is visible. The certainty of action is palpable, and if someone wants to call it *giving you lightning*, then I suppose it's perfectly acceptable.

Chapter 26

Things We Carry

I booked another trip to Soul Quest and began focusing on the nature of this mental wound. My nineteen year old son, Wayah, who had been struggling for some time with adolescence, pandemic, and anxiety, expressed interest in joining me this time. He would be both done with high school and old enough to legally join in, and Melanie and I talked about his coming at length.

We had tried so many things to help him find some peace with himself that we were willing to do most anything. Taking my teenager to partake in powerful psychedelics seemed to cross a line, but I knew there was so much more in the medicine than a drug trip. If he could get across the hurdle and into the space where he could receive the message from Her that he was a sacred vessel overflowing with loving energy, then he might find some of the truly positive change that I'd experienced.

It was just as likely that we wouldn't get the dose just right, and it would be just a messy, vomitous weekend like my first one. I didn't regret that weekend, but I didn't see it as part of the powerful healing I had undergone. I remembered what Granny had told me about my energy only being effective when I was close, and so I resolved to lean in and give him the best shot I could. Instead of just flying to Orlando, we would have a week-long road trip there and back. Whatever happened with his Ayahuasca journey, we would have that week together to bond.

The spring was hard with Wayah. While we had left behind the violent tantrums of his middle school years and found an uneasy truce, Wayah was deeply unhappy. Our attempts to enforce chores and school participation were rarely met with open defiance as they had been years before, but were often avoided, minimized, or agreed with and then neglected. It felt like a terrible puzzle where none of the pieces fit. While he was beginning to make progress in some ways, like choosing to end several unhealthy relationships, his lack of motivation towered over everything, blanketing his world in shadow.

Consequences for actions at home and at school were only mild inconveniences to him because there was no goal or desire that was being deferred. Video games brought him a sliver of joy, but that was a fleeting illusion. Taking away his phone and computer were the standard bargaining chips of our negotiation and also pulled him even deeper into the dark of isolation. Melanie and I were locked in a constant battle between his personal responsibility and happiness at a time when we were hoping that he would be managing that balance on his own. He always had all the resources internally and externally to excel, but without motivation, every piece of the equation was illusory.

A few times I considered removing him from the trip when I was angry and looking for any leverage to help him see reason, but I had a burning hope that if he could see any part of what She'd shown me, it might be the key to unlocking that elusive spark in him. I doggedly looked to our trip to Soul Quest in May with hard-fought hope.

I was meditating on my time in the hospital daily and preparing myself to turn and face the fullness of the memory in hopes of taking the bite out of it and removing the mental stopper in my lungs. It still nagged at me to imagine my mind putting a governor on my own body that way. My dojo had incorporated a yoga school the year before and so I was building a yoga practice of my own for the first time. In these slow, studious lessons I was able to dissect the feeling I had been having when I was pushing hard in my training. When I was swimming, or sparring, or doing a long kata, it felt like I ran into a wall when my exertion got to around eighty percent, and I had to stop immediately to recover.

What I learned in yoga was that it wasn't a block on my exertion, but a panic attack that came on whenever my breathing was challenged. I learned this upside down with my legs folded over me, compressing my torso and the lungs at their center. Suddenly I had to get out. Out of the pose, out of the room, just away. By the time I disentangled myself, I started to get it together, but the next time I was folded over, there it came again. It occurred to me that now that I could see what was happening, I'd be able to exert my mental control over it and make it go away, but no luck. Like with the armor of unworthiness, knowing what it was doing didn't address the root cause and didn't do anything to stop the attacks.

I went back to preparing to confront whatever it was about being in the hospital that had bound my mind in such a knot and created this insurmountable fear in me. I talked with Wayah at length about intentions and guides and dosage, hoping to get him into Her loving presence during his first weekend. If he could only feel that explosion of love and the recognition of his sacred worth, surely much of his internal conflict would resolve itself right there on the mat.

Caite and I kept communicating via international texting apps as she bounced around the world with her new passion of paragliding and we did the work of integration, trying to build practices out of revelations. It was often hard to reach her, and our communications slowed over time. She was healing, though, and our connection had been a good trial for being intentional about the shape of energetic connections with a relative stranger. We promised to keep in touch, but it was clear that those touches would be seldom.

I had scheduled the Ayahuasca weekend retreat for just after Cuong Nhu's International Annual Training Camp on Memorial Day weekend since Wayah would be done with school, and the business of summer camps wouldn't have started at the dojo yet. It looked like the pandemic had quieted to the point that we'd finally get to meet as a style again.

Two days before training camp, Wayah and I packed up all our gear for martial arts, camping, and the Ayahuasca retreat. Our road trip began with a stop in Nashville to stay with my cousin and see his music studio. The route to Raleigh, North Carolina from Little Rock, Arkansas is a journey of one road. You merge onto I-40 near our house, and then follow the flow of brakelights and tailpipes for thirteen hours until you exit in Raleigh.

I hadn't visited my cousin since he moved to Nashville, about halfway from Little Rock to Raleigh, though several family members had told me about his beautiful in-home music studio. Wayah had fought me and Melanie for years about his piano lessons, before finally realizing that he loved to play. This would be his first time getting to know my musical prodigy cousin, but as we drove along and he asked me what my cousin and his family were like, I realized that it had been a very long time since we'd really connected.

"I'm realizing that I really have no idea. The last time we spent any real time together I was in middle-school and he was in elementary school, asking me if my karate powers came from the devil. I don't think that's what he's about now, but I suppose there's a chance that in the middle of dinner, we'll just nod to each other and stand up and leave."

We found Jordan and his family wonderful. Smart, funny, loving, interested in our Ayahuasca road trip, and happy to dig into the cringy stories of our youth. Wayah spent the night in the studio area set up for bands to stay while recording. Back on the road, he told me with wide-eyed awe about the various amenities designed to augment the creativity of a visiting artist. The visit had ended too quickly, but we knew that we were off to a good start. We spent the hours in the car trading driving duties and albums to be the soundtrack of our drive. He'd choose an album to best introduce me to Kendrick Lamar, and then a discussion about a set of lyrics would lead me to ask if he'd ever heard Pink Floyd's *The Wall* all the way through. As he soaked it up and planned for another album to share, the words flowed in a way that they hadn't over the years of my parenting and his growing conflict with our parental controls. Now we were just two guys on an adventure in search of healing. We talked about life and relationships, work and meaning.

Cuong Nhu's International Annual Training Camp is my favorite weekend of every year. We gather for four days to train, spar, hold our advanced tests, and celebrate our history and love for each other and Cuong Nhu. We all stay together in college dorms and use the gyms for our classes. In the evenings we roam the halls between dorm room gatherings. Some are playing games, some are making music, most are telling stories and remembering times and people long past. It's hundreds of people I love all gathered together for one weekend of each year, and I can't think of anything I'd miss it for.

This year was the first year it had been held since it was canceled at the outbreak of Covid, and there was a shroud over everyone from the loss of Quynh, which we hadn't been able to mourn as a gathered family yet. The weekend included many toasts to him, stories of his gregarious life retold and amplified, and conversations held about how best to honor his life's work in our practice.

Despite the shadow of that loss, we were all so excited to finally see each other again that joy flowed all weekend long. After three days of balancing my breath with the classes I was taking and teaching, multiplied by nights up late reveling, toasting the fallen, and loving our friends, I was thoroughly exhausted.

Before leaving Raleigh, we stopped by the house of the old elementary school friend I'd called a year earlier. Taran lived in the midst of the tallest magnolia trees I've ever seen. You could easily climb a hundred feet in the air through their gnarled, easily accessible branches. I was a little shocked not to see the lower branches cut off since he'd raised a daughter here, but he just nodded and said, "Yeah, she gets way up there sometimes."

I wanted to talk to him more about what I was doing, but even more to ask him for advice with Wayah in his approach to the medicine. I wasn't entirely sure that it was appropriate for someone so young, partially because he didn't have as much life to dig through, and also because Beck had reported having Her tell him that he should live for a while before coming to see Her. He had reiterated the message to Wayah the night before at the closing festivities of training camp, and it was looming in our minds. Taran told me some about living with a group in Brazil that took Ayahuasca as part of their daily lives and as a regular religious practice. His wife had taken it while pregnant with his daughter, and the babies were given some to connect them to the Mother from birth.

I got the sense that he was talking about smaller doses than what I was taking since he said they would dance and play music together while "in the power." I can hardly stand, much less dance, during a journey, but maybe if you do it all the time, dancing is possible. Mainly his message was that Wayah's age wouldn't hamper the experience in any way. Aya knew how to meet everyone where they were when they were ready to do the work of healing. There was a steadiness to Taran and his hopeful message that set us off towards Orlando with light hearts and hopeful thoughts.

We visited Atlanta, where we were both born, and stayed a day with family and friends. We continued on to camp on a beach on the Georgia coast. We would decide each day where to go next. We just needed to be in Orlando by Friday afternoon. I wanted Wayah to feel completely ready. I told him everything that had helped me, the guides, focused intention, letting Her take control when She wanted to go somewhere I didn't expect. We talked about dosage, and boosters, and what I thought would be the best strategy.

Josh had been back several more times since the last time I'd been, and said there was some friction in the ownership that had been hard for him. It sounded like some of the staff and volunteers that we liked were thinking about parting ways and maybe starting a new place. I'd follow my favored staff members if they left, but for now I was counting on the fact that once I had the medicine in me, none of the trivialities of our host's personal lives could touch me, and I was determined to get Wayah to that threshold before anything interfered. We listened to a lot more music and talked about everything and nothing.

Part 5
Integration

Chapter 27

For the Love of Our Fathers

I'd booked a small one-room cabin for us. It was really a small shed with two single beds and a side table with a light between. A window AC unit hummed happily and cut the June Florida heat. We waited through the now familiar check in, different now only because I was here feeling parental instead of with my peers. I got a couple of comments from people waiting for their medical check-ups about how great they thought it was that I brought my son. I still had some reservations, not about the idea of him taking the medicine, but just that it may take time to get it right, and the one weekend might not get him the relief I so longed for him to have.

The doctors had suggested EMDR for working through my panic attacks. EMDR is Eye Movement Desensitization and Reprocessing. I'd talked to a few people that offered it and a few more that had been through it, and it sounded ultimately effective, but a very long and expensive process. It might be that coming at it through Ayahuasca would also be a long and expensive process. Here I was, about three thousand dollars into a weekend retreat with my son. Would it take all three sessions, three weekends, six? I had a lot of faith in the power of the medicine, though, based on what I'd already learned and developed. Whenever I entered the calculus of comparing the expense of the retreat to the deep love, joy, and peace that came out of the medicine, the dollars seemed trivial.

When Wayah and I went to our mats in separate lodges, I first went with him to be sure he got to the right place. I saw a familiar face in the lodge he was assigned to and felt enormous relief to see Brandon would be watching over him during his journey. I took a moment to give Brandon a hug and tell him what it meant to me to have him there for my son's first journey, and then hugged my boy and left for my own mat. I had some work to do.

The very owner who seemed to be the source of the strife was supposed to be in charge of my group. I prepared myself for that, but mostly planned to block him out entirely and focus on my process. I knew how to meet the teacher, I just needed the rocket boost of the medicine to launch me entirely into Her presence. A peaceful transition was helpful, but no longer necessary for me. About twenty minutes passed when we were supposed to be talking with our facilitator about our goals, but the contentious owner still hadn't arrived, and so all the waiting sojourners were sitting quietly, centering ourselves privately. Outside, I heard some thrashing and recognized our facilitator's voice.

"I shouldn't even need to be here for this! I should get to have a nap!" His voice rambled away from the building in sharp negative contrast to the peaceful and positive vibration of the place. I was thinking to myself that I really hoped he wasn't about to bring that kind of energy into this space, when another staff member entered and subbed in to pick up and carry on. Good. I was in the zone. I just needed my dose. I thought about Wayah a hundred feet away collecting his own thoughts, hearing other people's hard stories, and sent him my love and my strength.

Blessing the medicine, smoke cleanse, two tablespoons please, "Good journey, brother," waiting, waiting. We all drank, and I sat, fighting the medicine to keep it down. It had been harder each time to prevent the brew from coming back up. I had even developed a gag reflex when discussing the flavor or hearing someone else describe it. I was able to keep it in my stomach, though, and as the minutes ticked by, the wretched taste faded, leaving only an uneasy feeling of work happening in my stomach, that twisting that I knew would soon begin to take over my whole existence.

On it came, the bending, emergent transformation out of the world of fear and illusions, and into Her divine classroom. As usual, the process was so all-encompassing that when I came to the challenge of purifying myself, I had forgotten all of my goals and felt that this was the work itself. This time I was spitting out my sickness, searching the dark corners of my existence to find where the illness was still hiding. Only I had the power to commit to the hard work of purging, and when I was done, clarity returned to me.

She was there. I had never experienced Her so directly before. On my second weekend, She had come to me through my granny. On the third trip, almost a year earlier, She had made Herself known without using the trusted mask of my beloved grandmother. On that journey She was around me and near me, whispering in my ear, directing my attention to what I needed to see. Now She waited in front of me in the greatest wholeness of Her that my heart had yet experienced. She was like the multitude of femininity opening endlessly as flowering vines and prowling paws, an explosion of love and life contained in patient, undulating peace, a sphinx-like guardian waiting for the password that would unlock the vault where my final healing awaited.

"I'm ready," I said, very aware of where I was and what I was doing. I had meditated and practiced for this moment for months now, and I was fully ready for the battle in the hospital to come.

"Ready for what?" She wove playfully in front of me. She was a stern teacher and a playful lover, a challenging little girl and a loving grandmother. She wanted desperately to see me healed and also wasn't going to take any of the work off of me. The work was mine to perform, but She could point, guide, love, and exalt. I had to say all of the words. She wouldn't let me suggest and then fill in the blanks for me.

"The hospital. I'm ready to face the hospital and uproot the trauma that's there." She swirled there gloriously, everything all at once. I waited to be transported to that world of tubes and gloves and pain, but several beats passed with only Her magnificence.

"No." The wind was kicked out of me by the resounding weight of Her rejection.

"What?" My mind scrambled to find the thread that She was pulling. She had never just told me "no" before.

"That was the hardest, most painful thing you've ever been through." I could feel tears on my cheeks, partially from relief that we weren't going back into the hospital, but also from the acknowledgment of that suffering. "But you won. You beat it. You're not afraid of that at all."

"Then why can't I breathe?" I cried. This question that had plagued me for two and a half years came crashing into the front of my mind. I no longer had the slightest clue about how to search for healing, and I threw myself at the mercy of Her love.

"You can't breathe," She said with mortal certainty, "because you haven't let go of the fact that people you love and trust thought it made sense that you should be the one to get sick and die." I sat confused. Forgiveness is a great power, but I couldn't even imagine who She might be talking about. I searched my mind while She waited, looking on with her many patient faces. I only knew of people saying it didn't make sense that I got so sick. I'm healthy and vital. It had always been a confounding mystery that I was hospitalized when much more vulnerable people were barely harmed. Literally no one had ever said anything like that in my hearing. Telling my story had even caused people to rethink their position on vaccines because they thought only the old and the weak got sick. My doctor told people about me as his office's great Covid anomaly. Who the hell heard that I got sick and thought, "That makes sense, I bet he'll die"?

"Are you ready?" She said. I was. I couldn't imagine what She had to show me, but I was riled up and ready to fight. "He thinks you're weak." She faded away, and a figure approached me. A cold sweat broke out when I realized it was my father's father, dead now twenty-five years.

"Oh. We're doing this," I thought, and approached him.

"You think I'm weak? You think I'm the one who should die?" My grandfather had been a kind man, and a good man. He'd loved his family in the best way he knew and treated everyone right that he could. I hadn't been his kind of man, though. He had his own pew at church, but I had been disillusioned by churches and looked for holiness outside of them. He valued team sports, but I liked martial arts and hiked the Appalachian Trail. He thought a real man joined the army, but I won writing awards, studied anthropology, and traveled the world whenever I could. There had always been room in my mind for his way, but there was no room in his for mine. It had driven a wedge between him and my father at the end, and seeing the life drained from his body the night he finally gave in had made me sad, not for his death, but for the lost love we could've shared.

"You think you know better about everything. Why couldn't you join the football team? They drooled over you. They would've taught you what you needed to know."

"I tried it, remember? It wasn't for me. And don't even start with the army. You and everyone you knew in the army worked at desks and talked about heroism, but when my dad was in real combat it broke him! My whole life has been in the shadow of a handful of bullets. I would never put my soul through that."

"You and your father question everything, even the word of God!"

I was filled with a profound sympathy for this good man. He wanted so much to protect me from a future he feared. I remembered his cold, sad church building, with a dwindling congregation of increasingly elderly worriers. God was waiting for me in the forest where I learned my strength, and in the life that flowed between me and everyone I lifted up. We weren't really arguing, just blowing our values back and forth like so much hot air. I realized that there was no argument here to win.

"I forgive you for not seeing me. You did your best with what you had. Now it's my turn. I can take it from here."

"I don't think you're strong enough."

"I am. I forgive you for not seeing it. You can rest." He faded into the dark and another figure approached. This was my other grandfather, my mother's father. During my early life, we'd been around my mom's family, and it had always been uncomfortable. There was a lot of fighting. The one cousin that was about my age lived near them, and there was a long running agenda to build him up and diminish me since my mother had been the favored daughter, and they wanted the scales balanced by lauding my cousin and putting me down. By the time I was old enough to make decisions about what I let into my life, my mother's family was out. I didn't want that kind of negativity for my family.

My grandfather, Mac, had tried in the most pitiful way to bridge that gap and make me feel seen, but the moment anyone pulled his leash, he'd fall back into the game, teasing, making fun, pushing me out. I hated his weakness precisely because he knew he should do something and wasn't man enough to stand up to the bullies in his family. I was surprised to see him here, now, precisely because I hadn't considered my mother's family as part of my life for decades. Unlike my father's father, what any of them thought of me or my life was entirely inconsequential to me.

"I already know you think I'm weak. It doesn't matter to me." I said before he could speak.

"It matters to me." His face looked pained at my rejection. "I wanted you to be tougher, harder. You let everything get past you. You have to learn how to play the game."

"I don't. I'm stronger than you are. I can stand up to people that aren't right. I don't need to play games with them."

"People are going to take advantage of you." As he spoke I realized that it did matter to me. Unlike his family members that had so openly rejected me, this man's feelings mattered because I knew that deep down he actually loved me. I could feel my anger like hidden coals under a deep bed of ash.

"You love me, but you don't see me. You don't recognize my strength. I forgive you for not seeing me." I could feel the weight of my anger lifting.

"I don't understand," he said tearfully.

"You don't have to. I've got it from here. I have the strength to do what you couldn't." He walked away with his shoulders hunched and the old hat that I'd forgotten he always wore. The next figure I knew immediately.

"No, come on man. Quynh? What are you doing here? Did you think it made sense that I would get sick? You were my biggest cheerleader!" He looked like he'd been caught stealing. This powerful mentor that I loved so dearly brought himself into my crosshairs.

"I mean, you're a great martial artist, but you've never been fit like me," he grinned, half laughing as he spoke, his hand feeling the opposite bicep, swollen from a workout. "I mean, you do all right, but you don't inspire people with your fitness, you know. I want people to look at me and think 'that's what I can be.'" It was odd after arguing my way of living with my grandfathers to be hearing my teacher tell me he wished I had lost twenty pounds. Did he really think my lack of a six pack made me vulnerable to Covid?

"Brother, it killed you." I reached out to him and put my hand on his shoulder. "You died from this thing that made me sick." We looked into each other's eyes, and I realized that he'd been looking down this whole time because he was weeping.

"It's not fair, man. It's not fair." He cried and clenched his powerful fists. I wrapped my arms around him.

"It's not fair. Whatever you thought about me and my health, or you and yours, I forgive you." I could feel him wrestling with all he still wanted to do. He was so in love with his family and his children. He was really coming into his own as a leader and finding his vision for our martial art style. He had dreams that he knew he could fulfill. "The people you love, the martial art you spent your life on, I'll be here for them," I said, still holding him with both arms.

"Are you strong enough?" he said through his tears. I held him out at arm's length, smiling through tears at hearing this for the third time. Had I not practiced on my grandfathers, I might not have had the answer ready for him.

"I forgive you for not seeing it. I've got this. You can rest, brother."

I was sitting up with the walls of the maloca coming into focus. My face was drenched with streaming tears, and I began to breathe deep, humored breaths of relief. I could already tell that it was gone. I'd test it out, but I knew my lungs were mine again. Just one session was all it took. I shook my head, chuckling at the awesome power of this medicine, and what an odd, perfect cure She was. I never would've thought in a million years that I couldn't breathe because I needed to stand up for myself and forgive.

I drew slowly and steadily to my feet and went out to the fire. Almost everyone was still in the midst of their journeys. Mine had only taken about two and a half hours. I claimed a mat by the fire pit where I could see the door of Wayah's lodge. I wanted to find Brandon and ask how Wayah was doing, but I knew that since he wasn't out here by the fire, he was probably in the thick of it. I sat by the fire and thought about strength and forgiveness. How were my strengths so unusual that my elders had such trouble understanding them? She had taken great care to show me what they were and how they worked, and in the times between my weekends here, those powers had shown themselves to be true and consistently effective.

I watched the fire swirl and the sparks drift lazily in a pattern both predictable with the breeze and at the same time unique for each ember. So many wondrous sparks. Do they know how perfectly they swirl, each in their own perfect path? Do they fear that they might not find the great destiny of a spark to set off a conflagration, and through that fear miss the joy of flight? All around, people writhed on their mats. Some gently swayed and others were fighting much more physical battles. A few guys who needed to yell a lot in their trials were moved to a more private area so that they wouldn't worry those near them, but I could hear their muffled exclamations from a distance.

My mind floated back and forth between Wayah and his journey and the revelation of healing through forgiveness. I felt waves of gratitude washing over me. Over the next hour, people started to come out of their journeys, and some out of the lodge he was in.

Finally I saw the clear shape of my son, moving on shaky legs and supported by a helper in white. I rose smoothly and he saw me moving towards him and stumbled my way. I stepped around the still journeying people on the lawn.

"Can I talk to you?" he said with a teary, exhausted face. He looked more like my little boy in that moment than the young man he was becoming. As I opened and prepared to embrace him, figures in white stepped between us.

"You're his dad?" one said gently.

"Yeah," I said, ready to hold Wayah and hear what he had to say about his experience.

"I'm sorry, but the ceremony isn't over, and we can't let you have any contact until it's finished." It ached to be told not to respond to the cry of my child and a raw, uncivilized piece of me asked if they could actually stop me, but I knew these gentle caretakers were keeping our minds and spirits safe, and I retired to a chair to wait for the gong. I watched Wayah in another chair staring at the fire and looked for clues about how it had gone for him. He certainly seemed to have been through something.

When the gong finally sounded he joined me where I'd made space for both of us and told me a story far greater than my wildest dreams for his first journey. He told me about being transported back to when he was in fifth grade and how he walked all over the neighborhood for a long time. Then through the playground, into his school, and to his fifth grade classroom, She'd shown him the place where he first felt like he wasn't enough. In that moment he'd made a mask to replace himself. She showed him how this tough, unbeatable mask had changed his relationship to the world. He had to watch every painful thing he'd ever done while wearing that mask one-by-one, and see them laid out in a sprawling montage.

Then She condensed it down to a little opalescent marble to put in his pocket. She told him this was his past to learn from, but showed him a great empty expanse left in its absence to build his future in. We held each other and marveled at the healing we'd experienced and the freedom we felt. We ate a few lite snacks that would digest fully before the morning session and then returned to our cabin and did our best to sleep. I was only able to put together a few decent sleeping hours after writing everything down, but Wayah managed to sleep well the whole night.

Chapter 28

It Was All the Way

I awoke a bit rough in the throat, but more refreshed than I normally felt on the second day of a weekend of ceremonies. I reviewed the prior night's experience in my journal and thought about what might come up in the second session. I hadn't thought about a second problem to solve. I had been sure that recovering from PTSD would be a multi-session treatment. I hadn't pushed myself hard yet to see if the block was completely gone and I could access my lungs fully, but I really didn't need to. I felt clear in a way that I hadn't since the hospital. My body belonged to me, and there were no limits on my future self and development. It was still going to be a challenge, for sure. Almost three years without being able to push myself hard had left me out of shape and in my fifties, but the deep-seated knowledge that I was whole and healed made me feel light and eager for the challenge.

I woke Wayah, half expecting him to be sullen about being woken up, but he was ready to go and excited to see what she would show him next. I had never seen someone sleep well after taking Ayahuasca, but here again, he surprised me. He hopped out of bed and made for the outdoor showers lined up on a platform with curtains draping from shoulder to calf level so that people couldn't disappear into them and be unseen during a ceremony. My hope for him continued to swell. We made our way to the daytime ceremony yard. Not everyone that comes for the weekend does all three ceremonies, so the daytime ceremony is a smaller, single group. This was the same yard where I'd called the lightning and heard the thunder roll as I gripped the hammer high the summer before. I still missed the sweeping limbs of the live oaks where we'd had daytime ceremony the first time when I found myself in the womb, but the group had lost access to that land and now I could hear the saw and lumber sounds from that direction where an apartment complex was being built. A part of me felt intruded on by the attentions and noises of the builders. I knew that once the medicine kicked in, I wouldn't think about them again until it wore off.

Wayah and I spread out so as not to distract each other. This was normally a time of pensive focus, reading back to myself the litany of what I needed to accomplish and keep at the front of my mind no matter how much reality dismantled itself around me. Now I sat joyfully, happy for myself, happy for my son, curious about what She wanted to show me next. The ceremony proceeded as normal. A short speech, a smoke cleanse, the medicine blessing, the lines to get our cups. I chose one and a half, since there was a full double dose in me from the night before, and I wasn't really sure about my intentions for this journey. Wayah had experienced his perfect journey on a single tablespoon, so we had talked about dosage this morning and both decided to back off a little in order to hit the same place. He chose to take three-quarters of a tablespoon.

I sat on my mat and drank my medicine like a communion. I thought about those youthful times in church when I drank grape juice from a clear plastic thimble, and felt my own thoughts echo, reaching and waiting. I would strain to listen for God to speak to me through that silence, for some little sign that I couldn't deconstruct in my mind as a normal action of my thoughts in motion. How different this was, to taste the bitter earth in a cup, and to wait patiently, knowing that in just half an hour, startling revelations would come from outside of me directly through my heart whether I prayed for them or not. I was open to anything now like the first time I drank, except this time I was entering my developed practice in order to meet my loving teacher. I waited and glanced around at the other people, looking down and readying their minds. I saw my son past a tree, his head down and waiting, and I decided to scoot to where the tree would stand between us, just to remove the temptation to keep checking on him.

After a time it began. I could feel the world slipping around me, but instead of my body coming apart, I felt myself connecting outward to all of the people, the trees, the facilitators, the buildings. I began to be aware of Her in the light, the leaves of the trees, and the people around me. I wasn't adhering to my own rule about keeping my eyes closed, and I felt the two worlds mixing. She was there, all around me.

"What will you teach me today, Mama?" I called to her by heart, still sitting up on my mat. She was slow to respond. A woman on a mat near me with very large eyes was staring right at me, and I smiled. I was humming and swaying, feeling energy pass through me from all directions and from the source. Aya was present, but not speaking, and some time passed in pleasurable energetic vibration. I watched the trees and people and wondered at what She might reveal to me.

"You are healed, now," She said casually, in answer to my thoughts. "Take what you've learned and use it now in the world. You don't need to come back here unless you forget the lessons or who you are." I didn't feel rejected by this statement, but it was an odd diversion from what I had observed and experienced. There were people that had been coming for years and years and were still in the process. I had also just drunk a powerful medicine about thirty minutes earlier, and it was going to be at work in me for hours more. She seemed to spread out, and I could feel Her at work on everyone here. I felt like maybe I was intruding now, and lay back on my mat to just feel for a while. I didn't feel particularly nauseous, and I wondered if this time I would keep it in me, like a going-away present. I wasn't having the normal pre-communion experience of something weak or impure that I needed to purge from myself. I felt whole and stable, and in harmony. Thoughts swirled about what it all meant to put what She'd shown me into practice. I wondered if I would just think and feel through this entire experience, and if that would make it like any other hallucinogen, just me and my thoughts, without Her presence.

Oh, wait. I was going to throw up. My thought about keeping it for myself was kicked hard from behind by the urge to give it back to the others, to Mama, to the world. I surrendered to my body's noisy vomiting, though the purging didn't feel like a deep and personal dredging, which it always had before. Now it was like cleansing my soul and giving back. I drank some cold, fresh water and waited, still sitting, for the escalation that I knew would follow soon after. I imagined that She was focusing on the others, so I would do this one on my own. Maybe that's what being healed looked like.

Then She was there. She was feminine and sensual but also not human. There were vine-like limbs that all surged with life. She was many things at once, every aspect of femininity and energy simultaneously. I could see the playful girl, the sensuous lover, the patient teacher, the probing scholar, the fearless defender, the all-giving mother, the patient grandmother, and the knowing crone. It was clear to me how a person could experience this and then make a statue of a many-armed goddess in an attempt to convey the multitude of being. There would not be room for all the aspects in any painting of Her, no way to show them in energetic action. There is no way for the eye to contain Her, but having experienced it, I can "see" it in the part of me that knows.

"I will show you how the pieces all fit together." Her voice didn't come from any of the representations of a mouth that I was experiencing, but rather vibrated through me from inside with the root of what it means to experience the vibrating waves that make up all sound and light and energy. Before me and around me I saw all of the lessons I had experienced with her, all connected. She pieced them together with no detail left out, and I was suddenly aware how vital each experience was and the order in which they came. Even those ceremonies when I just felt lost or nauseous were part of a perfect whole, and now that I saw it like a map unrolled, I felt a sense of perfect wholeness rain down on me.

I could see in that swirling map of my healing how each piece was placed in exactly the place that it needed to be. Those first ceremonies when it seemed like I got nowhere showed me the chaos in my mind while teaching me how much of a dose of the medicine it would take to find Her. The middle session, when I approached the right dose and found myself in the womb with the power to assert myself on the future, was preparing me for the revelation that I was reborn and able to create a new reality.

By the time I went back, I was truly in need and knew the name of my suffering. I knew the dose to take and had the tools to successfully meet Her. In that meeting, though, we tackled the first lesson which was to mourn the death of myself and receive the full beauty of my existence in the loving fountain of creation that worked through me. The medicineless journeys that started the next night and continued for months built on what I'd seen, developed practices to connect with the power of my new self, and gave me the courage and certainty to embrace a new way of being.

On my third weekend, I had fully embraced the beauty of my existence, so she was ready to show me the power of that existence and how it manifested in the world. She wanted to encourage me to use my voice and my powers, and ended the weekend by removing the last trace of unworthiness from my mind. I still wasn't ready to heal completely, though. It took the act of pressing through my test with an empowered soul but an injured body, and then almost a year of testing those powers before I was ready. I couldn't finally heal my lungs until I was so certain of my potency that I could stand up to my elders and claim authority from them, while at the same time seeing them and their attempts to protect and love me, and forgiving any failures to see me. I prayed to have that same forgiveness from my sons and students and grandchildren one day.

Each of the lessons she taught me hung in the air, fitting together perfectly - the image of my healing as a completed puzzle with no extraneous pieces. Every moment was absolutely critical to the whole, both in its content and its sequence, and I basked in the elegance and simplicity of Her map of my creation. As I pulled back from it, brimming with gratitude for my healing and feeling powerful and sacred, I was still fully within the sway of the medicine, with quite some time left before the ceremony ended.

Our review was done and now She wanted to celebrate. For more than an hour of bliss, She swirled through my nervous system, danced in the energy of my chakras, laughed, played, and sang to the tune of my existence in the world. I was connected to everyone there through the pulsing energy, and overwhelmed with love and gratitude for my life, my friends, my family, that sanctuary, and all the healing souls that protected me there.

There were other things moving in the cosmic dance around me as well. As I was both in the world with my eyes open, and also on the other side with Her, there were entities that came to me, drawn by my position astride the threshold. Most just peeked and ran like fish in the water near a strange thing, subtle, unformed presences that only hinted at shape or personality. One lumbering being approached me with an elder confidence. He was a musky, heavy brute of a thing, and he asked me without fear, but also with some weariness, if he could come into the world with me while I was sitting on both sides. I couldn't see him with my open eyes, but my heart was very aware of his presence. He said it had been a long time since he had been able to breathe the air, and I could feel his deep yearning. He had been painted on horses before going into battle, called on to help hunt buffalo, danced in raucous ceremony, but not for a long time.

I could sense that he was a warrior spirit and his medium was the fight.

"Yes, you can come breathe with me." I said, not sure what I was getting into, or if there was anything dangerous about bringing strange spirits to the threshold of reality. It felt a little risky, but I resolved to be sure that I put him back before we finished, what-ever that meant.

He said, "You don't seem strong enough to fight me."

"I get that a lot," I said, unable to hold back the grin that spread across my face. "Bring it on, big guy." We wrestled and fought for a while, each exertion a powerful inhalation of the joy of being a physical being: the strain of muscle, the taste of blood, the dance to get ahead of each other's movements. It didn't feel like he wanted to dominate me, he just wanted an invigorating fight that would last as long as possible. When he had filled himself up, he thanked me and went quietly back. I kept celebrating until I began to feel the effects fading.

She held my gaze and said, "You're healed. I'm going to use my energy on healing others." I thought that was all but She said one final thing to me. "Tell Wayah to come back tonight. He thinks he's done but I have something special for him."

The celebration faded to the bright sun of the ceremonial grounds and I sat in my tears of joy, dirty, sweaty, and grateful for my healing. I looked around and saw that Wayah was out of it, too. Finding my legs and my balance gently, I lifted myself up, enjoying my height and my strength. We shared an exhausted hug when he rose, and then started walking through the grounds toward the house where the kitchen and food were waiting. The smell of brothy vegetable soup and bread lit the way there, and I listened to my son's account of how She took him back to the big blank space that She'd told him the night before was the rest of his life. She asked him what he wanted to do with the empty canvas, and he played music for her. He played his favorites, pieces he'd composed, and even tuned in with the ceremonial music to riff off of it.

I told him how she'd said I was done so I was going to sit out the last ceremony and I'd be better rested for the morning and the driving that we needed to do.

"Yeah, I'm feeling really good about this. I think I've gotten enough for one weekend," he said. I remembered the last thing she told me and grinned broadly.

"Interesting. She told me you'd say that. She said she had something special for you tonight so you should come back." I half expected him to double down. A week ago, he'd have resisted, just to not have to change a position he'd already declared.

"Well, all right," he said. "I'm not going to say no to Mama!" It wasn't even a battle for him. Something had really changed in this kid in less than twenty-four hours.

We ate and loved the feel of nutrients in our weary bodies. We talked about all we'd seen together and with others who were equally travel-weary and laid open. I was filled with an additional measure of gratitude knowing that I was healed and might never see this place again. All of the broken and searching participants, the broken and loved volunteers, the broken and steadfast staff, were able to come together through this medicine and ritual to experience the truth in love and healing.

Now I thought about my son and what he'd see tonight. What "special" thing did she have for him? Why wouldn't she say that to him directly? Perhaps it was to give me one last taste of the truth before going back out into the world to fight for it. I rested and the evening passed. They all prepared as I watched. Wayah waited in line for the smoke cleanse. Though it was usually a five-second procedure, one man was held up in the line as the woman cleansing him kept cleansing and cleansing. Wayah behind him looked back at me with a raised eyebrow and a shrug, but she wasn't stopping, and they rerouted her line to others.

Soon he was back in his lodge under Brandon's care. I was amazed at this man's ability to be in the moment with me and my kid. Even attempts to thank him for past help or talk about the future weren't nearly as interesting to him as what we were experiencing right now in the moment. He had appeared to Wayah several times during the daytime ceremony, holding just the thing that Wayah needed without his ever having asked for it (a wet cloth, scented water to spray on his skin in a cooling mist). Watching someone out in the world see and love my sons well brings a peace that dances magically with my own love for them. Few things can bring me down like watching my children lose sight of happiness. Few things bring me back like seeing them reunited with it.

I lay in my cot and wrote. I watched the stars come out as a few people journeyed in the open around the fire. I watched the staff and volunteers with gratitude as they looked after every need, spoke quietly, and sat in communion, waiting for the voice to say "now." After hours lengthened by seeing people finish their journeys and begin to walk away from the ceremony ground, I finally saw my little boy in the body of a man shamble slowly out of his hut. Those same eyes that looked at me in weary wonder when I eased him from his mother's belly sought me out with joyful determination. I had a cold bottle full of cucumber water ready for him, and we held each other silently for a bit while I waited to hear him tell his story.

He told me how he had hallucinated for a bit and thought it was all over. I nodded, remembering all the times I'd felt that way just before the lesson started. When he opened his eyes, another Wayah was looking at him from the mat to his right, and She was on the mat to his left.

"What's going on?" He'd asked Her.

"That's him." She gestured. "That's the Wayah you made when you thought you weren't enough. He's what gets in the way of your happiness and relationships."

Wayah swung his glance back to his other self, who lay staring at him on the next mat. He looked back to her. "Do I have to kill him?"

"Oh, no, dear one." She laughed. "You've been together for many years and the hardest of your life. He's protected you and been there with you through everything. When you leave here tonight, he's going to stay with me. You should spend some time together, you have a lot of history and stories together." And so he did. They remembered old times and talked about all they'd seen and done together. As the ceremony faded, he said goodbye and walked out into the fire-lit night and felt his other self melt into Her and away. I drank in his story, felt the deep truth of it, and looked at my son. He was free of his past in a way that had taken me many decades to accomplish, and I was in awe of his work, and the power of the medicine.

I told him we should get a photo with Brandon, and Wayah laughed that Brandon is probably too holy to show up in photos.

Sure enough, when we looked for him in the morning, he had taken an early flight out. I sat in my last integration, balancing my moment to speak, as mine was a story of empowerment and completed healing and many others were still in the throes of their struggles. Despite any misgivings I had, there was only love in that room, and the conversation was perfectly capable of containing their work and mine together. The man leading the discussion was Andrew, whom I'd judged and been humbled by on my first day here two-and-a-half years earlier. How perfect it was to see him so ably helping others heal. He had grown so much in those same years from someone who was bound with suffering but showing up, into a full fledged healer, giving good counsel and sharing love.

Wayah and I traveled slowly back home, taking our time, talking, listening to music. We were so light, and the years since then haven't dimmed that light in any way. A part of my mind will always want to question, but we both underwent deep neural reprogramming. A month later when Chris and Ming told me they wanted to move home to Atlanta to be near family, it didn't crush me the way it should have.

Even though my vision for the dojo and my future centered around passing the school on to him, I wished them well and reconfigured my business. This was a storm I hadn't called, but my power to wield the lightning was still there, and I took the swirling pieces and made something better out of them by rearranging schedules, incorporating another martial arts school, and developing a new program for creating teachers and leaders. Now the school is stronger than it's ever been through avenues that would never have opened if I had been able to follow my original plan.

In the years since, I've been able to talk to Josh and Darrick more about their experiences as they have continued to process them. While I'd feared that they were having trouble connecting as clearly as I had, they were undergoing powerful transformation that was difficult to communicate at the time. Just as it took me time to process all I'd seen and what it meant for my life, they had profound experiences that couldn't find a voice for months or years.

Darrick, who'd been tight lipped during the two weekends that I shared with him, has since opened up about the journeys he undertook with the medicine and how they transformed him. On his first journey, She'd taken him through the car wreck that took his mother, for which he'd always felt responsible even though he wasn't driving. She showed him each aspect and made him see and accept that none of it was his fault.

Over three weekend retreats, he watched himself die and release himself to wade in waves of ceaseless love, giving him powerful and lasting tools to reinforce his self worth. He was able to meet himself as a child, as a man, and in the eye of the divine. He learned how to be kind to himself and through that path, to forgive and seek forgiveness from others.

During the afternoon when Josh and I couldn't find him and first witnessed Shadow integration, he had tried going as deep as he could at the daytime ceremony with six tablespoons (three times as much as I ever had). During the resulting many hour journey, he experienced all reality, time, and identity dissolve in a terrifying break. Experiencing it all come gradually back into focus, though, left him feeling grounded with profound gratitude and peace.

On his third and final retreat he'd experienced an acceptance of his power and message of completion as he made peace with all his life of wrongs and all those who had wronged him. In the years since, he's broken through many barriers that used to bind him, and continues to search and grow.

Josh's experience with the medicine began with an overwhelming experience that there was more to this life than all the trivialities that worried him, and each time he returned, he gained freedom from his anxieties. He describes that in the months following each retreat, the anxieties would start to return, but the floor of those depths got shallower and shallower each time.

Pivotal to his transformation was when She walked him through his father and then his mother abandoning him as a child. He'd been able to dismantle the overwhelming anger that he felt for them and see them with divine perspective. He saw how young, afraid, and lost they were, and how even those things that hurt him had been their desperate attempts for love. He was able to reconnect and has the best relationship he's ever had with his mother. That tolerance has extended outward over everyone in his life and he's now able to start by seeing the good in people rather than being overwhelmed by their threats.

Eight months ago, Josh was diagnosed with Leukemia, and I found myself standing by his hospital bed, holding his hand in mine. Because of the deep knowledge we've both found along this path, I had the words to speak to his fear of death. I echoed her revelations to me and told him that he'd died the moment he heard that it was cancer and not just an infection. We mourned the loss of the old Josh and began to look forward to everything this new version of him would learn, whether that was about the rigor of beating cancer, or the exercise in love and connection that was letting go of his people in the world. His perspective on life, anxiety, love, and fear has blossomed into a truly new view of the world and his place in it.

He got a bone marrow transplant a month ago, and is at home resting, his voice stronger each day. We marvel at the synchronicity of our paths of healing as he fights for the strength to walk around the block or stand up through a shower. He's getting stronger each day, and soon will have the immune system to sit on the back porch with me, distanced and with masks on, to be sure I don't pass on an illness while his immune system is recovering, looking across the deck like a reflection in time's mirror.

Soul Quest has since closed. I was aware from the Netflix documentary that there had been a death from hyponatremia (drinking too much water) years before my experience there. After my final visit, the lawsuit against them by the family of the deceased was successful. It seemed likely to me that some measure of the increased medical presence and attentiveness during the retreats I attended may have been a reaction to this early tragedy. Despite my own strained impression of the group's founder based on passing interactions, nothing ever got in the way of my connection with the medicine. The genuine love of volunteers and facilitators was my primary interaction, but my experience was not universal.

It's difficult for me to tell you this story and not have in hand a ready pathway towards this healing, but for now, the truths that She revealed to me are all I can offer.

If you are yearning for teaching and healing from Aya or one of the other plant teachers, I urge you to seek one of the legal sanctuaries, guided by loving, certified healers with medical staff on hand. You can probably have some concoction mailed to your house, but this is both potentially dangerous and to my understanding far less likely to meet with success. Please follow an experienced guide into this wild country. I truly hope that in the near future you can experience the medicine in a clinic, covered by your health care, and watched over by well trained therapeutic and medical staff.

Lastly, while I experienced miraculous healing and revelation in a relatively short time, many people I have spoken to and met while in communion are on a very long journey of healing. Everyone I have ever spoken to, even if the weekend wrecked them mentally and physically, has experienced healing from it. I'm sure there are also people with negative experiences.

In a sense the journeys must begin in a great expanse of over-lapping illusion, and the first hurdle in healing is to let your heart be cracked open to experience the love bursting from beneath. Many people desperately want healing, but have a very hard time allowing the medicine to reach their core. The armor that protects your wounded heart is mighty and held fast.

My belief is that we build up armor to protect us, skills to thrive, and relationships to sustain us, but that we change, our situations change, and the world changes. At some point, our armors become maladaptive and we need to discard them, but our minds don't easily let go of things that have helped us before. This is the role of these adventures in our lives. If we can strip down to our core and test each aspect of ourselves in a true adventure, then we have a chance to shed those things that no longer suit our reality.

I, however, will never tell anyone they need to drink the medi-cine. It is serious work that you must choose on your own. It is death and rebirth. It is losing the world and confronting your darkest fears. I dread it every time. The taste, the waiting, the vomiting, the sore throat and deep exhaustion. But on the other side of that is love, power, healing, and truth. I can take my medicine for that.

In each small moment, I transform. The change builds and builds until my transformation has broken the label that contains me. The ways that served my past no longer serve my transformed self, and I must continually let go. Each transformation echoes the beginning even as it reaches its end. I begin again, to begin again.

I begin under a tree by a river. I begin after school on the play-ground where the teachers can't see. I begin on a torn hill in Vietnam. I begin in a roach infested apartment with a trusting dog. I begin, eaten up by love and wrong about all but one thing. I begin by taking a bow filled with the fear that there will be no applause. I begin on my knees with a bitter taste of vomit in my mouth and angels standing guard. I begin on the holy mountain top, on the desperate street, waiting for unlikely help, looking for unearned grace. I begin right now in the thread of light that strings these words between you and me.

The following lessons are discussions of each principle She taught me during my journeys. While the narrative of my healing story would have slowed considerably from what was often hours of discussion and instruction, the lessons are worth looking at beyond a few paragraphs of narration. While the order in which I experienced them seemed somewhat random in the moment, what She showed me on the last day about how and why they were arranged the way they were brought it all into perspective.

Lesson 1

The Gate of Mourning

*To begin this new life,
you must die to the old*

When I first arrived in Florida, looking for healing but entirely unaware of what I needed to heal, I was suffering on many levels. She would unpack them all for me over the next two and a half years, but first She had to help me understand how lost I was, and illustrate how beautiful and full of hope the next stage of my life was. I hadn't fully grasped the scope of my sickness, my transformation, and the degree to which things would continue to unravel around me, so my first session was about learning to take the medicine. How much did a teaspoon affect me? How quickly would it move through my system? How much would a second dose build on the one before? How do I purge?

Most importantly, I hadn't come there ready to undergo transformation. I still believed that my illness would quickly fade on its own. I assumed my strength would return soon after, and I would pick up where I'd left off. My first three journeys gave me a preview of the chaos that I was in the middle of, and showed me that in the midst of it all, I could build a new life.

After my second journey, I was talking to Robert and Elizabeth, telling them all I had seen with Granny about dying in the hospital. I could tell from his voice that Robert had reclined and closed his eyes as he was listening. He sat up and said, "didn't you say that last time you were in a womb, and now you're finding out that just before that you had died and were reborn? Interesting." I hadn't seen it until Robert pointed it out.

In looking so closely at the energy of a new life and spending time molding it, I was preparing myself to understand months later that I had been reborn. This infant was so weak and yet contained so much possibility. There were so many strands of life moving through it in the womb and I was able to affect them in so many ways. Some I smoothed out, taking out minor difficulties, and some I built up. That part was like tending a garden. The big choices were tougher, and many of the hardships facing this new life, I chose to leave there. Those hardships would be so much a part of building strength, identity, and character that I couldn't remove them. In making those decisions over and over in the course of those hours, I was readying myself for the idea of my rebirth and that there were both new possibilities and also new challenges that would define me in this new life.

By the time I returned for a second weekend almost a year later, reeling from Quynh's death, and seeing that my breath wasn't coming back and my strength wasn't returning, I cried out for help and healing. I was ready for change. She answered me expansively. When Granny sat above me showing me the entire nature of life as an energetic system and how I fit into it, She opened me up. First, by approaching me through my beloved grandmother, second by showing me the potency and urgency of my life's energy, and third, by making me give voice to the broken question, "Why can't I heal myself."

It's a bit contradictory in the sense that we did come back around to healing my breath in the end, but I hadn't taken the necessary steps at that point. A critical step towards that healing was to mourn all I had lost and acknowledge that my previous identity had died and a new self was born. I had to let go of the desperation to bring back what was lost, so She denied me healing until I embraced rebirth and the powers of my new self. I'd say that overall I'm stronger now than I was before I got sick. It's different this time, though, and I wouldn't have been able to get there without fully letting go of the strength of my past.

That single revelation of my death, and more importantly the experience of it in all its beauty (since just the words would never have convinced me), freed my mind completely. There were plenty more things to learn, and more hurts to cleanse, but I was freed from the tyranny of my past self. I could be proud of every little step I took forward out of the looming shadow of my own accomplishments. While others in my life might still need to grieve that loss and acclimate to a new version of me, I felt entirely whole.

Everyone I know that has found transformation on this path has had to pass this gate before any more discovery takes place. For me, the act of mourning was crucial to fully letting go, but the key element that presents itself to us is the breakdown of our conscious block on our own sacredness. It's taken a slightly different form for everyone that I've spoken with, but there's a moment of terror when the heart is finally made vulnerable. For some it takes the form of death itself with the fear of what it means to lose the self. For others it takes the form of a physical defense around the heart, and the terror is in taking it off and seeing what's left behind. Whatever form it takes, a flood of love is what comes next, and it's worth whatever it takes to get there.

I asked Her during one of our debates if every stage in my life had a death and rebirth. Did the child that was hurt by bullying and lost in depression die to let the version of me that would hike the Appalachian Trail and travel the world live? She told me that I could use that tool as much as I needed for healing. In a sense, we are reborn every day and every moment, but mourning each day in order to make way for the new one is unnecessarily consuming. That was the path of the holy man again, perfection beyond humanness. It's when my baggage begins to build up and I'm starting to suffer under the strain of my own identity that a life change or event will signal a clear breaking point.

We've built traditions spanning human culture to help us create these breaking points. Adulthood rituals in adolescence, college, marriage, etc., give us clear moments when we can break with the past and declare ourselves new. They often lack the cathartic mourning that helped me entirely let go, shocking me out of my dogged insistence on returning to my old self. We learn and grow so much all the time, but our responsibilities and our relationships want consistency and reliability from us. After a while we're doing things that are contrary to what we've learned, just to keep up old connections and relationships.

How many people have I known over the years who accomplished their great feats in high school, college, or their early careers, and still cling to those, telling the stories of their heroic past with ever growing multiplication? We can't fully take pride in the adventures and lessons of our adulthood without letting go of those old stories and mourning the death of that young self to make way for the new.

The Energetic Lattice

What Granny taught me after we died

For six months, "What Granny Taught Me After We Died" was the title of this book. The revelations from Granny and the enunciation of my death was the core of my transformation. I wasn't even halfway to healing, but the things She showed me had changed my life forever. Telling it to others was bringing them healing, too, so I had to start writing it down in a way that I could share. During my third weekend of ceremonies, I saw Her and realized that She had appeared as my beloved grandmother to gain my trust. I know that my actual Granny was there, too, but she was part of a much bigger whole.

The things She showed me were so big that words, especially written down, have a hard time containing them. I would never have been able to believe it without experiencing it. Nevertheless, I'll do my best to describe it. When I perform the breathing meditation I describe in lesson 4, I look for a vibration in the center of my body. I usually first pick it up near the solar plexus or in my dantian, just below the navel. As I continue the meditation I can feel the vibration pick up on its own, separate from my breathing. I hum to guide it to different parts of my body. Sometimes on my own, but definitely with the medicine, it expands until I can feel points all up and down my spine radiating a spiral, vibrating energy that continues to grow until my physical body gives way to the energetic self that pours through it.

It grows and grows, and becomes so powerful that my eyes cannot see and my ears cannot hear anything but the radiating energy. The vibration is greater than the matter of my body can contain, and I slip away from my material self like falling between the wide open spaces of my atoms. I can "see" my body, but not the material animal suit that is slumped somewhere in the physical world. I am deeply aware of the glorious portal through which my consciousness explores the world. I "see" in energy with my heart instead of my eyes, and my body is on fire with it. It courses through me from behind, pouring out into the world like an open fire hydrant in the summer street.

That first time I was shown this world with Granny as my guide, it felt like I watched this fireworks show for hours, but I can't possibly know how much time passed. Time had lost its regency over my experience of reality. I began to see that it wasn't just energy pouring through randomly, but it moved in a consistent pattern. I was being shown my personal pattern, perhaps similar to a few others, but exactly like no one else.

I saw how I would build up energy and get close to others, and the precise way in which that energy would take root in them, adding to their whole. This wasn't just a boost of caffeine. My energy makes people grow and transform. It's a living matrix that fits certain situations like a key, and I could see through Her examples from my life how I'd built the dojo in a way that allowed that key ample opportunities to affect people in its quiet, gentle way. This structure allows time and creates trust that allows for the nearness that is required for my energetic key to unlock potential over and over again.

Once I felt I had absorbed exactly how this energy moved, and how powerful and special it was, I became curious about where all this energy was coming from. It seemed like it was coming from behind me and going forward out of the front of my body, but I was no longer housed in my body. It took some experimenting to turn my consciousness separate from the normal process of muscles, and eyes, and space - to look "behind" (which would probably be better described as "deeper"). What I saw there was nothing less than the Source. I'm perfectly comfortable with calling it "God," though most people would attach a list of additions to that word that would distract from the core truth I experienced there. I'm also comfortable calling it "Heaven," since it exceeded every description I've ever heard of an afterlife and also answered all of my questions about how it would work.

It was at once the collection of all consciousness in and out of the world, curating the existence of love as it flows into the world. It had aspects of a waterfall, with endless souls intermingling and emerging, barely aware of their existence separate from the Source. It also had aspects of a tree trunk, interwoven like a thick bark of living texture. It seemed like a scintillating array of colors, except I wasn't really perceiving color, but energy. It was a bright swirling dance of a million kinds of energy: all of the patterns had their own individual signature, but were also deeply integrated with each other.

I was able to find individuals by searching for energy that matched the effect they'd had on me in my life. I looked for Quynh since I had a message for him. I was able to find his pattern, but it was hard for him to break away to see me at that time. Since others could have conversations with me and he was able to have one a year and a half later, I interpret that as an aspect of being recently returned to the Source. It felt at the time like he was still reaching out desperately to the world and all of the loving connections he had made there, not having fully accepted his return. It may also be that he wasn't ready (or I wasn't ready) to confront what would ultimately be the climax of my healing, but at the time, I didn't know anything about that and he just seemed overwhelmed.

While I was looking at the Source, I saw individual patterns stretch out from the waterfall-like surface and push through a membrane like the surface of an eye into "the world." They penetrated the surface while still being rooted in the Source, like energetic tendrils exerting pressure to stay in the world, and eventually relaxing to recede from it back to the Source. This process of birth and death was so easy and beautiful that it instantly removed all fear of death from me. Life was our great work but our energetic being came from the Source. It is impossible to destroy a soul since they are all part of that single great energy. As beautiful as every instant of the work is, it's work, and exposes the energetic being fueled by loving energy to a world tyrannically governed by fear.

Going back to the Source is like exhaling a long held breath, and letting the world of fear and illusion go. I was tempted as months went by to doubt all that I saw there as a mere hallucination. The energy kept flowing, though, and I've been able to access it ever since. It's hard for me to dismiss something that keeps being accessible and having a powerful effect on people's lives, so I hold it as a faithful depiction, such as my senses are able to contain it. Drinking the medicine doesn't seem to me like the singular pathway to this experience, but simply a boost that takes me farther, deeper, faster out of the dense trapping of my physical body and mind.

It was only the faint memory that I came in search of healing that pulled me back to my body enough to focus on turning my energy's power back on myself. It was a simple matter to redirect it back into myself but it kept leaping away just as she had described it was made to. It was after the third try that I realized that my Granny was sitting nearby watching me and guiding me. She became immediately and intensely present when she stopped the vibrations that had become the medium of my consciousness over the past few hours, and asked me what I thought I was doing.

In that moment, acknowledging the need for healing, I was ready to do the work. I could finally see that I wasn't able to heal myself just by learning more and getting stronger. I also was suspended in an ocean of accepting love and energy, just like the baby in the womb a year earlier. I had seen what was hiding under my bed, and it was love. I was safe and powerful enough to hear about my own death. Once she showed me that moment, let it sink in, and let me mourn until the tears ran dry, I had let the veil drop and could see clearly with new eyes. She made me proud of who I was instead of ashamed of what I'd lost. The change in how I felt about myself was powerful and immediate.

What she showed me about how my energy works seemed personal to me, and teachings from other journeys backed this up. Her assertion that my energy was not for healing myself but for building up others has been questioned by other healers that I've met since who have access to this energy. Their position asserted that the energy can certainly heal you and a variety of other things that my Granny didn't mention. They suggested that it's possible that my Granny was interpreting through her own background. That sounds off to me for a couple of reasons. Firstly, she felt like an enlightened version of my Granny. She knew more, accepted more, and feared nothing. Secondly, I saw later that it was Her, using my Granny to help gain my trust. She showed me what I needed to see at that moment, told me what I needed to hear so that I could heal farther down the road. She showed me that my healing was an elaborate temple with each brick gently placed when and where it needed to go.

Lesson 3

The Still, Small Voice

Truth, Illusion, Gratitude, and Grace

One of the tools She gave me was the revelation of truth and illusion. This came during my first journey without the medicine, no less potent, but shorter and with some urgency.

There are two True acts (that are more like categories):

The first is the truth of gratitude. This is anything that helps you see and feel how sacred it is that you are here in this moment. This could be something as simple as enjoying a beautiful view, playing an instrument, enjoying a cup of coffee. It's not really important what the thing is as much as how you do it. It's about being present in the moment instead of thinking about happy or troubling things in the past or future. This state pulses with gratitude, but specifically, it's about gratitude for the present. Feeling grateful that something will be happening in the future or happened in the past pulls us out of the present moment just as much as worrying about it. This gratitude is fully in the moment and paired with awe at how fortunate we are to be the sacred vessels of consciousness right now. It connects deeply to meditative practices that observe the movement of the breath, the experience of the senses, and the awe of our spiritual connections spreading out to people and projects all around us. It's important that the gratitude for these people and projects doesn't draw us into the future or the past, but that we can be in awe of what they are right now.

The second is the truth of grace. These acts are anything that takes that built up gratitude and energetic love, and transfers it to another person. Implied in this is that if you aren't living in the moment and experiencing the sacred truth of immediate gratitude, you won't have this built up love to give. This isn't just the love of good feelings and intentions, but the disarming, terrifying love of intimacy without expectations. This could take a million forms from sitting at someone's death bed, to giving your seat and a kind word, to asking someone to be your partner. Again, how you do it is key.

The truth of grace eludes us when we're looking for someone to help. The looking is ruled by expectation and desire. When we seek out a person to help, what we're really doing is seeking help for ourselves. Think of people longing to start a relationship. Their desperation and expectations mean that they are never in the moment with people. When they stop looking, give up, and move on, they suddenly meet someone.

This truth requires that you are fully in the moment and at peace. When your mind is calm and perceiving your surroundings with love, you will be able to hear the Still, Small Voice. I first assumed this was Her voice, but if She is just a representative of a Source that connects everyone, then the voice is coming from those in the world around me as much as from within. Souls call out for connection and complimentary patterns can "hear" the call. It is very quiet and only says one word, "now." This word "now" is certainly my own interpretation. It could easily be described as a ping on my consciousness that comes from an individual in my presence. I hear the word "now" because it embodies the urgency and direction implicit in that ping.

There are several characteristics of the truth of grace that are common. First, it is immediate. "Now" means "now." What you need to do isn't known, but in the moment that you hear the "now," your attention is drawn to the person that it applies to. What·are you supposed to do? Take a step towards them and open up to the present, with no pre-conceived idea about what comes next. Hold on to the signals of the moment and respond with your unique powers. Those are what the call is searching for. The second common characteristic is that it is highly uncertain, maybe even frightening. "Why are you telling me 'now' when I glance at an attractive young woman? I'm happily married and she'll think I'm a creep." "Why are you telling me 'now' when I see that weight-lifter with the big protein shake? He doesn't look like he'd want help from me or take the offer the way it's intended."

In that moment, you act, or turn away. This situation feels unsafe. It is. It feels like your help might be rejected. It might. The truth, though, isn't about success and failure, but about love. You can only heal people with love. Even when they turn it away it sticks to them. Your ego is the victim you are worried about. The past and the future are where the anxiety comes from, not the present. Your lack of expectation is key. What you are doing is not really for you, and there's not an outcome that you're searching for besides letting that person feel love. Is it thrilling to be in that moment? Sure. When you see that the person in front of you actually does need the love you're uniquely able to deliver and opens up to be moved by it, do you feel the love in the world increase? Definitely. Can you just go around trying to give love to everyone because you like the way it feels? Nope. That's not about being present and listening for the voice anymore. It's become about your ego again. The voice is the only guide for this truth, and the only way to hear it is by being entirely in the moment.

So far, every time I've answered the voice, it has been received. Every time there was a palpable change in the other person's energy. Every time it led to greater love in the world. I also have to acknowledge that this may not be entirely true. From my life of martial arts, I don't see anything as a failure. Every attempt is part of an inevitable drive forward that has no end. In that context, an attempt might look like failure to one person, but part of the path to success to me. Even acknowledging my dogged optimism, I'd say that reactions to the voice are overwhelmingly affirmative. It's key that I'm not looking for it. I have no expectations besides that love will flow outward from me. I think that it's disarming in its sincerity and allows people to open up in ways they otherwise would not, precisely because I'm clearly in the woods with them, discovering what will happen as we go.

Most of the time, though, we are too scared to answer the call and we let the moment of the Still, Small Voice pass without acting. This leads to the category of acts on the other side of the truth - illusion. Illusion encompasses our elaborate plots and plans to build a safe and convenient way to recreate that moment when we heard the Voice. We think, "I looked at that teenager with the soccer ball and heard the call, and I knew that I should ask to play with them. That would've been weird. I'm not wearing the right clothes, I'm on my way somewhere, they'd just make fun of me or call an adult and say I was harassing them." It nags at us. We know that we missed something important. We decide to start a program where adults mentor teens by playing sports with them. It never really takes off, we have some good relationships, some things are really hard, and we eventually let it go because it runs out of gas and its time is done. Alternately it becomes a big program and a decade later we're receiving an award for all the work we've done for teens, but the feeling of pride is short-lived and in its wake we wonder what's next. Something about it still seems less-than-enough.

All of that work and effort wasn't wrong, but it was part of an illusion we built to attempt a safe and controlled version of that missed moment of truth. It doesn't break anything and actually makes the world a better place and prepares you to be more brave in the future. In the deepest root of existence, though, the call that you heard was for your energy freely given in that particular moment when that one specific teen was in need of your specific energetic gift at that specific moment. That's the name of the hollow feeling in your gut. There's nothing evil about illusion. It constitutes most of our time in the world and runs the gamut from noble enterprise to heartless mayhem. The reason that these illusory pursuits don't scratch that deep itch is because our desire for control pushes us relentlessly into the future and the past, away from the present moment where we actually have a shot at experiencing the truth.

She had a great urgency about the truth of grace, which was out of place with an infinitely patient entity. I felt that it was because we don't live that long, and that the entire purpose of our presence in reality was to connect to the truth. This made me fearful about all the calls I've missed, and She showed me what it would be like to answer every one. It meant no home, no possessions, no relationships. It meant not knowing where you would sleep each night or what you would eat next. All of these attempts to create predictability and safety in the face of our biological, mental, and spiritual needs, are illusory constructs. They take us out of the purest experience of the moment to different degrees. Discarding all of these illusions to follow the truth isn't destitute homelessness, but an experiential existence fully in the moment, overflowing with the truth of gratitude, and offering the truth of grace everywhere they go. It was the vision of every holy ascetic I've heard of from traditions all over the world: the total release of control over their lives empowering their holy connection.

She laughed with me at the idea that I might live like that at this point and said, "You just want to listen as much as you can. Have as much gratitude as you can. It's hard and scary. We know that. There is only love, not judgment." As I thought about this in later months, it seemed like my martial arts school was an interesting tapestry of moments of truth and projects in illusion. Many risky aspects of its creation were awe inducing experiences of the truth, but most of the day-to-day work was the pursuit of illusion. That day-to-day work, though, set up ample opportunities for moments of truth as long as I didn't get bogged down by it and was present to the moment.

Likewise my marriage, which also included day-to-day work that was based on a mindset in the future and the past, was well balanced to offer a high frequency of experience with the truth when I was able to be present in the moment. There is definitely daily work that can create opportunities to be present for the truth without trying to force it. My belief is that the work of human development, whether in a direct relationship, or with a flow of people in search of transformation, allows this balance. The key is to be present to the human element of the equation whenever possible, and not to try to figure out the easy way. The truth isn't easy.

In later conversations, I asked her if resisting or thwarting the voice was what we call evil. She said, "There is no evil. There is only love which leads to truth, and fear which leads to illusion." I pushed back on that, asserting that there are some pretty awful urges, and actions, and forces in the world that really feel like they deserve the name "evil." She showed me that if I kept pulling away the layers of these acts that I wanted to call evil, I'd just see fears that lead to constructed illusions meant to gain a feeling of control. Take a step back from the murder to see what illusion was being protected, what overactive piece of childhood armor was leading to a life or death struggle for control. Underneath the manyfold layers of fearful illusion on top of fearful illusion, all compounding to distort this soul away from seeing the human in front of them in the moment, is the soul aching for connection. The mind has wrapped itself up in so many distortions that it has identified this victim as the obstacle to be overcome so that it can start to regain control and find love. Often there were many many layers of illusion, and the exposure of one would just lead to the creation of another layer to protect the exposure. Underneath all of it is the desperate need for love and human connection.

I Am the Medicine

If I had just had my first conversation with Granny, I would've considered all of this worth it. She had completely revolutionized how I saw myself, helped me understand how sacred and needed I was, and given me a measure to both pursue and discern meaningful experiences in my life. That was the fourth of my nine journeys, but what came after was what transformed this experience from a revelation to a practice.

I had signed up for two more journeys the weekend I saw Granny, but after that first night I would become nauseous whenever I thought of drinking the medicine again. I thought hard about whether sitting out the rest of the weekend was the right thing to do, since I had gained so much from the first ceremony and had paid a lot to be there for two more. I wanted to keep going and had the energy for it, but was experiencing a hard block somewhere in my mind or body that kept giving me pause. I was surrounded by voices claiming that She would show me exactly what I needed to see, so I was prepared to see the rejection as a message from Her, but even when I take a step back, it was oddly specific that my body's reaction to the flavor of the medicine changed so dramatically as to render me unable to even imagine drinking it on that day.

That night I had an experience that was unique amongst all the people I could find. Twenty-four hours after drinking the medicine, I followed my breathing and meditation back to that energetic space from the night before where She was ready to teach me, and where pain and fear couldn't touch me. It was definitely a shorter journey, perhaps thirty minutes, but no less potent. Having the lesson that evening hinge on abstaining from the ceremony was too strong of a coincidence to ignore. If it had stopped there, I might even assume that my mind was creating a dialog in that moment about hallucinating without drinking the medicine. The fact that it introduced a recurring effect that continues to this day, and introduced me to mental tools that remain effective, leads me to believe that there was an intelligence that drove those events with my healing as the ultimate goal.

My journals chart the next few months of trying daily under different circumstances and in different settings to make the connection. There were only a handful of times that I was able to have a teaching journey (my name for the times when Her voice came through clearly as separate from my own and gave me instructions or information that didn't feel like my own mind's work). A handful more put me in a liminal space where I felt connected and had thoughts rush into my head that didn't feel like my own, but there was no external voice and I was aware of my surroundings in the midst of the vibrations encompassing my body. Sometimes I couldn't get anywhere at all. Today I can reliably find the vibration and gently hum with it, helping relieve pain and anxiety, and observing the energy from different chakras as they vary day-to-day.

When it was first suggested to me that I was experiencing chakras, I watched a couple of videos that perfectly matched the vibration, humming, and location of what I was feeling. I was shocked to see that this was not only something known, but ancient. Not because I felt like my experience had to be novel, but because I would have thought that I and everyone else would know more about this if it was so accessible. Once I was tuned into it, I found that there were some people who <u>had</u> known about it before, but until that change in attunement, I was unable to sense it so they seemed like they were just wishful thinkers. I also found a lot more people that claimed to be in tune and didn't seem to have any access. It's possible that they know something deeper than I can connect with, but also possible that they're struggling in their illusions.

Investigating and reading about chakras brought up volumes more information. Colors, tones, hand positions, and all sorts of terminology are associated with them. Thousands of pages are written about each one and there are other systems with more and different chakras. Oddly, studying more didn't help me as much as I thought it would. If I added the hand gestures or thought about the colors or sounds that were supposed to be associated with them, I started to lose touch with my ability to feel them. I naturally wanted to develop more and learn more, but was always brought back to what She told me several times in different ways. "I'm not teaching you how to cast spells. I'm showing you what you already do every day." I'm not creating new energy, I'm just diving in deep to be able to experience what's already there.

To date, the most consistent way I've found to enter into the state where I can connect to the energy is a modification of Wim Hof's breathing method. I was amazed, when I saw it, that it so closely resembled what I was intuiting from my interaction with her, and hoped that this more refined method would help amplify what I was already trying. After following a guided breathing video a few times, I started doing it on my own with a timer. Once I became reliably able to enter the state, though, it was too hard to pay attention to the timer and I abandoned it. My connective breathing session generally goes like this:

∞   I take 30 deep breaths fairly rapidly. I have big lungs, so this takes some work. I like to start out seated on the floor.

∞   On the exhale of the 30th breath, I stop and don't inhale. I focus on gratitude and track the movement of my blood and muscles and skin. I wait to inhale for as long as I can, but without thinking about holding my breath. I just enjoy not needing to inhale and focus on my surroundings and my body.

∞   When I have to inhale, I breathe deep and hold it in for a few seconds, then repeat the process from the beginning with thirty more rapid deep breaths and continue through the steps.

∞   During the third or fourth round I find the vibrations. I'll usually adjust to lie flat on the floor and continue. I'm entering a much deeper relaxation at this point.

∞   It is usually the fifth round when I become fully immersed. I lose track of rounds, breaths, and time. I can dwell in the vibration and watch how energy is moving in my body in that moment, humming to assess and energize different chakras. I'll hum in different keys as I continue long slow breaths.

The bulk of the teachings that I'm placing under the heading "I Am the Medicine" relate to our nature as energetic beings living in a physical body and our deep desire for the truth which is sacred gratitude, love, and present human connection. These teachings came to me in sessions where I had broken through or reached a liminal state where a voice outside of myself began teaching. Each time it would expound on different aspects of our existence as energetic beings longing for truth. This great consciousness that we are part of has spent billions of years working its way to the surface of reality through living things in order to create this vast, balanced network in which to experience truth. Every piece of it plays its part, from bugs and fungus, to animals and plants, to us. Experiencing it in motion by being in nature is one of the easiest ways to build our gratitude since it is incomprehensibly complex and beautiful, and we fit into it elegantly and truthfully. By letting go of the past and the future, we can let it sink in and fill us with peace.

Experiencing the world through this complex vehicle of muscle, bone, and tissue comes with a suite of ills and difficulties. To grow, thrive, and replicate in a dangerous environment, we've had to be adaptable in the extreme which requires a multitude of interwoven systems, redundancies, and ongoing adaptation related to each of the perils the planet has used to snuff us out in the past. This also creates endless opportunities for misalignment and suffering. So many things can go wrong in an adaptable human body without destroying it that our bodies are always a collage of beauty, power, weakness, and confusion. We take in enormous amounts of information through our senses that we interpret in order to navigate and communicate, but in order to reach our higher purpose of gratitude, love, and connection, we have to survive and stay healthy enough not to be mired in instability.

These survival functions work incredibly well, but also overreach or linger past their usefulness and bring us pain, suffering, and fear. We want to analyze the past while imagining future scenarios in order to create better outcomes. Our bodies are hyper-alert to change and stress, using a polar pain and pleasure system to tell good pressure from dangerous impact, nutrients we need from those that will make us sick, and a smooth running body from one that is out of balance. All of these overlapping signals lead to us being in a perpetual state of anxiety. We're distressed when nothing seems wrong. We're in pain that no one can find the source of. We flip from joy to distress back to joy in moments.

None of this is the real identity of our consciousness, though. Each of us, deep down, represents a unique pattern within a sacred whole. This energetic pattern surfaces through the body as a vehicle, but it is not the body. It has no gender, no physical and mental skills and attributes, and no memories in the way that our fear and reward based mind records things. Our pattern certainly has gifts and powers that are unique to it, but they could be expressed through any body that nature conjures for us out of the lush garden of human reproduction.

It was easy to see from the other side how people fall into male, female, and a variety of joyful combinations in between and on the outside edges, since gender is a combination of reproductive biology, cultural roles, and hormones. These systems might align in a simple way, or include combinations that fall outside the most likely crossovers in the Venn diagram of gender. More importantly, gender has no impact on the viability of the human spirit. Underneath the physical, social, hormonal body and mind is the surging energetic consciousness, untroubled by the body and its overlapping, sometimes contradictory systems.

The mind likewise is part of a wide spectrum of overlapping processes within the body, but doesn't belong to our energetic selves either. The mind functions as the operating system for the body, and its processes can create a great deal of happiness and despair on their own as it navigates the world. The mind has strengths and weaknesses that are genetic or developed during a lifetime, but these are different from your energetic self. They might form a unique combination with our energetic signature that creates new possibilities within a single lifetime, but they're still separate.

Much of the follow-up work that I did after my visit with Granny was about making the most of the combinations of this body's mind with my energetic self and, in doing so, healing my physical body. Even memories can be divided into the memories of our body (reflexes, tastes, preferences), of our mind (fears, hopes, anxieties, daydreams), and of our energetic self (connections with the truth that still we feel in our bones like they happened yesterday). If the records of our physical and mental selves live in the body, I believe the records of our souls (energetic selves) connect to others and back to the source like a stitch in the fabric of reality. This is the very reason that we spend difficult time here, to build and maintain these deeper connections that carry through even into other lifetimes, like a tapestry of love that trancends time and space.

One of our most consistent interactions with illusion comes when we feel the draw of human connection and conflate the whisper of the truth with our body's hormonal drive to reproduce more vessels for consciousness. We feel the deep desire for human connection, which is an energetic connection, and then conflate it with sex, or physical domination, or social domination. These interactions feel like creating safety and control for our physical form. Sex can indeed include this deeper interaction, but is often performed without it. The act of being taken in past all the walls of social protection, adornment, and physical boundaries by another is one of the easiest ways to be connected to the moment. Both bodies press close and vibrate with ecstasy. When fully present and swept into the delight of yourself and the other in simultaneous communion, this human connection is a nearly perfect act of truth. That's often not how it's done.

When sex is about social obligation, to cover or hide from something, or to seek an identity, then it is part of illusion. We use sex in an attempt to create a feeling of control, thinking that the sexual act means the validation of our designs since it checks off our most basic, animal metric of success. This is why people can have encounter after encounter and still feel hollow. Sex done right contains truth, but it's not much easier to find the truth that way than any other. It still requires gratitude, love, and human connection while listening for the voice and being one in the moment.

More often, sex, or the looming specter of sex, stands in the way of connection. Our energy is genderless, and the voice is just as likely to call us to connect with someone of a gender that our body has a sexual attraction to as not. When answering the call of the voice, one of the first filters that two people have to sort through is animal hormonal defaults. If I, as a fifty year old large male am standing in a coffee shop and look over at a woman in her twenties reading a book and hear the voice, that first interaction will almost certainly be taken as a sexual advance. To approach her and offer a moment of truth requires that I become entirely vulnerable and remove all expectations. This is putting myself entirely in the moment. I can't carry with me my fears about her response or what others watching might think into the interaction.

This is a difficult state to accomplish, but is surprisingly effective. Most of us are innately good at reading other people. We can generally tell a person in distress, from a person who wants something, from a person that has no expectations. Being present to another human with no expectations, entirely in the moment, with only loving acceptance in your heart allows you to feel the sacred presence of the truth. Even if the other person turns away from the encounter, you still get to experience it, and they may still benefit from it. When they do engage with it, though, you create a true human connection that will stick with you for a long time. These True moments are the key frames of our lives and our purpose for being on earth.

The Power You Wield

Your sacred tool for healing through grace

This section felt particular to me, but for all I know, my power is yours as well. After months of teachings on the energetic nature of humanity and learning to see and interact with that nature, I returned, expecting to go even deeper. Going deeper was my idea, however, not Her's. The vibrations which had been the hallmark of every journey with her so far never appeared. Since all of my journeys and the meditative exploration in the six months between was focused heavily on the nature of these vibrations, I had come to think of them as a stepping stone in connecting to my energetic self. I now had the sense that the vibration was part of a separate teaching, and that it was time to move on.

Now it was time to learn about how my unique energetic pattern had combined with this particular body and mind in this specific trip through life to create powers that were needed in the world around me. She chose a symbol that I knew well to manifest these powers to my mind. I saw Mjolnir, Thor's hammer, as it looked on the silver pendant I was given as a boy. My mother had told me it was a traditional gift for a Norwegian boy (which I sort of am, a couple generations back on one side). In the decades that had passed since I'd worn the pendant, popular movies had portrayed a Marvel superhero Thor with a blocky version of Mjolnir made popular in the comic books, and I had come to think of him and his hammer this way as me and my young sons gobbled up the movies.

It was a surprise to see my childhood pendant writ large, hovering above me, with her charging me to pick it up. Rather than being a hammer that only those pure in spirit could wield, it was just heavy, painful, and intimidating to hold. She called it the Hammer of Creation and Destruction. The hammer can tear things apart or build them. When you face the challenge to hold it up high, you can change the world, but if you let it down, it inverts into an anchor shape, weighing you down. I had never heard it described this way, but when I looked into Mjolnir more online, this idea of the thunder god's hammer being used to create as well as destroy is definitely already out there.

She made me drill and review two powers related to the hammer over the course of two journeys. The first was to Call the Storm. This aspect of wielding the hammer is destructive at its core. It is the fearlessness to instigate change. It means to walk into a system that needs renewal, and without being able to see how all the pieces will fit in the new version, dismantling it to make way for the new. The storm tears down houses, lightning burns and kills, floods wash out roads and drown. But the ashes fertilize the soil for new life, the water nourishes and feeds, the void that is created holds the opportunity to come back stronger than before. It is, however, terrifying and uncertain. People naturally recoil from bringing it on themselves, so wielding the hammer of destruction isn't something people are lining up to do.

The power that was paired with Call the Storm made the destruction less terrifying. It is to Wield the Lightning. This means that when all the pieces are flying around in the midst of the storm, you find peace and look at how the storm moves, what it reveals, what is enduring, and what is frail. The seemingly chaotic power of lightning becomes something you can direct. As the pieces swirl around, you begin to guide them into place and build a greater future that most people can't see while the storm is raging. In fact, only other lightning wielders will perceive anything other than instability until it is nearly done. People that can't see it, though, can still see the changes and the work, and take some comfort in that, largely based on how much they trust the lightning wielder. They may not fully appreciate what's happened until after you've finished building, but they know deep down that the situation is being worked on. If they've seen you do it before, they can have faith in the process, even when still uncomfortable from all the change.

She made me hold the hammer exhaustingly through hours of ceremony, practicing how to use the pair of powers to change lives and empower people and things. Over and over She would stop and tell me to hold the hammer up, and I would realize that I'd let it slip lower under the weight.

When I'm in the world and I hear the voice say "now," it's usually the Hammer of Creation and Destruction that people need. It's important not to assume because it's heavy and breaks things. But that is one of my unique powers.

In the spectrum of actions broken out into truth and illusion, the work of the hammer could be categorized as a method and also a medium. As a method, it is a tool to use when meeting another soul. They may need the lightning which tears down old things that have outlived their usefulness. It may be that they need a question that challenges the broken aspect of their life that seems inescapable. They may need support, knowing that the hammer is raised and being shown a vision of what life will look like on the other side through the change. Both come from the combination of calling the storm and wielding the lightning.

As a medium, these powers are neither truth, nor illusion, but a lifestyle pattern that best uses my gifts. It creates opportunities to hear the voice and be my best self. It can easily become frightening or exhausting, leading me into illusion, but overall, I get more opportunities to be present for people when I'm using my powers.

The Hurt That Won't Heal

Armor that must be cast aside

Once I was ensconced in my powers, feeling mighty and sacred, it was time, finally, to begin healing. I'm familiar through my work as a karate teacher with how often a person will think they're doing all they can, while being miles away from their actual capability. A large chunk of that is the discomfort of effort and people's belief that the discomfort means that they're on the wrong path. But there's another aspect to it, where your mind will hold back what it allows you to do in order to protect you from injury. I see this, for example, when someone thinks a movement will hurt them. They can't summon nearly as much force as they will after they've succeeded once and they see that they're all right and it's safe. People also imagine an arbitrary maximum, and that level feels impossible to cross. Once they see someone else cross it, suddenly they can, too. People tend to accomplish pushups in even tens. If they manage to push themselves to fifty, they'll stop, rather than trying fifty-one. Their mind was set on fifty. If the person next to them does fifty one, then suddenly more seems possible.

A variety of mental mechanisms hold sway over what our bodies can and will do, but I am still amazed at the biological limits I was able to disentangle on my final journeys. The first (recognizing the death of my past self) created a perspective shift that made growth possible again. The second was more of a mental disentanglement (removing the message of unworthiness) freeing me from decades of self-inflicted suffering.

Since the time in my life when people began to remark that what I was doing was impressive, I had experienced an immediate negative reaction to praise. At first I thought I was being humble to refuse praise, or to deflect the praise to the circumstances that allowed me to do well. As the compliments became more elaborate and focused, I felt severe discomfort and even angry distrust.

For example, after a martial arts test or demonstration, if someone approached me with praise about my performance, I was sure they thought it was embarrassing and were trying to make me feel better. The praise affected me more negatively than if they had just said nothing. If they dug in, describing what they admired or recounting particular moments that impressed them, I would become increasingly agitated, feeling that since the performance wasn't worth noting, they must have some ulterior motive for buttering me up. I would try to escape with a joke just to not make a public rebuke of their rudeness. A few minutes later, wrapped in confusion, I would recall that I'm very good at martial arts and recognize that the person's praise was perfectly genuine and that I had offended them a little by brushing off their compliment.

No matter how much I reasoned it out, it still sat in front of my vision like a suit of armor that everything had to work its way through before I could start thinking clearly. On the third journey of my third weekend retreat, I asked Her to free me from it. While I remembered the event that She brought me back to, I didn't think that it was the lynch pin of my feelings of unworthiness. She brought back everything from the week leading up to it and multiple details about that day that I had forgotten. She showed me every detail that made me open to the message of unworthiness and even showed me the vulnerability and humanity of the man who planted the message.

I could see from a safe vantage point how a healthy, happy child, under strain for certain, but well loved, could wrap this armor around his own perception that filtered out anything that suggested he was exceptional and twisted it into self loathing and distrust. The wall was an armor that explained to him why things were unfair. It explained why the good things would pass him by, and helped him make peace with his unexceptional life. He was surrounded by kids who were worthy and brilliant, and he was lucky to be there but didn't belong. It was ok to leave that opportunity and go somewhere more unassuming. To settle for far less challenge. He would need to stay away from teams in order not to let others down. In karate, he just wouldn't advance if he failed, but no one would get hurt or angry about it. This was the protection offered by the armor.

It was armor that made the world make sense, but I had learned over the years that it didn't fit the person I was becoming. On the Appalachian Trail I had been able to open the visor and see past it, but it was still there. For almost thirty more years I would have to filter through that armor, even knowing that it was ridiculous. When She showed me how it was made, where it was attached, and let me see the unfettered boy that hadn't put it on yet, I was able to connect with him and take the armor off. I planned in my diary of the event several ways to stay connected with him so that the unworthiness wouldn't come back, but it hasn't been necessary. It's just gone.

These traumas throughout our lives make us don armors. These armors filter our perception of the world and change how everything looks and what parts of our body and mind are accessible to us. Since our access to our own physical potential can be controlled in the same way, these armors can change the way our bodies work by altering what we think is possible and what we expect out of interaction. Even after we become aware of the filters, even if we know the source of the trauma, removing the armor is immensely hard since it has protected us and made the world feel safe and make sense.

It defies healing precisely because you aren't injured. What is required is respect and gratitude for the armor you wear. Only then do you have the option of taking it off. I know that Shadow work is directed towards this very idea, and other therapies are effective over time, but I was shocked that Aya removed it in a single session.

A Battle of Forgiveness

Unsettled business at the core of our identity

My final journey in this process of healing was much different than I anticipated. Based on all my experience to that point, I was sure that this step was essentially to return to the traumatic experience of the hospital and let Her give me perspective on it like She had months earlier with my feelings of unworthiness. I'd even seen people discussing how they treated their PTSD with Ayahuasca, and it was exactly like that last experience unraveling my unworthiness. Having Her tell me that there was no fear there was a real shock. Realizing how deep the forgiveness had to go into my past, as well as making me stand up for myself in order to accomplish it, finally opened the way to real healing.

Each of the three instances of forgiveness that I had to take on was hidden deep down. The barbs were sunk deep inside and I would've told any therapist that I had grown past any hurt from these feelings and, in my grown-up strength, had no ill effects from them. Yet those feelings in combination with this instance of weakness (nearly dying of a sickness that was barely felt by anyone around me, even my elderly relatives) was enough to cut off my full access to my lungs.

When I discuss forgiveness with my classes (It's mentioned in several of our martial arts philosophies), I make sure everyone understands that forgiveness isn't letting someone off the hook for what they've done as long as they apologize or make things right in some way. We call that justice. Forgiveness is a personal exercise that you take on to free yourself of the obligation to play the part of judge and debt collector. It means letting go of both the wrong-doing and also the justice for what was done. It doesn't require the consent, or involvement, or even the knowledge of the other party.

With all three of my wounds, the perception of weakness was unspoken. In life, all three men would make suggestions, react more to certain acts than others, or make a point of demonstrating certain aspects of their own lives. They all had power over me and wanted to use that power to guide me to what they thought would be the best version of myself. Their comments and attentions were meant to be instructive, but they often conflicted with what I knew about myself. Instead of guiding me, they created a pattern that told me how they feared for me because they thought I wasn't measuring up. All three of them loved me, though, and wanted me to succeed and to be loved and happy.

The first step was to go ahead and have that conversation out loud. The words had to come out into the open so that we could feel how the air moved around them and remove all shadows. Now stated, the second step was the clash. All of them still believed in their position despite seeing that my way was succeeding where they thought it would fail. They had to make their points and let me make mine. I had to stand up to their position, and when they told me they still thought I couldn't do it my way, that was the moment that my heart was fully ready to let go. The third step was to tell each that I forgave them for not seeing me, for not understanding what I was doing and the heart that was in it. All of them struggled with legacy and what would come after them. It was important to tell them that they could rest easy and know that I was strong enough and prepared for all that would come next. Forgiveness is an act of bravery, so it was necessary to struggle with it and come to the same resolution for my future over and over. Each act of forgiveness required me to stand taller and lift my head higher. It was important not just to stand up for myself, but also to pledge myself to answer all of their doubts in my own way.

About Tanner Critz

Tanner is a lifelong seeker, storyteller, and teacher whose path winds through wilderness trails, martial arts dojos, and deep journeys of the spirit. At twenty-one, he thru-hiked the entire Appalachian Trail, an experience that reshaped his young adulthood and ignited a lifelong hunger for meaningful adventure. Thirty years later, after surviving a near-death illness that left him unable to continue his life's work, he found healing and transformation through the ceremonial use of Ayahuasca. His memoirs—End to Ending and End to Beginning—bookend these two defining journeys.

In both works, Tanner explores what it means to step away from the life we're handed and move toward the one our soul demands. With an eye for poetic detail and a reverence for hard-earned truth, his writing illuminates the path from breakdown to rebirth.

Tanner is the founder and head instructor of Unity Martial Arts, a community dojo that weaves together Cuong Nhu, Brazilian Jiujitsu, and Tai Chi to develop power, presence, and deep connection. His teaching and writing share a common thread: transformation through discipline, vulnerability, and the courage to walk into the unknown. He lives and teaches in Little Rock, Arkansas with his wife and two sons, where he continues to explore the sacred space between endings and beginnings.

END TO ENDING

An Appalachian Trail Thru-Hiker's Story

Chapter 1

Wayah Bald, North Carolina

117 miles down and 2,051 miles to go

"You must leave now, take what you need, you think will last."

Bob Dylan

When I awoke March 25th, I began to notice little things that weren't quite right. My bed was harder than usual, my pillow strangely dense. There was a ghostly fabric looming a foot or so from my head. I became aware of a spoiled, oddly familiar smell marinating the air all around me. Recognition began to seep in, and then like a spray of cold water, understanding. I was in my tent, not my bed. I was in the woods, not my house. This would be my tenth day hiking the Appalachian Trail, and my fifth day of being alone.

I stared at the roof of the cocoon-like tent for a while, watching sunlight patterning on the thin, stretched nylon. The mountain dawn was a bright, crisp white since the sun had been up for a while before it came over the ridge. I could hear the chatty spring a few yards away and listened to the loud absence of walls around me. During the night my heavy bones had slowly settled into each other and forgotten where they began and ended. I soaked up the syrupy warmth of my sleeping bag like a chrysalis and tasted the chill, moist air of the tent on my face.

When I moved, I did so carefully, mindful of my weary feet and legs and back. I was growing used to the fact that, though I ached to the point of stinging before going to bed, the night would leave only soreness in its wake, and most of that was dampened within the first hour of walking. Nevertheless, I always wondered if my body would eventually wear down and break, and I tried to imagine how I would be able to tell that pain from the daily aches that came with eight or nine hours of carrying my hefty pack through the mountains.

There were many ways to break, and differences between the pains of damage and those of hard work weren't always clear. Three years earlier I had been hospitalized when an ulcer in my stomach had bled me nearly to death. At the time I hadn't been able to distinguish that pain from the dull ache in my abdomen after the normal aches from a karate class. I had ignored it for a week, blaming each symptom on being kicked in the belly, doing crunches, or having a stomach cramp. Finally I collapsed during a tournament from anemia.

After several blood transfusions and conversations with confused doctors for whom I was far from the profile for peptic ulcers, I was released and declared recovered. Two years later it happened again. At the time I was in the process of planning my thru-hike and my parents and doctors were very concerned about what would happen if I started bleeding again in the woods. After the second episode a theory was being kicked around the medical community about my ulcers being the result of a bacterial infection instead of stress and eating habits, as I was a very relaxed and fit teenager. I was determined to hike despite the threat, so they sent along a vial of prescription acid-inhibitors and a vial of antibiotics to carry with me in case I had an episode in the woods.

My current pains however, were decidedly more leg, back, and shoulder related. Despite the pains and the growing loneliness, or maybe because of them, I felt centered. What I was centered on was harder to say. Through the soreness, the climbing, the dirtiness and the quiet, an air of pleasurable weariness hung around my head that made me very comfortable in the base motions and movements of the hike, the camp, and the cook-fire. Katahdin was so far away that to think of it as a goal made me feel very small and lonely, so I focused more tightly: getting up, breaking camp, climbing the next mountain.

My sleeping bag and its warmth came off reluctantly, but once out of it, I wasted no time in leaving the tent. The little one-and-a-half-man tent was too small for me to even sit up straight in and barely afforded room to get into my shorts and heavy fleece pullover. I crunched my knees to my chest, turned my feet to the door, and unzipped the mesh internal door separating me from the rain fly that was the outer shell of my shelter. My big, black boots wouldn't fit entirely inside the tiny vestibule of the tent, but even if the toes had to hang out under the flap, they could resist any rain that might come along. Where the toes had been exposed to the night air, beads of moisture clung to the leather, the crisp drops beading on the pristine, water-repellent surface reminding me of how new they were. Before the Trail I had only hiked twenty-two miles in them. One overnight backpacking trip. Of course the same was true for the rest of my gear, and me for that matter.

I had spent the month before the trail hanging out in the local outdoor equipment store. I finally had enough money saved to buy equipment and interviewed the employees at length about each piece. Two of them had hiked the A.T. before, and were happy to discuss gear opinions and strategies for hours on end. My feet slid easily into the well-fitted boots and dropped into the snug socket around the heel. I laced them up soundly but lightly, not wanting to cramp the flow of blood through my ankles as my feet swelled later in the day, as per the recommendations of the staff at the store. I felt solid and steady in the mountain boots. They still smelled like new leather, and once I laced them up they pleasantly contained the growing reek from my socks. I had three pairs, but three days of constant hiking in each pair had left them all pretty ripe.

A few days earlier I had tried to wash two pairs with liquid soap on a frosty afternoon in a high mountain stream. The icy water that sloshed over my already cold hands made them numb almost instantly, and as I hastily scrubbed the socks, dipping them now and again to try to get the suds off, the numbness warped into a hard, crushing ache. Before I was halfway finished I threw the sudsy, wet socks across a rail, rammed my hands into my fleece and curled my body around them to fight back the feeling that my hands were lost for good. When in the morning the socks were solid with ice, I was further fortified in my decision that the stink was a better friend than the cold and let the socks smell how they wanted after that, planning to wash them in the distant warmth of summer.

I brushed some of the dirt and moisture off the inside of the rainfly that covered my tent's vestibule and pushed past it into the frigid mountain air. Climbing out of the tent is one of the great rewards of camping. It's like being born every morning. The warm, soft, musky shell with all its layers is pulled off, and you stretch out to more than twice its height, reaching your arms to the trees and letting every joint, tendon, and muscle unwind to its fullest. You let your bones separate and the crystal talons of the morning air invade your pores as you breathe in the pure, high mountain air and realize that the whole world starts beneath your feet and extends down and away forever. For that moment before you breathe out, you, too, extend through the brook and the earth and the trail, beyond the trees and the horizon and the sky. For that moment you have no bounds and no limits, and there's nothing you cannot do.

Slightly less glamorous is the next part of the morning, when the countdown begins for you to find a suitable spot to dig a toilet hole. It was not an uncommon decision on particularly cold nights for me to ignore my colon's suggestions in favor of uninterrupted warmth, leading to a fairly dynamic morning rush. After filling in my ditch and putting away my trowel, I settled down on a log near a blackened old fire pit and cooked up a small pot of water on my little camp stove for tea and oatmeal. The oatmeal was routine by this time, but the tea was a new experiment on the trail.

I felt very cosmopolitan with the tag hanging out of my flimsy plastic cup, and the hot tea nestled very comfortably between my chilly hands. I thought I must have looked like a picture in one of those camping magazines, except dirtier and with no hair. I felt the steam flow past my face as I looked out off Wine Spring Mountain. I had made my camp last night at the very top of the small, winter-stripped mountain and the view into the valleys beyond was cluttered by the gray-brown skeletons of trees and the arching green boughs of rhododendron around the spring. It hadn't taken long to get used to staring past those gray, southern trees and to wonder where among the valleys and hills the trail would lead each day. My body was almost getting used to the abuse of hiking with the sixty-pound pack all day, and though climbing mountains would never become really easy, I was beginning to feel the world around me instead of only feeling my legs and feet and shoulders and the pounding of my heart.

I had been hiking alone for five days and hadn't seen a soul for three. I crossed into North Carolina from Georgia with Bob the Postman on day six, but he had gotten ahead of me that day, and I never saw him again. Even though I grew up as an only child with both parents working, I was used to having people around for some part of the day. The solitude was beginning to reach me on a very personal level.

The laughter, posturing, aches, and general camaraderie of the hikers I had met during the first few days had been a welcome distraction. It felt like we were all in the classroom without a teacher, and no one knew quite how to act. We just watched each other having our personal problems with feet and gear and spirits, and wondered quietly who would make it all the way and who would limp off to town at the next road crossing. One man hurt his knee the first day and decided to stay behind in the shelter the next. One woman was starting to lose toenails the third day. One girl had a dog who wasn't adjusting well to the chaffing from its little dog-pack. Our packs were heavy, our days were hard, and the task ahead was Olympian. One in ten people that start a thru-hike finish it. It was less a question of who might quit than who might make it.

I had virtually no idea what I was doing. I spent a lot of time watching other hikers and trying to pick up useful tips from them, but the experience seemed to have even the two Eagle Scouts among us at the end of their wits. While they knew some tricks about how to use their packs and looked more comfortable with their tents, they weren't any more used to the effort and the isolation than the rest of us.

On the second day I lost most of my nylon cord while trying to hang my food out of reach of bears as I had seen in drawings. The knotted system of branches and cord that I improvised proved to be not only bear-proof, but hiker proof, and I spent the first part of the morning jumping in the air with my knife and whacking at the only part of the cord that was in reach where I had tethered it high around a tree trunk. As far as I know, the rest of that cord is still up there, prompting hikers to wonder what alien intelligence managed to bind two trees together at such a height.

There was one guy who was pretty relaxed about the whole thing. His trail name was Sir Renity, and I met him on the way up Springer Mountain the first day. Most everyone I met already had a trail name that they had chosen before starting. I had read about these names that hikers go by on the trail, but hadn't thought of anything fitting for myself. Trail names were easier to remember than people's real names, and often had some sort of story behind them that said something about the hiker. Sir Renity ate fancy food and carried fresh eggs and all sorts of cooking toys with him. I would pass him during the day, napping on a hillside or reading by a cliff. I suppose I was too caught up in struggling to hike at the time to notice that he was having a bit more fun than the rest of us in spite of his heavy pack and blisters.

Five days ago he had hitched off the trail to a hostel with everyone else I had met to resupply and do some laundry. In my planning I had worked from the data book to set my resupply points based on the miles in between them and the distance off the trail that I would have to hike or hitch to get to them. It turned out that many of the best hiker services like the hostel that my fellow hikers had all known about were mentioned only in the Thru-Hiker's

Handbook by Dan "Wingfoot" Bruce. Somehow I hadn't caught wind of this trove of hiker information during my preparations. I had sent my mail drop based on mileage alone to the post office in Franklin, North Carolina, a couple of days farther down the trail than the hostel, and had to keep moving on by myself in order to make it there before I ran out of food.

I hadn't anticipated the impact of five days of complete solitude. Normally to achieve such a level of isolation, one must be stranded on an island or locked in solitary confinement. Not only were there no people, there was no contact with society at all. No television, internet, phone, music, or books. I had charts and maps and read the occasional sign or mile-marker. It was surprising how quickly the loneliness turned to resigned singularity and how quickly the dialogue with myself became an elusive give-and-take instead of a series of one-sided pleas and reminders.

I was hiking longer days than most so I could catch up to the schedule I had set for my own resupply points and not run out of food in between them. Since the boxes of food arrived at certain towns on particular days, it seemed like a tempo that couldn't be interrupted.

I had estimated the distances from the comfort of my mother's living room, poring over maps and the data book in an attempt to chart twelve to fifteen miles a day, but take into account steep climbs and the locations of shelters. It had all been very academic then, but now some of those days were hard to live up to, and I was a little behind. Sitting on a log holding an empty teacup wasn't getting me there any faster, either. I needed to start breaking camp and get my body moving.

I suddenly realized that a used tea bag weighs a great deal more than a new one and, if deposited in my zip-lock trash bag with my regular trash, would make quite a mess once I crammed it into my tightly packed gear. I pulled the dripping, mottled sack out of my cup and hobbled over to the fire pit to deposit it under the half-burnt logs where it could be consumed in the next fire.

My idea no longer seemed clever when I found dozens of bits of food and trash strewn through the pit. Thinking perhaps to squeeze the juice out of the bag so it would be lighter and less messy, I placed it on a large rock by the pit and used another rock to flatten it. When I opened the press, though, I found the tea bag had been reduced to a wet, flattened, torn mess of herbs and paper marinated in an inky, brown juice. I hesitantly picked up the now very light and empty paper tatters by the string and placed them in my trash bag, kicking the mess of herbs into the dirt.

I pulled my green cap out of my pack and secured it to the oily, two-week-old stubble on my head. I had shaved my head a few days before starting, and now my big, pale scalp would grab onto any fabric that passed near it. I had never been bald before, but it seemed somehow fitting to let go of all of my hair and start fresh. I had done it myself with an electric beard trimmer one night during a moment of courageous romanticism, starting before I could talk myself out of it. The trimmer wasn't hefty like clippers, and a courageous moment turned into hours of etching my thick hairline slowly backwards, a gesture transformed into a lengthy meditation.

I was already growing used to my gear, and packing it up went rather quickly: break down bedding and tent, secure tent on pack after shaking out and brushing off dirt and moisture, tent sections poles and spikes in their respective sacks. Arrange the stove, pots, and food in the main pouch, and the toilet supplies in the right side pouch near the spare fuel and first aid supplies. Zip the main pouch up and I was nearly ready. In the narrow pouch on the outside of the main section, I pushed aside my journal and pulled out the maps and my data book.

I already knew I was seven miles behind schedule. The night before I had decided that I needed to stop at the spring on top of Wine Spring Mountain because there was no way I was going to make it to the shelter that day. To catch up to my schedule now I would have to do a nineteen mile day to Wesser, North Carolina; a little rafting outpost by a state road. There was supposed to be a restaurant and bunks there. I unfolded the map and followed the zigzagging line of the profile display to find where I was. This two dimensional chart showed the line of miles at the bottom, and the profile of the elevation changes moving along that line as they passed up and down through the 1000 ft elevation lines. I rarely even looked at the directional map. All that mattered were the changes in altitude. The up and down didn't look so bad, but nineteen miles would be daunting even if it was flat. I had done nineteen six days ago when I hiked with Bob the Postman and it had damn near killed me.

The trail in Georgia had only been a seventy-five-mile chunk. On the sixth day it had felt good to cross the state line into North Carolina, marked by a pipe nailed to a tree with "GA - NC" painted on it. Now in the second state on the trail, it would be hundreds of miles before I would cross another such line. The goals I set for myself would have to be daily ones, and nineteen miles wasn't so unreasonable, especially if I could buy a hot meal that was anything other than macaroni and cheese and Ramen noodles at the end of it. The only way to know for sure was to start walking.

I put away my maps, pulled my water filter out of the left side pouch and filtered some more water for the day ahead from the babbling spring smelling the thick rhododendron leaves hanging low and resilient. I put the two water bottles in the mesh pockets below the side pouches where I could reach them without taking my pack off, and finally took off my warm fleece pullover to pack it away, zipping everything up and making my pack fully ready. It was cold on the mountaintop but being cold was motivation to start hiking and warm up. I felt strangely at home with the chill, and hefted the cold pack on my back, the pads still damp from yesterday's sweat. As I tightened the hip belt, the weight stood up obediently on my back and seemed to disappear into my own for a moment. Leaning our combined weight forward I started down the trail, stepping over the brook and pushing away a rhododendron branch weighed down by the morning dew.

Among the many benefits of sleeping on top of a mountain is beginning the day with a nice, cool downhill to get the blood flowing. A tough uphill at the wrong time could put a stop to all productive thought, but an easy morning stroll into a sleepy, mist-laced valley always got my mind working. In the five days I had been alone, I had plenty of time to think. A few days earlier I tried to think of all of the dozens of houses and apartments I'd lived in. Then I tried to go through everyone I had ever known. Since all that only took a couple of hours I went on to try to remember every-thing that had ever happened to me.

Over the long hours of climbing I had struggled for produc-tive thought, tried to look over my life clearly, discover something new, remember something lost. There were many subtle impli-cations before setting out that I should discover the meaning of life on such a journey, and I was doing my best, but my thoughts were running thin, and now I was just tracking the pulse of my own consciousness. At twenty-one years old, I could only reflect for so long before redundancy set in, so when I could spare the breath, I would sing as I walked. It made me appreciate long songs and their ability to make the miles disappear. That morning I decided to sing "A Hard Rain's Gonna Fall" as it would carry me quite a ways.

I was following the trail along the shaded side of a ridge with

the moist, leaf-covered ground rising to my right and a valley dropping away to my left. The shadow of the ridge made a dark crescent
in the valley, and the gentle mist clung to the shelter of the receding
shade.

"Where have you been, my blue-eyed son? Where have you
been my darling young one? I've stumbled on the side of twelve
misty mountains." I paused for a moment, wondering if I had
subconsciously chosen the song because of the fitting lyrics. "I've
stepped in the middle of seven sad forests." I continued walking
through the winter-stripped trees, and singing on I began to
examine the lines of the traveling song more closely. I began to see
more and more in the verses of the musical poem and, with the
reflection of my life fresh on my mind, began to make connections.
The people and places and moments of my life rolled through my
mind with the words, and I stitched each note into my life's fabric.

Even where a line seemed at first to have no connection to me,
the fast spinning loom found a fit and wove it in. I began to trail
my life behind me like a long quilt of images and feelings as I sang.
Instead of a thought coming to mind and then passing away, the
heavy fabric held them all at once to be seen in a single observation, and the weight of it pulled at my neck, growing as I continued.

"I've been ten thousand miles in the mouth of a graveyard." The
words came slower and slower as with each new verse my mind
was filled with the forces that had moved my life for better and
for worse. The words of the song went on alone, measuring themselves with the falling of my feet as my mind began to race faster
and faster, my thoughts overlapping and threatening collapse.

"I saw a newborn baby with wild wolves all around it...I saw
guns and sharp swords in the hands of young children...I heard
the sound of a thunder and it roared out a warning...I heard one
hundred drummers whose hands were a blazin'... I heard the sound

of a clown who cried in the alley...I met a young girl and she gave me a rainbow...Oh and what'll you do now my blue-eyed son? What'll you do now my darling young one?"

Breathing out sharply as my eyes teared up, I became aware that I had stopped on the trail and goosebumps rose all over my body as the forest fell silent, awaiting reply. The pulling tapestry of my life snapped free and fell gently into the leaves. I turned to look out into the valley and smelled the richness of the earth, the dying, dry chill of winter trying to hold on while deep in the valley was a sparkle of green so bright that its light was the cry of a newborn child and below it, running away into valleys beyond, was a brilliant spring throwing light into the dark woods as it ran.

For a moment I could see it wandering far down the valleys, meeting other streams and creeks, growing and changing, becoming greater and faster until it spilled into the ocean, and the whole world lay out in front of me. A cold breeze blew up from the valley and brought me back, and I turned and hiked lightly along the trail.

I had reached the end of the valley and now looked up at the mountain ahead, walking steadily to meet it. The uphill was strangely welcome, each step pulling me higher and higher. Questions shot clearly into my mind as if I were climbing up into them. The questions were big, and they washed over me and through me and away. Why am I alive? What is power? What is love? What will I do with my life? I stepped through them like layers of mist, and when I had risen above them, they lay in the roots and rocks by the trail for people to see and wonder who had discarded them. Who am I? What am I doing here?

I broke out of the trees into a wide clearing with a strange tower. It seemed very out of place and I approached it with some caution. Beside the tower, a sign explained the history of this mountain named Wayah Bald. Wayah was the Cherokee word for the wolf spirit, a symbol of great power and strength. The mountain was the ancestral home of the wolves in Cherokee legend, but the wolves had been driven out and killed long ago. The stone tower sat on top of the bald mountain like a mushroom with a staircase on one side, and I wound my way up to the stone cap where the view stretched all around.

The world faded off to its lacy cusps, and I was entirely at peace. I shrugged off the pack and felt the cool wind catch the sweaty middle of my back as I leaned my pack against the short guard wall that encircled the rim. Opening the zipper, I pulled some nuts and granola out of the bag of snacks that was positioned closest to the top of the main pouch on top of my cooking gear. Sitting on the cobbled stone wall, there was nothing in the world but the wind, the tapestry of North Carolina, and the tiny bits of granola and nuts crunching lightly in my mouth.

Something broke the stillness below. I could see two figures making their way quickly up another path, a concrete walkway from a community parking lot. One was a short, plump woman with a camera and wide, black sunglasses. The other was a tall man who pulled his windbreaker tightly over his shoulders and looked at the ground. As they neared, I heard the woman's voice announcing their presence to all of the wildlife.

"There it is! It's not much farther now!" She was looking straight ahead at the tower, glancing down now and then at the path. As they got closer I realized that words flowed from her in an endless stream punctuated only by bursts of exclamatory laughter that did nothing to break the tempo of her speech. The man was perfectly quiet and never looked up.

"Yeah so I read in this magazine that they were gonna start puttin' wolves back in the woods, and I said to Murray that he'd better... Hey! There's somebody up on the tower already!" Her words gave way for a moment to a heavy, panting grin.

"Already?" the tall man glanced at his watch as she led him up the steps.

"Howdy!" said the woman as she drew close and ascended the stairs, her cheeks red and her movements quick. She introduced herself and the man but I didn't listen to their names as they flew by. "Who are you?" She asked. The question seemed to echo around the tower and over the mountaintop. I looked back to the quiet woods where I had left the question in the rocks where the trail broke from the trees and it peeked out at me again. I turned back to the pair and found them unmoving for the first time, waiting uncomfortably long for my answer.

"I'm... Wayah," I said, looking her coolly in the glasses.

"Oh?" she chuckled. "Are you from around here?" She seemed amused.

"Yes." I said thoughtfully.

"So are we! We're from Haysville. This is my brother. He sells insurance. How 'bout you?"

"I'm hiking the Appalachian Trail."

"Oh, really?" She looked at the tall man and crooked her brow. The man shrugged. "Don't you remember? That's that trail Muriel likes to hike. Goes clear to Wesser."

"Where's that?" said the tall man.

"It's that rafting place on Highway Nineteen. Oh look, it's almost eight. We'd better get moving." She shuffled back to the stairs, breathing sharply a few times and peering through her thick sunglasses. "You sure can see a lot today. Have a good one." She began to drop down the steps and the tall man nodded, following her. I watched them plod down the path as inefficiently as I'd seen anyone move in ten days. The pack weight would never forgive that kind of shake.

"Thanks," I said quietly, nodding and smiling as they disappeared down the concrete walkway. My body felt light and mobile like a leaf on the wind and I squinted into the sunlight smiling, suddenly feeling out of place on the tower. I was ready to move, and I packed my granola away and hefted the pack back onto my shoulders and hips. Sliding smoothly down the steps I said to myself, "I am Wayah, the Wolf. I'm hiking the Appalachian Trail from Georgia to Maine." I thought of the southern terminus marker on Springer Mountain in Georgia, only ten days past, and of the northern terminus marker on Mount Katahdin in Maine, veiled in the tint of old photographs and the cold uncertainty of the months ahead. I looked at the two-by-six-inch white blaze on the tree next to where the trail dove back into the woods and walked on down the path, gently touching the blaze as I passed and dreaming of my dinner in Wesser.

◇

End to Ending is both a raw first-hand account and a time-traveling reflection—a vivid memoir written by a young man who walked the entire Appalachian Trail in the 1990s, and now reissued with the clarity and insight of three decades gone by.

At nineteen, Tanner heard whispers of a footpath stretching from Georgia to Maine. At twenty-one, he shouldered a heavy pack, said goodbye to his father at the trailhead, and stepped into a world where hunger replaced comfort, and solitude peeled away everything but the truth. The original manuscript—penned soon after his 1995 thru-hike—captures that experience with the voice

of someone still buzzing from the wild. It tells of firelight conversations and snowbound missteps; of trail magic and tumult; of
Vikings with trail names and minds cracking open in the mountains;
of becoming one with the woods, not just walking through them.

Now, thirty years later, Critz returns to that trail—not with his
boots, but with the reflective lens of age, fatherhood, and loss. This
anniversary edition includes new chapters and commentary that
deepen the meaning of the original journey. He stands at the mirror
of time, no longer the boy who hiked into the forest—but the man
who walked out.

End to Ending is a book for anyone who has stepped into the
unknown in search of themselves, or who wonders what becomes
of the seeker when the trail ends. Poetic, gritty, and soul-searching,
it reminds us that some journeys don't stop when the walking
does—they echo for a lifetime.

www.ingramcontent.com/pod-product-compliance
Lightning Source LLC
Chambersburg PA
CBHW021706120626
46545CB00004B/1435